SCARRED BEAUTIFUL

My True Story of Finding God
in Despair and Beauty in Imperfection

ANDREA CASTEEL SMITH

outskirtspress

DENVER, COLORADO

The opinions expressed in this manuscript are solely the opinions of the author and do not represent the opinions or thoughts of the publisher. The author has represented and warranted full ownership and/or legal right to publish all the materials in this book.

Outskirts Press, Inc.
http://www.outskirtspress.com

ISBN: 978-1-4787-4674-4

Outskirts Press and the "OP" logo are trademarks belonging to Outskirts Press, Inc.

PRINTED IN THE UNITED STATES OF AMERICA

Contents

Introduction...i
Chapter 1 1
Chapter 2 11
Chapter 3 25
Chapter 4 34
Chapter 5 43
Chapter 6 49
Chapter 7 58
Chapter 8 66
Chapter 9 74
Chapter 10 84
Chapter 11 91
Chapter 12 101
Chapter 13 111
Chapter 14 120
Chapter 15 133
Chapter 16 143
Chapter 17 153
Chapter 18 160
Chapter 19 168
Chapter 20 183
Chapter 21 194
Chapter 22 200
Chapter 23 210
Chapter 24 215
Chapter 25 222
Chapter 26 231
Chapter 27 238
Chapter 28 248
Chapter 29 256

Chapter 30 266
Chapter 31 274
Chapter 32 280
Chapter 33 289
Chapter 34 300
Chapter 35 304
Chapter 36 310
Chapter 37 324
Where They Are Now 334

Introduction

*"For as the heavens are high above the earth,
So great is His mercy toward those who fear Him;
As far as the east is from the west, So far has
He removed our transgressions from us."* Psalm 103:11-12

Getting away to Coronado Island in California was just what we all needed. Walking the beach, breathing the ocean air, beholding the splendor of each wave as it collides and collapses with such awesome force, is truly healing. I am mesmerized by the ocean's beauty. Watching the water break and stretch up its beach reaching high, then slowly retreat, regaining its power as it swells full and deep, becoming massive and grandiose once more. It truly is an example of life, its falls, its swells and its breaking; yet its procession is truly breathtaking. Its majesty causes me to exhale, releasing out the pain, fear and sadness that twisted tightly around my heart. It's been years since I really felt I could just exhale.... Today I can.

Having to live just twenty days where time stood still, I had to reflect on everything, my thoughts and memories inescapable. In moments of total darkness, as each second moved languorously by, the things in life and people that matter overwhelmed me and gave me new and real perspective on my true priorities. In the rat race of the outside, these priorities can easily get lost and set aside due to life's constant shuffle.

My incarceration was hard and at times broke me, yet in truth, I am grateful for the renewed perspective it has given me. I now recognize, in a deeper way, what is most precious and cherished in my life.

I am blessed to have a beautiful heritage of grandparents that gave their life for the very Message of compassion and grace they learned from the Words spoken by their Savior. I am blessed to have each of them personally speak over me and teach me through their life examples. I do not deserve the lineage I am part of. As Scripture describes the great cloud of witnesses, I know they are there.

I am grateful for my friends who showed generosity to my daughter on her first day home. I needed to feel the celebration of her arrival and they lovingly did that for me. These same beautiful women kept my head above water with their relentless encouragement and words of love when I was drowning in my own despair. I had no idea how much I would need them, but they actually saved me from myself.

My brother, Michael, and sister-in-law, Beth: They have made choices each day unselfishly, determined to put the lives of their family above their own. I am in awe of them and am honored by their love and support that they have shown and continue to show me each day of my life.

My sister, Esther, who is my rock and inspiration: She has believed in me when I didn't believe in myself. She would not let me fall, but called me strong and told me to hold myself and my head high as someone who overcomes. She has stood by me, loved me and defended me without fail. I love her and am so grateful that God has given to me this woman that I can watch, admire and rejoice in her life and her beauty. I love that God has parted the clouds and shines his light on her like no other; her calling is unique, special and as her name states: she is royalty.

I am grateful for my beautiful parents who kissed my face and wiped my shame away. They held me and said they were proud of me when my spirit was stripped of all dignity. Their lives, their journey and their love is a beautiful example of the character of my Father in heaven.

My husband, a man of God, who has been my strength and my protector all seventeen years of our marriage. He has loved me and carried me through hard times and good. He has kissed my scars, comforted my broken heart and shown me that I have so much to be thankful for in him. I love him deeply, passionately and look forward to growing old by his side. You still take my breath away.

My children: I may not have given birth, but I labored greatly for them both. As a mother, there will never be a night that I don't reevaluate the day and question my parenting. The entrustment of my children has been great and I carry the weight of that in my heart and my every day. Their biological mothers were beautiful women. I truly pray that my kids understand this and keep this truth in their heart. They loved them deeply and were willing to lose their hearts to see that my two could have a chance at greatness. My two… my children… they are the fruition, the gift from God, which was the answer to my unrelenting prayers.

I pray my children know throughout their life, that they are truly my life's greatest love. They will never know the depth and length I care, or how much they matter to me. They will love and live and make mistakes, but I will love them always, and forever be their greatest fan.

Finally to the One who was and is my first love, my God, my Jesus: I have learned that as Scripture says, "the wages of sin is death." Since the fall of Adam and Eve, we are born into death. My back, although I was but an infant and formed in my mother's womb, was a product of being born of sin, a symbol of the surety of death even at my birth. It was ugly, yet death is ugly, but God you have taken away death's sting through the cross. You took my ugliness and changed it to beauty. The scars still remain and they will never be gone, but You can change that which is ugly and make it beautiful in spirit. You, God, can make good out of evil, You can heal the brokenhearted, bring life to the barren, You can turn mourning into laughter. You gave me a man who sees not my scars but a beautiful woman. You took my barren body and placed in my arms two children. You gave me hope and perspective when I was alone, cuffed and emotionally beaten. To you my God: All I can say is "Thank you."

Chapter 1

"Out of the depths I have cried to You,
O Lᴏʀᴅ; Lord, hear my voice!"
Psalm 130:1

CHECK IN, HOUR ONE

August is such a miserable time in Tucson, Arizona. It is an annual spell of extreme heat, with no break. The monsoons have passed; a gorgeous, dangerous season, where rainfall hits the desert with such force and majesty, you can watch the clouds unload a sheet of water and move from north to south, east to west. The clay soil is too dry and dense to drink its unrelenting force, causing the water to become a wall of rushing river through the desert, down the mountains and hills, into the streets. Although the heat is hard and penetrating, the sudden rain cools the air in an instant. Now it is August, the rains have gone north and Tucson is left with the sound of the miserable cicada bugs and unrelenting heat. The cicadas: they come buzzing and clicking every summer. Their noises are amplified by their multitudes creating an overpowering and menacing hum.

My heart is pounding and neck pulsing with each beat; making an agonizing loud, incessant drum in my ear. The heat, although only eight o'clock in the morning, was already intense. My palms are wet with sweat from the combination of the sun's sting and my mounting anxiety. I watch the shadow on the sidewalk move symbiotically ahead of me; its silhouette taking each step toward the inmate entrance of the towering and terrifying jail that loomed ahead. I didn't want to acknowledge that the outline ahead of me was a reflection of myself. The person I was, the person I am, shouldn't be here. How could this happen to me? My shadow reveals my feminine frame, slender and small; causing a strong shiver of fear to strike through me. I have thought in spirit I was strong; but in body I knew I could easily be overcome. Now my spirit was weak too. The jail's steel door, the inmate entrance, was now visible up ahead; a buzzer or doorbell is perched proud next to it. Behind that very door was my sentence, waiting to be realized.

I hate Tucson. I hate its heat, its culture, its bugs. I used to love it. I would take off by myself to hike its canyons and dip into the ice cold water, created by the fresh melted mountain snow. I could sit and admire the rugged, barren, gnarly terrain, with its cactus and thorns reaching to the sky, warding off birds and prey. I became mesmerized, as I gazed at the rock formations blistered, beautifully beaten, into rustic and grandiose sculptures from the waterfalls that spill through its stone; a rock that appears impenetrable, yet their strength had to yield to the force of the water that cut through. But now the joy I once found in the desert is gone and the cicadas annoying bitter song is an appropriate chorus as I walk to my punishment. It's like a trumpet sound as I march to my judgment.

Through the bugs, I can hear accordion music in the distance. The accordion is accompanied by Spanish singers harmonizing a jubilant tune. I look to find its source. Far in the distance, across from my new "home", the Pima County Jail, is an automobile repair shop. Several men are working, in this tiny carport structure. It has a primitive painted sign, devoid of fluff or fancy. I am struck, suddenly, when I realize the men are looking at me... yes, me... walking toward my punishment. These men watch and know my fate. I drop my head and look away, ashamed. The beat of the music fights the horrible hum of the cicadas and the pace of my walk. I have a deadline... but I walk with apprehension and dread. No joy in my step. I walk alone; very alone.

It was only moments ago that my arms were wrapped around my heart: my son and my daughter... a sad goodbye embrace. I feel a lump in my throat gather as I envision their beautiful faces and the intensity of remorse that my farewell brought. I was leaving not because I loved them less than my own life, or loved anything or anyone more. My mind now imprisoned by the image of them holding their teddy bears as I drove away. The teddies we built together at the local Build A Bear...

which I am eternally grateful for… because it was something I could give them to hold during my absence.

I am now steps away from the steel door and its nearby oversized bell. After dropping off my car at the jail parking lot over two blocks away, the walk to the inmate entrance was long and intimidating. The fence and structure of the jail imposing. Its commanding image, only augments my escalating fear of what's to come. It is a colossal structure of metal and concrete that sprawls an entire city block. There are many layers of fencing that is littered with large warning signs and notices of its electricity, topped with barbwire curled and tangled to ward off any escapees. Despair grips me and depression's fangs take hold of my heart, my body and my soul.

"It's time: I am here," I say to myself as I stop face-to-face with the steel door, then stare at the industrial buzzer. Reluctantly, I reach toward it and push. Immediately I get a response: "Yes?" the female voice on the other end is bored and annoyed.

"…Umm…, I am Andrea Smith, Inmate Number……, I am here to check in?" I say.

Silence… Then the sound of the intercom rings.

"Do you have your judgment order and ID?" Click.

"Yes." I respond.

Once again there is a high pitch ring, "Read the sign next to the door. Make sure you understand it and someone will be at the window to your right at their convenience." Click.

The sign above the buzzer is a warning against being caught with contraband and the grave penalties if found. There is no actual window that I can see. There is, however, a wall with a large steel shutter and steel counter. The entire area is cement block, met by concrete sidewalk, next to asphalt. I stand for a while, then lean up against the wall and try to find some shade. I feel the accordion music and the cicadas are now laughing at me, deafening my thoughts… mocking me. I wait, linger and watch for the shutter to roll and unveil the face of supremacy.

It is getting hotter… really hot. Beads of sweat trickle down my forehead. Being wet with perspiration doesn't make me feel any better about the impending strip search that is to come. Anxiety and trepidation regarding the level of humiliation that awaits is overwhelming. I begin to reminisce of a happier time, the first time Chad viewed my entire body, my breasts, my shape. I recall standing in the bathroom, looking at myself in the mirror. I was wearing a white silk nightie, my long blonde hair spilled all around my shoulders and fell down my back, hitting my waist. I was young and pretty; with soft, sweet features. I was so fantastically innocent, so incredibly naive and so very much in love. I was excited, nervous, and not loving the awkwardness of the moment. I took a deep breath, knowing he was waiting on the other side of the door. Then reached for the handle to leave that room a virgin and to lose it in the arms of the man who had just vowed to love me until death. It was our wedding night.

I am pulled away from my thoughts by a drop of sweat that ran down my scalp under my hair. My hair is now shoulder length, with an edgy severe cut, Asian style bangs, layered in light brown with highlights of blonde at the tips. A look I chose to get me through my sentence and give myself a stronger appearance; intentionally taking away any softness or flash. I glance around and suddenly notice the video cameras watching me; realizing, rapidly, that not only am I being watched, I am probably part of a joke that is played out daily by its viewers, at the expense of its enforced and depraved caller. I was on time for my court ordered "check in". I look again at the window. Panic takes over as I grasp that once again, my life and my ability to establish the truth is out of my control. I have no way to prove that I arrived on time. I could only rely on the honesty of the person or persons behind this buzzer. Sadly, in all my recent encounters with those in authority, honesty was not upheld. My faith and trust in people, especially those in power, was not only shaken, but has made me become aware of how at risk and vulnerable I really am. No matter what type of citizen I was, what my position was in society, how many charitable causes and/or governmental services I performed, it was my word against a deputy. The deputy, who had his own record of abuse, continued to change his story of his accounts of the night; where in contrast I had no record, not even a traffic ticket, nor did my story ever change… because it was the truth. To this day, I can say I was factual and honest in every way; but lost. It was his word only, mine was of no relevance; nor was the evidence, or the fact that his arrest wasn't in accordance with the law. Now, I was afraid of everyone. My genuineness held no value in court… held no value to other deputies, who took the position of backing a fellow teammate. Now I sit waiting, aware that I face a new potential penalty if I am reported as tardy, which will equal more court dates and more days in jail; more days away from my kids. Here I stand in front of this intimidating steel door and worry that the eyes behind the video cameras will stall, in jest, as I pass my judgment deadline to further their joy of watching my anxiety mount. I know this delight, this power others relish in. I have seen the smirk of self-satisfaction a tyrant with a badge had at his ability to make me small. It was fun to humiliate me, as I was driving my sports car convertible in my own neighborhood, a guarded country club. He reduced me and enjoyed every moment: arresting me in my driveway, in front of my home and family.

So much time has passed and my legs are tired. I decide to sit on the sidewalk curb next to the asphalt, giving up on any hope of shade. I can feel my upper brow bubble. What a pathetic sight I must be, I think to myself… as the bugs and accordion continue to heckle. The asphalt in Tucson gets so hot that every year in August the local reporters like to televise cracking an egg onto the street to show it sizzle and fry into a hard and broken breakfast. I feel the burn of the asphalt begin to melt the rubber of my flip flops. My required time of check in has long passed. I am the fool, and am sure I am not the first fool the car garage has watched sit and sulk as deadlines pass. They seem unamused; awarding me a little grace, by ignoring me and going about their chores, unconcerned of my low state. God bless them.

I am wearing sweat shorts and a white t-shirt, listed items I have been allowed to bring and sleep in. Earlier, I had submitted a clear grocery bag of items such as: underwear, wireless sports bras, more white t-shirts, and additional sweat shorts. Confiscated, not really sure why, was one grey sweatshirt with no draw string or hood, deodorant and soap.

I jerk, startled, at the thundering sound of the steel shutters roll, quickly I stand to my feet and walk to the window. Behind the shutter a tempered glass window is revealed, along with a very sour young woman, whose brown hair is pulled back in a bun, looking uninterested and irritated. In a monotone voice she asks for my judgment order and ID, not willing to give me the time for eye contact or to lower herself to even move her head in my direction. A drawer pushes out and in it I place my paperwork, then the drawer disappears. Shutters sound and the window vanishes once again.

I stand feeling confused and look back at the spot on the sidewalk I just left. Unsure if I should go back and sit down or wait for the shutter to roll again. I stand dumbfounded until I hear buzzers ring and locks release. The steel door opens... exposing a long concrete hallway illuminated by florescent lighting. The hallway is partly painted, crude and intimidating. No warmth or welcome. It looks cold, sterile; not the feeling of a hospital, but the obvious look of a dungeon, devoid of anything but the pathway to lock-up.

In the doorway a woman dressed in her Pima County Jail guard uniform, tan and double knit, with a badge and a large black belt riddled with contraptions such as: a baton, flashlight, cuffs, pepper spray and some type of walkie talkie. Under her uniform shirt, is the outline of a bullet proof vest; her womanly frame distorted from its padding. Dread overtakes me as I realize the depths of her need for such padding. She is armed and equipped to protect herself from the very people that I am to live with… and from me.

Her dark hair is also pulled into a bun, although older than the other female. She appears to be in her mid to late 40's with a pleasant face, which comforts me for some reason, and I smile at her hoping to get some reassurance that everything is going to be ok. She doesn't smile, or look at me, but past me; she too is affected by her position. The little hope I had for a fragment of consolation now crushed. I feel my eyes well, but breathe hard and strong to suppress their force, "just breathe" I say to myself, "breathe".

With paperwork in hand and in a hostile, aggressive tone she demands I follow her with one hand on her baton. I can tell she relishes in the power her uniform provides. Her badge has conditioned her to psychologically separate humankind: she and her associates superior, versus me, the incarcerated vermin.

She has me walk past her into the hallway, then follows closely behind. The hallway is well lit, but the block cement walls are dark, partly
painted in grey. With her heavy boots, she stomps loudly on the concrete floor, keeping me keenly aware of how close she is with each step.
The steel door, now behind me, shuts loudly. I jump from its strength
and my body becomes cold as the blood in my extremities falls and
drains making my fingers and toes tingle. I can hear the door seal with
an industrial clank. Panic sets in and I began to breathe fast. I want to
run back and bang on the door and call to the cicadas to let me hear
them once again. Their sound has been silenced. In their place is the
deliberate thump from the guard's boot hitting the hard floor, which
echoes down the barren and colorless hallway. Her stomp is accompanied by a persistent and ominous whine from the lights above, yet all
is dulled by the intensity of my heart's beat and the panic of my breath.

In spite of myself, I walk the path directed. The hallway opens up to
a large concrete sunken floor. The sunken space looks as though a pit
filled with metal benches lined up one after the other with about 50-
60 detainees, each wearing miscellaneous street clothes or jail issued
fashion, all sitting… eerily quiet. I glance at them but quickly look away
when my eyes meet theirs. They look menacing, criminal. I am frightened. The block walls and inmates' hardness makes my oppression all
consuming, while my spirit absorbs that this place is my penalty, this is
my value to society.

Just beyond the sunken pit are glass and steel holding cells, lined
up, one after the other, all numbered and each filled with the accused.
The guard has me turn just before the pit. I exhale in relief that I was
not having to join those sitting on their benches, their images intimidating and clearly not the people of whom I belong. I swallow hard as I
quickly recognize my relief was foolish; the pit was shown to me so
that I would see my fate and the reality of exactly whom and where I
do belong.

We walk past guards' desks and stations erected on the other side
of the pit. They sit in view of all the incarcerated on their benches, as
well as those in their cages. Their floor is elevated high, higher than

the path I am on and towering above those in the pit, to ensure there is nothing to obstruct their view of the criminals they are responsible to impound and control. Several deputies are mingling, leaning up against their desks, laughing loudly, jesting and glowering at me and the other inmates, who clearly are unlike their grander selves.

In the distance, I can see the nurse's office whose door is propped open. Her conversation with an inmate can be heard by all. I conclude that inmates no longer have any right to medical privacy, hence the door propped open and her loud projecting voice. Close by is another group of deputies, who are hanging by a camera, talking loud and eating breakfast burritos.

I am directed to stop in front of a door. The guard pushes something and waits until I hear the door buzz and unlatch. Once open, I am led through it into a large room, enhanced with extreme security at every corner, which includes chained wrist and ankle cuffs attached to the walls, resting on a concrete bench and floor. Once again the door shuts loudly behind me followed by the sound of its locks that clank, sealing me in. How low have I fallen to be one and among those who need to be restrained and leashed with chains? The officer directs me to sit down on the bench and wait for my check in, explaining that I am not to stand up or move from until my name is called. She then leaves.

I sit on the cold concrete seat as I absorb the room, void of color or natural light from the outside. There are four numbered windows in front of me with a group of annoyed and young workers who idle around behind each. I can see the same younger female who apathetically greeted me at the shutter just moments ago; she is sitting with a few other young women and one pale and portly young man. They are not wearing uniforms, but casual work attire. Their floor is also elevated. Each employee has contemptuous facial expressions, while slowly pushing paper around and appearing as though they detested what lurks on other side of the glass. The windows were crucial to separate them, the elevated, from us, the depraved.

The room was actually icy, in spite of the tremendous heat outside. The layer of perspiration I accumulated as I waited outside was now quickly working against me and causing an acute drop in my body temperature. I begin to shiver.

Sitting near me was a man who had long stringy blonde hair, slender and tan, but not in a good way. He looks like he has been through a lot in life; his face worn and tired, his hands quite beaten. I sit upright, not leaning back against the wall, because there is a line of grease, very visible, that runs parallel to the bench from years and numerous arrestees who have deposited their residue. A woman, who also has blonde hair, sits across from me, her hair is short and permed, her face is smudged with eyeliner from dried tears. She is wearing pink shorts and a floral shirt. She sits without pose, dejected and tired. I feel bad for her. I can only imagine her night. Like her, I have learned, everything can change in an instant. She appears as though she just witnessed her entire world unravel into ruin. Above the woman is another tempered glass window exposing a lounge space for deputies. There inside a guard lolls with a deputy sheriff. The glass is sound proof, making the jovial conversation private. Clearly it is the place to hang out if you are among the privileged, such as them. They undoubtedly are talking about those of us who are sitting on the bench, because they point and gesture at us, while laughing at our expense.

Anger builds as I look at their pathetic yet haughty faces. One of them is holding onto the few hairs that remain on the side of his head, and doesn't seem self-conscious about his flabby waistline, and gut that hangs over his uniformed belt. The badge that gives them so much power is probably all the power in life they will ever have. Without that badge, they are common and nondescript. I start to count and measure the areas of my life and my accomplishments that outweigh any of these people who now belittle my existence. Yet, quickly I stop myself, recognizing that what I am doing is stroking pride that I no longer have a right to and trying to mend my heart by mentally depreciating these men the same way they are me.

My heart sinks, dejected and depressed once again. I replay in my mind my farewell to my children and my husband. I was in our kitchen, on my knees with my seven year old son's arms wrapped around my neck, my four year old daughter's head pressed against my chest. They smelled of strawberry shampoo. My daughter's brown curls were soft as I kissed her baby head. I turned to look into my son's sky blue round eyes; I melted in their beauty.

I whispered, "I love you."

He answered back, "I love you too, Mommy." My eyes stung as I heard those words.

My four-year-old then asked, "Are you going there for work?"

"No it's not for work." I answered softly.

Then he asks, "Are you going to be with friends?"

I gently responded, "No I am not meeting friends, but I may make new ones though."

I hadn't told them that I was going to jail. This was at the advice of the child counselor I had met, to hear his guidance on how to explain my absence to my children. The counselor encouraged me to wait to tell them when they were old enough to understand. He was concerned that they would confuse law enforcement's role. I want my children to feel safe with those in authority; I want them to feel law enforcement is there to protect, not to harm and not to be feared. So, for now, based on his counsel, I was just going away… but will be back.

I stood and kissed the top of my son's head. He had smooth blonde hair that had brown undertones; warm with golden streaks from the sun.

"I am going for a while because I need to, but I will be back. Without a doubt, I would much rather be home with you, take you to school every day and tuck you into your beds at night. Please remember, I will miss you terribly every morning and every night especially," I said tenderly, holding back my true emotions.

I looked at the clock reluctantly and realized I needed to go. I let my arms relax from pressing them tight, which in every way felt unnatural, like I was tearing away my heart from my chest, and took a few steps back. I looked from the kitchen toward my husband, who was in our family room and called to him, "I am leaving. Good bye Chad." He heard me but didn't get up off the couch, nor did he turn his head toward me. Without affection he muttered, "Bye." The sting to my spirit and the dagger to my heart was felt. Immediately my body drained of all warmth as I walked to my car and to fate's retribution.

Chapter 2

"Naked I came from my mother's womb, and naked shall I return.
The Lord gave, and the Lord has taken away;
blessed be the name of the Lord." Job 1:21

JUNE, 1995

I officially met my husband at the gym, but prior to that he had seen me, and I him, at my father's church. Our church was very large. Average Sunday service grossed more than a thousand people, at times up to two thousand. I sat with my father and mother on the front pew. I worked for my dad and typed and printed his sermon notes. I loved the Scriptures and I admired my father who was such a studied theologian in both Scripture and Biblical history. I felt it a privilege to have such access to his research and notes. I was twenty-one years old and still lived with my parents, worked with them and for them, believed in their ministry and the message they lived and preached. My first love was my God, my Savior, who consumed my every motion, thought, and desire. I refrained from anything I felt might be the slightest Biblical infraction that would cause a distance or barrier in my relationship with Him. Our church was charismatic, Pentecostal; which meant, we sang and worshipped with dancing, clapping and raising hands. I spent many hours every week dancing at the altar with great elation for the loving God who I adored and who caused my spirit to be light and full of joy. I wasn't tempted or curious to venture out and see life or experience "the world"; I felt my soul was full of joy and peace, and was content. My home was tender and loving. My father was a man of honesty and integrity. He was and believed everything he preached, never relaxed, and worked hard to live his life holy. My mother: a passionate, affectionate, spit fire of a woman, never conformed to the church people's image of what a "Pastor's Wife" should reflect. Her hot temper and trendy clothes were just not what they expected or wanted her to be. My father needed her though, he relied on her, she was his strength and he loved her. She lived her life by her truth and walked a path of uprightness. She would never scribble or scratch outside her moral guidelines which she built in her life based on Scriptural principles. They loved God wholly, dedicated themselves to His Word and His Message. They believed… I believed.

In addition to typing my father's sermon notes, I also typed and printed the Sunday bulletin and was the Youth Coordinator, which meant, I planned, budgeted and oversaw all youth activities, retreats, camps meetings and events. There was no budget, so in response, I turned everything into a fundraiser so that we could have pizza occasionally and maybe bring some help to our church expenses.

I worked hard, really never had a break, because I worked at the church office and worked at home. In pajamas, our family would plan and brainstorm, together with my parents and my sister, Esther, on how we could reach more children, youth and adults with the message of Jesus Christ. Esther was the Children's Pastor and also lived at home with my parents. She too was a true believer in my parents' life's work and its message. Esther was a beauty queen, literally. She had won the Miss Tucson pageant and a few other titles I can't recall, because she never invited us or wanted us there. It was her secret life or conquest and only after she won did we learn about her achievement. Esther was stunning: tall, amazing figure, blonde shoulder-length thick, full hair, a movie-star face and the most gorgeous smile. I was the opposite of her: tiny, petite, a bit too skinny, small features, sweet. My hair was a warm blonde, not naturally, which fell down to my waist. Although physically opposite in every way, Esther and I were very close. She was my best friend, my safe place, the person that I knew would have my back, and I hers. I loved that she was beautiful. Because our appearances were so different, our suitors were never interested in the other. We attracted different men and likewise was our attraction to them, so there was never a competition between us. We could yell at each other and then in minutes laugh and comfort one other. Only twelve months apart,

Esther the elder, we grew up together fighting, getting into mischief and defending one another.

However, there was one young man that I introduced to my sister and immediately became concerned that his affections would steer toward her instead of me. This was the first time I felt a bit of panic and competition. That young man's name was Chad.

Chad was magnificent; in every way my type. He had an athletic body, chiseled and defined, his blonde hair was short, cut clean and preppy. His eyes, dark blue and striking; his smile, masculine and flirty. I had a few male admirers at the time. For some reason I seemed to be a package that some young men felt they wanted; probably because I was so dedicated and absorbed in the ministry, they felt that my innocence and dedication would make for a good wife and loving mother. I, on the other hand, was not that interested in any. They all took me on dates, played their Christian music and talked lofty about their goals to be pastors of their own churches one day. I was turned off by their ambition and their insincere presentation of themselves. Chad didn't conform to any of these politics.

His father was a new member to our church and had greeted my parents while I was sitting near. Chad was standing next to his father. I felt Chad's eyes on me, not leaving me. I pretended not to notice him. In fact, I purposely wouldn't look back at him. He kept looking at me, in a way that made me feel uncomfortable; it was aggressive, penetrating. I intentionally did not return his gaze, but kept a peripheral view. It was unsettling… but I liked it. I wanted him to think I was unimpressed and ignored him resolutely. He made me nervous though. He was incredibly handsome, young, and strong. My parents and his father's idle chatter ended and they walked away. I exhaled so loudly that my parents looked at me, both shocked and confused. I had been so private about any emotions or feelings about the opposite sex, I think they felt I was asexual.

I gasped without control and blurted, "Who was that?"

My mother cried out, "Andrea, what has gotten into you?"

My father quickly looked back at the boy he hadn't paid attention to while in front of him, now intently watching walk away as someone of noteworthy. I felt silly at that moment, but was uncontrollably smitten.

The next day my parents left town to attend a church leader's conference. That evening I went to the gym to work out. I didn't go to bars, or have many social friends beyond church group events. I went on dates with boys a lot, of whom I really didn't have any interest, but gave them all my best effort. I thought possibly I would feel something more if I just got to know them better. Tonight I had off and decided to work out in my hot pink workout gear; my hair with big curls and full of AquaNet, leg warmers and lip gloss. I was set. I grabbed my two pound dumbbells and began my routine at the large aerobics and weight training facility. I couldn't get through one set without being propositioned or introduced to a beefy boy who took notice of my ninety-five pound nothing frame and my big fake blonde hair. I guess I enjoyed all the attention. It probably was my Christian version of a bar scene; a place to socialize, be noticed and get a date, around a treadmill. Most of the guys seemed mentally simple. They projected loud and wore crop tops to expose their 12 pack abs. I wasn't interested. I was friendly though, it wasn't in my nature or heart to make anyone feel bad, so I smiled and thanked them, then explained that I needed to go back to my church service later and wouldn't be able to go out for dinner. That ended their interest. It turned out that this night, Chad and his buddies saw me enter the gym. They watched the countless men approach me and one of his friends made a comment regarding me. Chad warned them, "I am going to marry that girl." They laughed and told him he was crazy. He turned and walked toward me. I was oblivious of him being there, oblivious to the significance of that night. He was wearing a tie-dye t-shirt; one that he clearly wore frequently all four years he attended college; of which upon graduation, should have retired along with his books. I heard a man introduce himself to me, "Hi, I am Chad."

I turned and almost fell over at the sight of him. I had expected another muscle bound mindless gym rat, wanting the blonde girl's phone number; yet it was not who I predicted it to be at all. In fact, it was the gorgeous young man I saw the day before who literally stole my air. I looked at him stunned, frozen.

He continued, "Our parents know each other. I go to your church."

"Yes, you are John Smith's son. My family is really close to Ruth, who just married your dad! I didn't know your dad had kids." I rambled.

"Yes… a son…." he smiled and reached out his hand. "Hi, I am Chad."

"Chad?" I said as I shook his hand, as though I hadn't already taken great inventory of who he was, his name and many other details that I pretended to have no knowledge of.

"That's me…" he said playfully.

He had a flirtatious smile. It made me uneasy. "Well it is good to meet you," I said politely. "Funny we bump into each other here."

"Yes. I was surprised when I saw you walk in. Do you work out here a lot?" he asked.

As we talked, I realized his friends were in the background and that we had an audience. This made me nervous. "I try to, at least five to six days a week." I answered.

"Wow, sounds like you are dedicated," he commented. Consistent maybe, but my routine was less than strenuous, I thought to myself.

"I wanted to introduce myself to you. I have been going to your church for six months and have been watching you. I like watching you," he said boldly.

I was uncomfortable once again. He had a way of making my stomach become full of nerves and my body weak. His confidence and directness was unnerving and made me uncontrollably interested.

"I would like to take you to dinner," he followed without hesitation.

"…Umm," my heart began to pound! "I would like that," I responded with a smile, but inside I was doing all I could to suppress my jitters. "Can you call me at the church office to arrange a time?" This to me sounded detached and not too excited; it also alleviated me from writing down my number and exposing my shaking hands.

He smiled and said, "I will. I am going to let you go back to your workout, but we will talk soon."

"Ok, I… I look forward to it," I answered.

He walked away and I waited until there was enough distance between us to let out a significant exhale. I then tried to lift another set of weights and realized I was trembling. In the corner of my eye I could see another gym rat coming my way; I decided it was best to go. As soon as I was home, I threw myself on my bed. My head swimming from excitement, butterflies dancing in my belly and my heart full of exhilaration. My phone rang, my mother was checking in.

Before she could say hello, I blurted, "Mom, you will not believe who just asked me out?"

"Oh no… not that Chad Smith boy?" she murmured.

"YES!" I cried with elation.

JAIL: DAY ONE, HOUR TWO

I hear my name called and look up to see a bored young man at window four, beckoning me in an irritated fashion. I get up and walk over to his window. He seems to appreciate the fact that his floor is elevated, causing him to look down at me. He asks me to verify some questions about my identity, my social security, address, date of birth, etc. I am looking at him without looking away, more so than I usually do, because he isn't looking back at me. It's as though he is too put off to acknowledge me and easier to look side-to-side while questioning me, to show me how insignificant I am. Since he doesn't look at me, I take a good inventory of him. He is fat, young, and unattractive. His fingers look soft, like he has never washed a dish or done anything with his hands. They are pudgy and smooth. His face is plump and also smooth. He either gets waxed, shaves his hands and arms, or he has yet to hit puberty. It turns me off. He is very pale white. I don't think he leaves this florescent illuminated space or his sofa at home often. He feels very imperious to me. This job gives him a sense of superiority as he sees the low-life examples of rock bottom, which lessens the ache of his own pathetic existence. I am answering his questions as though on auto pilot. Much like the night of my arrest, but I don't want to think about that night right now.

I decide to occupy my mind by looking at him closer. He has a few freckle-type moles on his face. His brown hair is very short. He has a lot of hair, but he clearly is young, probably in his early twenties. He was most likely teased in school... His eyes are green, like mine; although not eye-catching... not saying my eyes are either.

I don't think my eyes have ever been the part of my body that I would consider most appealing. They are small, as are all my features. They fit my face though. I think they are pretty because they are soft and sincere. I am not young, but still get attention and propositioned at times. I have learned to love my body and now I realize how beautiful it is. I have a 5'4", 105 pound frame; yet my shape has become more attractive as I approach middle age. I love to dress up and feel put together. Never in flats, but obsessed with high heels of every kind. Today I am in sweat shorts, my hair cut short, no make-up on, wearing flip flops and no bounce in my step. Very soon I will wear jail-issued rubber shoes and a red jump suit. I have been stripped and soon to be strip searched. I guess it is all fitting, a chubby twenty something boy who shaves his arms and hands is treating me as though I am repulsive. I think to myself how tragic, for the first time in my life I have felt truly beautiful and not just a mask to make people think I feel that way. Truth is, I have had a secret. I present myself as self-assured and secure, but in reality I have had my own private ugliness... my own secret shame that I just overcame.

"Have you ever considered or have you ever attempted suicide?" questions the man with no arm hair.

Jarred away from my thoughts I ask, "I'm sorry?"

He projects his voice at a louder volume and repeats the question slowly being cruel to the imbecile he feels I am, "...Have... you... ever... considered... or... attempted... suicide?"

"No," I answer.

This is a lie. I have been prompted by people that are familiar with the system, to lie regarding this question. If I were to have answered "yes", it would mean that I would have tests and be locked up in a medical health room to be "observed." I feel a little pang of guilt for lying, but pacify this feeling as justifiable after some self-talk.

The inimical young man begins to ask me medical information such as, am I current on my tetanus shot, etc. I conclude this is Pima County's way of reducing their liability from any infection that may occur after the injury or rape that may result during my stay. Then he asks me what personal possessions I had on me. I had none; only the items I had submitted earlier that morning in a clear plastic garbage bag, which are no longer with me.

"He broke my cell phone!" was the comment that distracts me from the annoyed and bitter male in front of me. To my left, at window two, is the woman in pink shorts. "What are you guys going to do so I can get it repaired?" she questions with her voice raised.

Next to her stood the Sherriff Deputy who was in the hang out room earlier; the few hairs on the side of his head were still there, but I am sure won't remain there for long. He is standing with his chest puffed, antagonizing her with the lack of space he is giving her, while she answers the questions from window two. He has her cell phone and some other items in a zip lock type bag which he places in the slot of the glass window. The look on his face shows he is amused; he is enjoying this. I hear him threaten the girl in pink saying that he would report that she is being "combative." The woman quickly responds, "I am not trying to be combative, I am just concerned that you took my cell phone from my hands and dropped it. It is completely ruined now. I want to know how I am going to get it repaired, since you are the person who broke it." The woman behind the window responds in a rehearsed answer. Because of my distance and the window, I cannot hear clearly, and instead her answer sounds like a muffled yap.

"I think you are being combative. Don't you think she is being combative?" the officer says in a mocking and merry tone to the woman behind the window. The deputy is a white male, with a considerable double chin. His eyes are small, piercing, showing great pleasure in the moment.

"You can have a seat," says the morally-bothered young male.

"Ok." I respond and move back to the bench I was sitting earlier. I glance back at the woman in pink shorts. She is now rattling off her basic information regarding social security number, address, etc.

The inmate next to me, who has blonde stringy hair and weathered hands, seems to have been agitated by something and begins to yell, "I am a veteran!"

"I served this country at war!!"

"I have watched my brothers die next to me."

He stands up and continues, his voice cracking with emotion, "I served to protect you. I do not deserve this. I am a veteran of war…"

Out of unknown locations are several jail guards surrounding the man with excessive speed. He is being forced back into a sitting position, which he fights. They have wrist and ankle restraints and he is quickly seized and muzzled. I look away. I want to give him some respect, not appear to be gawking while he is demoralized and beaten down. In the corner of my eye I see a guard, good looking, dark skin, well built, who is part of the action. From my peripheral, I can see him stand back to survey his efforts and if he needs to give the other guards his help, tighten the ankle restraint or manipulate the facial cover further. He seems satisfied, as do the other guards standing around the inmate, now subdued undignified. He walks past me and gives me a big grin. I think he thinks I am impressed. I am horrified. I do not look back at the veteran, not wanting to add to his shame. I am sad, very sad for him. The other guards, men and women, walk away, without a word, smug and proud.

"Andrea Smith?" I hear my name called.

The older female guard is back at the door looking at me with my paperwork. I stand and follow her out of the room. She leads me to a concrete closet with a half wall sporting a red "X" painted on the floor. My heart freezes when I realize this is the strip search area. The half wall gives some privacy from the other inmates in the pit, but also allows access necessary for other officers to join in the fun without limitation of number. I take a deep breath, "here we go" I think to myself. She has me stop and stand on the red "X" and face the wall. I am told to place my hands up and against the wall and spread my legs. The good looking guard comes over and stands next to me and the female guard. The two guards start laughing, not sure why. The older female guard begins to pat me down, while asking me if I have anything in my pockets or on my body that she should be aware of. I answer that

I have nothing, as she and the other guard chatter. It feels so awkward and I am thoroughly embarrassed, as though I am on show. I hate that this guy has to be looming over me and watching, and I question why this is done in front of all the other inmates in the pit, other than to add to the inmate shame tactics this jail seems to thrive on. Her pat down is done, she then asks me to go behind the half wall and turn around to get my next instruction. I turn the corner and rotate around. I can't see where the male officer went or if he is still on the other side of the half wall. I fear he is waiting to come in once I am asked to take my clothes off. I have read, and reread all Pima County Correctional Facility booklets. It clearly states that male and female guards have the right to search and even strip search inmates at their discretion, without regard to gender. Originally, I was so afraid of what hazards I may fall victim to as a result of having to live with accused and convicted criminals. After I researched the Pima County Jail assault charges, I learned the incarcerated were not my major threat; on the contrary, the majority of recorded assault charges were from the deputies and guards assaulting inmates, not inmate against inmate or inmate against guards. These men and women who have been given authority and ability, by record account, have been abusing their authority, taking advantage of the circumstances of those who are in their custody and have been criminally violent with the very people under their care and oversight. The tone and behavior I am now witnessing is a type of culture they all have been indoctrinated into. I am not surprised these criminal charges exist as evidence and a result of their intense hate and prejudice.

Knowing this, I stand ready to be stripped, afraid… afraid of the men and women who I must now surrender and succumb my body, my safety, my freedom and rights to. This causes my trembling to become uncontained.

"Take off your clothes, with your back to the wall, facing me," the female guard commands in a rehearsed tone.

I begin to remove my clothes piece by piece while she stands and watches. As each item drops, I become a spectacle laid bare to unkind eyes. I can't think clearly, my humiliation too great to envision a moment more shameful than this. The tension of my nerves cause my

trembles to become visible and my head becomes light from mortification. I am now completely naked, cold and ferociously shaking. She
then tells me to turn around. I turn and become even dizzier from the
little dignity I have leaving my spirit and body. Naked I stand and wait.
I shudder in one large quake as my hair stands from the instinctive
feeling that the male officer is now behind me. I am staring at a block
wall, cold, shivering, humiliated and dizzy, fearing there are more eyes
upon me. The female officer says something, but not to me, then I hear
a response. It is him... I am paralyzed. My eyes begin to burn, but I hold
the tears. Although I have no remaining pride to conjure, I won't show
weakness to them or anyone; I must be strong for my survival. I exhale
into a long sigh when she orders me to put my clothes back on, but
am confused why she directs me to keep my shorts off. I turn around
to grab my clothes and see I am alone with the female officer. I do not
know where he went or what he saw. My trembling becomes even more
severe as I quickly put my sports bra (required in jail), t-shirt and underwear back on, the only items at this moment I am permitted. I keep my
eyes fixed on the opening, as the female deputy leaves. I wait, feeling
foolish and vulnerable as I stand in a room without doors in my panties.
She returns with white, elastic waist, double knit, pants. "Put these on."
Printed in black on the right pant leg is "Pima County Jail." Dark smears
are all over the pants, and on one leg there is a foot print from a shoe.
She hands me the soiled pants. I am sickened. Then directs for me to
put my shorts in a plastic bag she has laid on a bench. With that I am
escorted out. I can now see the other male officer has since moved back
to his breakfast burrito in the mug shot area a few steps away.

Relieved to be dressed, I am led to the open sunken area that hosts
fifty to sixty other inmates, who seem a little less intimidating. It's the
guards who terrify me now, not the inmates. As I sit down, I am told that
I am not to cross a certain section within the sunken area that is designated, without any markings, for male inmates, nor am I to talk to them.

I am still lightheaded from the strip search, yet quickly recognize
that those in uniforms like to talk loud, laugh loud and cackle frequently in their lofty heightened space. At the moment, they are shaking their
phones, and showing each other the image displayed on their screen. It

appears they are playing "Fat Face" or one of those picture programs that distorts the person's picture once you shake your phone. This seems to be fun for them as they group together in this highly productive action.

Across from me is a small woman with long bleached blonde hair and three inch dark roots at the crown of her head. She appears to be in her thirties, but I have a feeling she is much younger; most likely a hard life has taken some of her youth and beauty. She, like me, is wearing jail issued clothing; however, her white ensemble includes a top as well. She has a pretty face, but it is weathered; her makeup is smeared, and she is violently shaking, clearly withdrawing. She looks at me and I smile at her; she attempts to smile back, but stops at a smirk. I can tell she is suffering. My heart quickly wants to reach out to her, she seems so lost, so sad, so sick. I don't know what I can do to help her, but I want to figure out how I can. I look to my right to see if anyone else is concerned and see a Caucasian girl in her twenties. She is a bit overweight and not interested in the girl across from her. Her hair is long and dark, her face very pleasant, with round large eyes and full lips. She seems frustrated and antsy. I feel the same, but am in no hurry, I guess, as I have nowhere else to go… not for a while. She flips her hair back and forth and runs her fingers through the top at her scalp. There are several women that appear to be American Indian. Tucson is next to several Indian Reservations. They all have extremely long dark hair. They huddle together in a pack. The last female in this area is a girl who seems to be very young. She has light brown hair and an attractive face. She is still in her street clothes, t-shirt and jeans. Her hair is shoulder length with big curls that lay loosely around her shoulders.

That is all the women I can see. The men definitely outnumber the females, and monopolize the majority of the pit.

I look back at the girl with long bleached hair. Her entire body shakes profusely and the agony of her withdrawal is apparent. She rests her torso on her legs and lets her head fall forward; her hair spills down the sides of her legs and rests on the floor. I want to soothe her, but feel helpless and afraid that any act of kindness shown to her would result in severe penalties to me by the guards.

I am startled by loud shouting, muffled groaning and a big scurry of guards grouped by the very room I just left. All of the inmates, including me, jump in our seats and look over to see what is going on. The older female guard who strip searched me was backing up through the door with a video camera in hand, propped in position. I see the other guards, a total of four male and female, holding and restraining the veteran, twisting his arm and pushing him to walk. He is shouting but his face is muzzled. The guards are forcing him to go to the strip-search area, while the older female guard keeps the camera on the soldier. I can tell the veteran is fighting, and getting quite roughed up in the process. I watch with my jaw dropped as they push and pull him on the other side of the half wall and into the closet. I can no longer see him but do see the "camerawoman" turn the corner into the strip area maintaining a good view of the soldier, while continually aiming the video camera on him. I can hear him, he is being stripped under duress. He is yelling, moaning, and there are sounds of wrestling. Other guards walk over, go inside or peer around the wall to watch. His humiliation is far beyond mine, with a male and female audience. The blood in my face drains as I think of him in there and what he must be enduring. I recognize the guards have to protect themselves, as well the other inmates, but I don't understand what this man has done to have to suffer this level of degradation. I am truly grieved that one of our country's heroes is being disrespected and belittled in such a demoralizing way. All I saw him actually do is stand and begin to talk. He was never addressed or asked to sit and remain quiet, warned of the penalty of such an outburst, just tackled. I am greatly disturbed, disgusted and afraid. The thought of my long duration under the care of these people causes me to shudder again, from my nerves, from the cold room, from fear of what is to come for me, for my heartbreak for this soldier.

The veteran's groans become quieted and then he is silent. I see him reappear a few minutes later from the half wall. Although being manhandled by the group of guards and still the focus of that camera, he now walks passively, dejected and without mettle. The guards are aggressive with him, but the veteran has lost all fight in his spirit. He is taken past the pit and into a numbered cell, of which dramatically locks with one loud echoing clank.

The sound of my breathing is loud in my head. I realize my chest is heaving from my emotions. I turn my gaze from the locked cell and glance back at the girl who was withdrawing across from me. She has fallen asleep. She is sitting, but her torso is slumped over her lap and head bent forward, hair spilling all around. Her trembling has quieted and I am thankful that she was able to get some relief from her suffering.

I take a deep breath, realizing that my own safety, my physical rights, and my life are in the hands, not of my own, but of these guards who sit over me. Like the woman across from me, I begin to shake once again.

Chapter 3

"Do not hide Your face from me;
Do not turn Your servant away in anger;
You have been my help; Do not leave me nor forsake me,
O God of my salvation." Psalm 27:9

JAIL: HOUR FIVE

"Fuck you." a guard says in jest to his associate at the desk.

"Hey, You!!! Porker!" another guard yells, pointing to the pit and at the inmate to my left. "Porker!!! Yeah you! Get your feet down." This provocation ignites his colleagues to double over in laughter as the guard roars pointing at the young woman.

I sit stupefied. She has one foot propped up under her leg. The pathetic look on her face, makes my stomach sick. She stares at the guards shocked, horrified, looking pitiful. She immediately pulls her foot out from under her leg and places both feet on the floor. Disgusted and feeling bad for the young woman, I look at her and whisper, "How rude!" Our eyes lock as she scoots closer to me on the bench. She is still running her fingers through her hair at the forehead and back; probably a nervous reaction to her current desperation. Since she is now closer, I mouth the words, "I'm so sorry." Her eyes become full of tears, but she holds her face to the side so the guards are unable see her defeat.

"They were mocking me during the strip search about my weight, saying I am fat and calling me 'Porker'." she says to me in a soft whisper.

Her eyes were wet and teary, her voice trembles and cracks with emotion. She stiffens and runs her fingers through her hair in an effort to hold in the tears. I am horrified.

"That is terrible!" I say in response. It really was terrible. "They have no right," I say... but in reality I guess they do... However, in my anger

I continue my venting. "Just look at them. They're fat, AND ugly. They mock you, but let's be honest, they're the ones that are repulsive. I am sorry they did that." I lean in closer, "It takes more work and energy for them to be this rude than it would for them to just be professional," I say.

Every word they speak, every action they make is overtly hostile, even startling. I am shocked at how deliberately they sneer, the energy they put into their tone and depths of their great hatred toward us, complete strangers, yet they feel justified in their hostility. They intend only to degrade, taunt and provoke. A dramatic contrast to the jovial and sociable demeanor they have one to another. It is like they turn on and off a switch; one moment they speak and spit with an insolent and ferocious tone, adding their glares and snarls with great force and then instantly shift back to pleasantry as they joke and jest among each other. How does that work? How can they modify their personality so dramatically in seconds? Most importantly, how can they treat another human the way they did this young woman? They took pleasure in insulting her for her weight while they stripped her down and intentionally humiliated her.

Tucson has a high violent crime rate. Being so close to the border and the extreme level of drugs that travel through our city brings serious offenders, with crimes far outweighing our city size. These guards and deputies are at risk, so I appreciate the need to have tight control and safety. However, their behavior incites, even provokes. This makes very little sense in safety and control. I have myself, a non-volatile person, felt my own blood boil with the aggressive and cruel demeanor they all have adopted. If they could show professionalism and calm control, they would be more powerful, more respected and would see less inmate reaction.

I look into the eyes of this stranger, yet a new friend made out of shared misery. Her eyes are watery and show that her spirit is injured. "I am sorry," I say again.

"Hey, you ladies, keep it down." says the same guard who just asked the young woman to move her foot.

I freeze, startled and swallow air. I was only told that I was not to talk to the men. I was not instructed that I could not talk to anyone. My alarm intensifies as the same guard begins to walk toward me. He is looking straight at the young woman he called "Porker" and me, taking strong deliberate steps for effect as he approaches us. His keys and contraptions on his belt are loud and jingle as he walks down the pit's stairs. This is not good, I think to myself, as my blood drains from my head. Not sure what I have done, but his theatrical stomp as he heads in our direction is clearly for our benefit. The young woman and I sit frozen as we watch him march toward us. Fear envelopes me, realizing how truly powerless I am and will be every day I serve. I lament that I have to surrender myself to these vicious men and women as my penalty. The guard intentionally and dramatically stops right in front of us, ominously hovering over, looking down at us while puffing his chest. Only inches away as he stands, glaring, his face exuding excessive stern to ensure we understand the impact of our behavior. He laughs at us and turns, pleased with himself that he got the desired frightened responses he so had hoped for and anticipated. He then walks over to the sleeping woman, whose trembling has subsided as she rests. The act of tormenting us had clearly emboldened him and he relishes in the sovereignty he has over each person who sits in this pit. At this point he has decided to direct his attention to the blonde addict. He bends down, leaning over her, with his face close to hers. Her sleep has caused her upper body to fall down to the side and her head is now resting peacefully on the bench, unaware of what looms above her.

"Hey, wake up!" he booms in her ear. "You can't lay down. Sit up." he says with great force.

She wakes startled, disoriented. He continued to stand above her, menacing, with all the authority given to him as he glares. A strong quake of tremors strike through her body as she comes back to reality and aware of his commanding presence gloating over her. He dramatically throws his arms in the air, exasperated by her disoriented movements and condition. With a loud groan, he barks at her, "Come with me!"

Without a word, she awkwardly stands up, having been jolted out of her sleep. Her body joins the assault, as violent trembles erupt again while being led by the supercilious guard up the steps.

"Where the fuck you taking her?" another guard in the elevated desk area yells.

"Cell 5, I guess." says the other with his hand gripping the woman's arm.

"No, not 5, take her to 3." I hear ring back.

"3? Ok." he answers, enjoying the spectacle he has made of the girl and the audience he has in his captivity.

Off they go to the windowed cell number 3 reserved and designated for the lowest and most wayward. I say a silent prayer, hoping she can freely lay down her head and find rest from her agony and reality of the cage she now is locked.

My heart groans for her… and for the Veteran. My family has given their lives for those suffering, down trodden and beaten. I was raised to reach out to those who suffer, to help, to minister, but here I sit unable to help anyone.

My parents were kids of missionaries, then on to be missionaries themselves and finally pastors of a large mega church in the desert. Life for them has been one of hardship, destitution, but also blessing. They have comforted people in sickness, desperate poverty, and horrible loss. My father and mother have dedicated themselves to preaching His Word, but also sharing that Message through compassion and care. My father had a specific theme as he taught and that theme was "grace and compassion", of which he even named his church.

My father's compassionate heart was a reflection of his own father. When he was a teenager, his father and mother felt that it was their calling to go to the mission field, specifically led to Cuba. My grandfather was a military technician with five children, living humbly. With Cuba as their believed assignment, they reached out to their local church in California to receive blessing and an endorsement from the Pastor and his congregation. The Pastor asked my grandfather if he could rent my grandparents' house as a way to support them while ministering in Cuba. My grandparents felt this proposition was an answer from God, as a source of income while they served, and with that they left for Cuba immediately. With my father's help, my grandfather began their

ministry by physically building and constructing small church buildings throughout Cuba, and preaching to anyone who would listen. My
father, extremely intelligent, picked up the Spanish language quickly
and began interpreting for his dad. The family immediately fell in love
with Cuba and its people. The warm, humid climate, fertile soil and
beautiful beaches became their home. I would sit at my father's feet and
listen to him describe gentle plains, green mountains greeted by white
soft beaches that touch a deep, dark, beautiful sapphire blue ocean. My
mom would reminisce of the large avocados that she would just salt
and eat alone with a fork, tomatoes that were as big as grapefruit and
royal palms that peppered the brilliantly magnificent and tranquil land.

My mother, Deborah, was also brought by her parents to Cuba as a
teenager. Her story very different from my dad's. Deborah's father was
a successful executive; her mother, a registered nurse. Coming from a
more influential social status, they left their comfortable income and
gave everything they had to proclaim the Message they believed in.
Deborah was, at the time, a popular and beautiful sixteen-year old, who
wanted nothing to do with leaving her very handsome hockey playing
boyfriend or her many dear and much-loved girlfriends in Vancouver,
Canada. At first she wouldn't commit to becoming part of Cuba or its
lure. She continued, instead, to write letters and strategize with her boyfriend her big escape back to Canada, which they acted out with great
failure. Her good-looking knight flew into Cuba, with a predesigned
time and place she was to meet him, at which time she ran from her
home and met him with a small bag of clothes. As Deborah and her
champion walked excitedly and hurriedly through the airport doors,
they felt shock come over them and stood paralyzed. Before them was
her mother waiting at the airport check in. Instead of flying off into the
sunset with her man, she was escorted by her mother, who said not a
word, back to her family car. The hockey playing knight; sent home
never to have contact with her daughter again; a devastating blow to
my mother's love affair.

My mother's mother, Naomi, was the core of her family. She was
tiny in stature, but her strength was foundational and relied on by all.
Naomi, a good mother, was not affectionate, but she was comforting.

She ran a structured home, put a lot of emphasis on manners, made sure every meal included proper linens and freshly polished silverware. She loved her daughters (my mother's older sister was twenty and newly married in Canada), but warmth wasn't how she expressed it. She was beautiful, had a heart for people in need and used her nursing skills to help those who were sick or injured. Sam, my mother's father, was a hardworking business man who loved the center of attention and was talented at getting an audience. He was a skilled speaker, driven, focused and successful in everything he did. He particularly loved being catered to by his wife and daughters, happy that his conservative wife, who preferred him to shine, allowed him to focus on his business or now his ministry. Sam was confident that Naomi would always keep things in order as he directed his attention on his newest passion: speaking the Word. They had heard from some locals that a young missionary kid had picked up the language and was interpreting for his father. With this knowledge, Sam reached out to my father's parents, to see if their son would also interpret for him. They agreed and sent my father on a new scheduled trek that he was to take daily to translate Sam's message.

I think my mother fell in love with Anna, my dad's mother, before she ever fell in love with my dad. Anna was the complete opposite of her own mother. Anna wasn't much worried about housekeeping, instead focused on the comfort food which she served her husband and each of her four children; her eldest fifth child at the time married and living in the States. Her hair was red; she was round and indelicate, took little stock in make-up or fancy dresses, in comparison to Naomi's starched and pressed skirts and perfectly trim waistline. Anna's house smelled of apple pie and each kid was kissed and hugged by mom and dad as a required greeting no matter how many times they were seen that day.

My mother had her first meal at Abram and Anna's and sat and watched the kids plop down on their chairs at the dinner table with forks in hand as Abram went from child to child and kissed each. Anna and Abram adopted everyone, Abram was called "Dad" by all. Even when I was an adult living in Tucson, the entire church only knew my grandfather as "Dad." On this day, my mom sat at the table and Abram leaned in and gave my mom a warm sloppy kiss before he took his own seat at the table. This action didn't surprise the other children, they appeared so accustomed to it, yet my mother was stunned and had never known such affection by either of her parents. Anna then presented the meal, which was boiled eggs piled in a large bowl with hot melting butter that ran down and pooled at its base. My mother had not seen eggs served for dinner, let alone smothered in butter. She told me that that meal was the most delicious dinner she ever had. Like the warm butter, her heart melted and she was home.

My mom made it a habit, from that day forward, to go visit Anna regularly. She would sit and talk to her, listen to her life stories, feel her warmth, soak in her affection. My mom loved to watch Anna with her kids. She would giggle from Anna's sweet banter with her husband, who always outwardly and unabashedly loved them all with her whole heart. Anna was sassy like my mom, having a quick wit that they all cherished and enjoyed. Their home was as humble as they were, with holes where daylight would shine through the walls. They were living on basics, what they could find, scavenge, or grow, with absolutely no income coming in. The local people fell in love with Abram and Anna's family. They, although destitute themselves, would bring to the family fruit, vegetables and meat that they had handpicked or just slaughtered from their own gardens and livestock.

The pastor who promised to support them and pay rent, never paid, and was living in Abram's home for free. The rent was beyond past due, they had little money and the outcome became very grim. A letter came from the church at the dire hour, which was exciting to the family who had prayed and hoped each day for that check to arrive. They believed that inside that envelope was the payment for all past unpaid rent. My dad was hopeful that what was due would, that day, be finally received, but he also feared that his family was being taken advantage of not only by a friend, but someone who claimed to be a minister of the Gospel.

Regrettably, my father's fears were soon realized. There was no money in the envelope, only a note from the Pastor declaring he had no intention of paying them past rent, nor would he in the future. If Abram wanted to take possession of the house in California, he would have to come back and do so in person. My father felt his rage build, yet stopped when he heard his father cry out, "God be praised!..."

My grandfather was on his knees with his arms raised to heaven.

"God be praised!" Abram cried louder, "I praise, You, my God!!" he shouted again as his tears ran down his face, still on the floor, looking up to the ceiling and calling out to his heavenly Father.

Now Abram forced himself to stand, jolting my father with astonishment when Abram jumped, again he jumped, and continued to shout, "I WILL praise You my God."

My father stood stunned as he watched his precious dad drive himself, force himself to dance... and he did, he danced.

My grandfather dancing is something very familiar to me. He danced all the time. I especially remember him at the altar at the church dancing his determined stomp, a precious sight I watched too many times to count. Today, it makes me miss him so desperately. My grandfather, Abram, danced, with true abandonment to God; which is why I was the first one at the altar to join him.

"God be praised, for clothing me, for the roof over our head, for Your faithfulness and love, for knowing every hair on each of our heads. God be praised!!!" Abram chanted into a song, stomping in rejection of his current forecast.

My father watched as his mother wept, yet with a sincere smile of endurance on her face, signing on to Abram's faith; he turned back to his father, in the mist of great despair, and watched bewildered as Abram did nothing else but praise his God.

With that Abram pulled together their last remaining pennies and purchased a boat fair to return home. When Abram arrived in California, he reached the front door and knocked... knocked at the door of his own home and the fruition of his entire life savings. In a matter of minutes what came into view was the face of a surprised and obscene so-called minister standing comfortably and contentedly inside.

In my grandfather's hand was an envelope that he had pulled out from his jacket. Abram said nothing, but handed it to the offender of my father's wrath. With that, my grandfather turned and walked away.

When Abram returned to Cuba, my father questioned him, "What did you say?"

"I said nothing," Abram answered while putting away his clothes from his suitcase.

"Then what happened?" my father pressed.

"I handed him something," Abram said without emotion or pause.

Frustrated my father demanded answers. "Dad, what did you hand him?"

"Did you give him a legal document or some forewarning of a potential suit?"

My father felt that at this point the best avenue for him and his family to find justice was legally.

"No," was Abram's answer.

"Then what did you give that man? "WHAT?" my father begged.

Abram responded, "I gave him the deed."

Chapter 4

"Have mercy on me, O Lᴏʀᴅ, for I am weak;
O Lᴏʀᴅ, heal me, for my bones are troubled." Psalm 6:2

JAIL: HOUR SIX

"Andrea Smith?" I hear my name called. The good looking guard that was busy eating a burrito the last time I saw him, was now calling my name. The sound of his voice causes my hair on the back of my head to stand, reminding me of its sound when standing naked in the concrete closet. He smiles and waves for me to follow him. I get up and do as I am told. He takes me to the mug shot area. First he places his hands on my shoulders once in the general area and moves me to stand facing a large computer-type device with my back to him. It has a lit screen, which lays flat like a table. He is behind me. I feel him move in close and his body presses against mine; his chest, torso and hips touching the back of me. He slides his hands down my arms to my hands, grabs them both with his and begins separating my fingers tenderly. I stiffen scared, while his breath heats my neck. I panic, confused what to do. Should I jump away and incite his fury, releasing the powers of the authority he has over me, or endure his touch? He then puts each of my fingers on the screen. I realize I am getting finger printed. I relax a bit, relieved for the moment that this is part of the check-in process, yet still sickened by the way in which he touches me. The guard leans in closer. I feel uncomfortable and scared once again.

"Your hands are so tiny. I've never seen such tiny hands," he says breathy, causing goose bumps to rise on my neck from his words.

My hands are small, but it is entirely unlikely that he hasn't seen any comparable or smaller. He releases his grip and backs away. This makes my anxiety dissipate as his body is no longer against mine. He directs me to sit in a chair and he wraps an appalling grey blanket around my shoulders and neck. I see the camera and try to make a pleasant face. I am there a while and before I know it, I realize that I have been looking around, distracted by the interactions of the guards. With utter disgust I watch them, and whatever expression I was trying to hold is long gone. The two guards are chatting, they stop, and the camera man gives the other the ok. The blanket is taken off of me and I am told to stand.

The two guards say something to each other, which inspires the cameraman to lift his middle finger at us as we walk away. This makes the other chuckle. As we approach the pit, the same guard who uses terms such as 'Porker' yells, "Jesus Christ, how long does it take you to get her processed?"

"Shut up, just doing my job," says the guard who breathed on my neck.

From his elevated desk, the other continues, now looking at me, "How long have you been waiting?"

I hesitate. I don't want to be included in their banter. I stutter, "… I… Uh… I have been sitting here for three hours," I respond as I am motioned to sit down.

"How 'bout we reach a new record for length of time to process," he says to the other guards provokingly. Then he looks at a younger, female guard who is sitting at her desk nearby, "What's taking you so long. Can't you do your job and get this young lady to her block." He jests and smacks the side of another guard. She rolls her eyes and smirks, then goes back to her paperwork.

A group of young people file in, led by a man wearing a cheesy Hawaiian shirt. He walks with a strange geeky bounce, hips forward and belly out, and his head wobbles with each step in a very pompous manner. Each are given a hanging guest tag, then a quick explanation of the rules from one of the guards. The teenagers look around and observe the depth of the space and its crude setting. They take in the gravity of this hell, which reveals their relief that they are only visiting. The adult with the Hawaiian shirt has a strange grin on his face. I recognize him, and he recognizes me. I look away as my eyes and face burn with humiliation. They are a local church youth group doing an "outreach". The youth are respectful, they do not look at the inmates. The adult, however, is very brazen as he gawks and ogles with his head shaking back and forth, chin high in the air. He stares at me, yet I continue to look away as he gloats. He enjoys the irony, as I too have been part of jail ministry "outreaches". I have spoken about my experience of attempting suicide in this very jail, where I am now being processed. I watch the kids walk by, each feeling so far from the inferno of where I am now, just as I felt back then. With that, they are gone, off to the Chapel, where they will share their stories and hope to save those whom are wretched and lowly, people like me.

The detained young female near me stretches and moves in closer. I think she has something to say to me....

"Fuck!" a male inmate yells, then stands up.

He is young, hair braided into cornrows close to his head, wearing street clothes, long athletic pants and a t-shirt. His hair is long, but shortened by his braids. His eyes have dark lashes that naturally outline his eyes as though wearing eyeliner. He is a beautiful boy. He reminds me of my nephew, with a striking skin tone. He must be of both Caucasian and African-American descent to have such a lovely golden color to his skin. He is wearing tennis shoes without laces. His shoes sit open, with the tongues hanging out looking strange and awkward. A guard storms over to him.

"Man, I was just telling this guy to back off and was trying to find a place to relocate," he appeals, yet to the guard there was no conversation required. He was immediately escorted to a tempered glass cage.

The boy indeed said a bad word and got 'locked up' for such; yet this was on the heels of those very standards supervising guards who had just shouted, "fuck" repeatedly, called people "ass", sacrilegiously used, "Jesus Christ" to emphasize their frustration, all while using their middle finger as their preferred form of sign language.

Another hour passes and I try to reposition myself, having been sitting in that one spot for a total of four hours, without resting my head, ensuring I kept both my feet on the floor.

The young girl has inched even closer. I look at her and smile. Instinctively I lean in and whisper, "Are you ok?", but then quickly look back at the guards, realizing speaking to her was probably not a good idea.

"No… not really," she whispers. "I am here for a traffic ticket I never paid!"

Oh my gosh!... I look at her in disbelief. "Really?" I ask.

How crazy I think to myself. I knew an officer could arrest such violators, but didn't know the infraction required actual jail time.

"I am so embarrassed. The strip search was so bad," she says, still whispering.

A strip search for an unpaid traffic ticket? I nod and agree, then look at the guards, afraid of the consequences of my quiet conversation.

"I think the rule is, if you sit close and whisper you are ok," she explains.

This possibility could be true, but doesn't explain what I was doing wrong when whispering with the girl on my left.

"My mom is picking me up. I thought I paid my ticket. My family is really upset with me. This place is terrible. I never want to ever come back again," she says in a sporadic sequence of thought.

"Agreed." I concur.

Her sweet face makes me want to hug her. I want to hug her for her mom who is probably waiting in the parking lot now and most likely has been for some time.

"How old are you?" I ask, wondering if she is in the right place.

"I am nineteen," she answers.

Her hair is soft, with round curls like my daughter's. Her skin and face reveal innocence. I know the moment she is out of these doors, in the parking lot and looking at her Mom, a flood of tears will surface, and the family that she was so worried about will hold her and console her. Her punishment has been far beyond anything they could add.

This makes my heart and mind think of my own parents. My father hugged me just the night before and kissed the top of my head in the same manner I did my own children as I left this morning. As I began to turn away, my dad grabbed my shoulders and turned me back to face him square in the eye and said, "Andrea, I am proud of you."

His statement stung my eyes, throat, and caused my chest to fill with air. He is still proud of me? A beaten, humiliated woman being sent to where only the criminals go? My beautiful dad, my precious father, my heart truly thanks you for those words! I then turned to my mother. She held me and sobbed; I sobbed with her.

"Can we take you there and drop you off? I don't want you going alone." My mother pleads.

This kind offer was not proposed by my husband, which also stings. I know it is best that I not have my parents take me. My emotions need to be in check, as I have to be strong for what is ahead…. There's no crying in jail, or so had I hoped.

A guard calls someone's name. The young nineteen-year old girl stands with excitement. It looks like her stay, for however many hours, has now passed and she will be in the arms of her family she fears will never forgive her. Her eyes fill with tears which begin to fall down her cheeks as she walks the long hallway to her freedom. A harsh lesson, a terrible experience, yet now soon to be just a memory.

Daniel and Deborah, CUBA, 1959

With my mom's love and admiration for Anna, and her frequency of visiting my grandparent's home, she and my father quickly become true friends. I believe my mom became enamored by my father's deep intellect and his unwavering conviction. My mom and my dad soon began to share long walks along the exquisite country side of Cuba and its tropical landscape, while visiting local friends to share fruit, vegetables, or to help where needed.

Their hearts for each other began to run deep as they roamed the gentle paradise. As Columbus said when he saw Cuba, "This is the most beautiful land that human eyes ever beheld." My father became friends with a local male prostitute named Paul. He was younger than my dad and had no other way to survive, so he did what he needed to. My father and grandparent's accepted Paul as their own. The boy would come around to hear my father translate a beautiful message of hope, grace and forgiveness. Abram and Anna never gave any illusions that life would be easier once you believed, or that prosperity and perfection awaited. They too lived each day by faith, and were sometimes hungry. Their message of grace was felt and became true to Paul too. Soon Paul was wearing less provocative clothes. He started helping out in the church, such as building, cleaning and even translating. The Word of God became so real and so transforming, he decided to leave his only known source of income and began sleeping on the floor of the church. Anna set a chair that waited for Paul at every family meal, and Abram greeted him with a kiss.

My mother and father became enraptured in this mission, the people they were serving and each other. All of this came to a quick end when Abram and Anna announced, for the safety of their children, they needed to leave Cuba and go back to the States.

While both my father's and mother's parents reached out to serve and work with the Cuban people, the Cuban environment became increasingly hostile and threatened by its leadership. Student riots and demonstrations became frequent and aggressive. To overpower the growing discontent amongst his people, Fulgencio Batista, Cuban elected President, decided to increase censorship of all media, while empowering his anti-Communist secret police to carry out wide-scale violence, torture and public executions; ultimately killing anywhere from 1,000 to 20,000 people. These actions became a catalyst to the resistance led by Fidel Castro with his urban and rural-based guerrilla support.

Both my grandparents and the local people supported and believed that Fidel Castro would be the answer to their suffering. They had no way of knowing the actual monster he was.

The casualties of the escalating battle and the atrocities being acted out by the regime were too dangerous for Abram and Anna to continue their work in the country. They felt that they could not continue and allow the four children in their care to be in harm's way. So they decided to leave Cuba.

My mother's parents chose to stay and continue their work. Sam, my mother's father, passionately and with great conviction, proclaimed that he would preach the Gospel through any danger or threat Satan would throw his way. He would not be "deterred from the Great Commission, even in days of great tribulation."

This was the end of my parent's romance (or so they thought); their last moments together were passionate and grief-stricken. Before my dad boarded the boat to take him to the States, he confessed to my mother that he felt he should cut off all contact. His heart and spirit tested by the passion of their last moments. My mom was devastated. Her love for him was unbearable and she became completely inconsolable that God was causing them to be divided not only physically, but now, due to my father's conviction, in spirit too.

Abram, Anna and their children were gone. My mom was left heartbroken and full of despair. She not only lost her heart's flame, but a dear friendship and a place of warmth she found in Anna.

Sam continued to preach with fervency, and the family's dedication to endure touched the Cuban people. Sam began to minister alongside a new found friend, Stephen. Stephen and his wife had a jeep, which they, with Sam, would take from village to village deep in the country conducting evening services under a small light and packed audience.

On one such adventure, Sam and Stephen, with their wives and children, drove the jeep into the rural countryside to conduct an evening service, where locals were congregating for a compelling lesson in the Bible. In addition to the four adults, there was also Stephen's four children, and my mother, all packed in the jeep. One little boy, only four years old, had fallen asleep on the vehicle's floor by my mother's feet. She softly picked him up and pulled him onto her lap so that he could rest his little head on her knees, rather than her shoe.

Suddenly, the jeep was under fire! The sound of ringing from metal hitting metal, as bullets ricochet, and glass broke. No one breathed, no one screamed, even the wind seemed to have stopped. The car sat motionless, the only noise was that of bullets penetrating, bouncing, singing. Stephen was hit in his right eye. He slumped over the gear shift, blood everywhere: on the window, steering wheel, and dash board. My mother then heard her own voice moaning as her body jolted and moved. Then the sensation of warm liquid ran down her legs, pooling at her feet. She looked and saw both of her feet were shot, her heels are completely detached. The top half of her shoes still on, yet the backs gone, showing bone and flesh. My grandmother turned toward her daughter, without expression, saying nothing, and began to tend to her daughter's feet. The children were now all awake. The four year old boy was sitting up, pressing tightly into my mother's arms, yet he too remained silent, scared, without breath as he watched his father's blood drain from his head, unconscious, and the fragments that remain of my mother's feet. Sam scrambled for his Spanish Gospel tracts and leaped out of the jeep. Sam called out to the group of young guerillas to declare that they are merely missionaries, not military. The rebels, realizing their grave error, ran to the jeep to aid and help the wounded. Sam handed them his Gospel tracts as evidence of their nonmilitary status, and then asked them if they would like to accept Jesus as their Lord and Savior.

The confused rebels stopped, looked at each other, then implored Sam to get in the car and drive his daughter, wife and friends to the hospital; but Sam instead began to orate, recognizing the significance of the moment, remembering his previous declarations, deciding first his devotion needed to be demonstrated.

My mom began to cry, "please… daddy." She heard herself groan as an acute and deep ache began to take over, along with the smell and taste of metal, evidence of the bullet fragments that had lodged in her body that were now scenting her nose and flavoring her mouth.

Sam continued to proselytize, his voice getting louder, his enthusiasm rising at the significance of the moment. My grandmother yelled, "Samuel, your daughter is shot! Stephen is dying!!!"

"Prisa, Prisa! (hurry, hurry)" the guerillas called.

Sam was relentless, his passion for the lives of the young men equaled the gravity of the situation. The guerillas became moved by his fervor and relented to his requests, took his tracts and accepted Jesus in the middle of the scene.

"Prisa, prisa!!" they yelled.

Deborah and Stephen were bleeding and both hanging onto life, but were now finally on their way to the nearest hospital, hours away.

My mom's feet were reassembled by the Cuban doctors and her legs and feet casted. Remarkably Stephen survived. His right eye removed and his face unrepairable, but he lived to continue his work and be a very present father to his children. His little boy's life also miraculously spared. Had my mother not picked him up just seconds before the attack, his entire body would have resembled what remained of my mother's feet.

The jeep had sixty four bullet holes and not one of its passengers died.

My mom now laid in the bed of a third world hospital. Her life, her future, now in the doctor's hands and in him was her only hope to ever walk again.

Chapter 5

"My harp is turned to mourning,
And my flute to the voice of those who weep." Job 30:31

JAIL: DAY ONE, SEVEN HOURS

My name is once again called. This time it is the female guard that rolled her eyes when being teased. She asks me to follow her. I was relieved to be leaving and was looking forward to a bed, or somewhere I could relax; yet it won't be long before I wished I never left that pit. She takes me from the main building to another building. It's a much smaller building resembling a gymnasium without windows. This smaller building was much cruder than the previous. The block walls are not painted, there are no cells, just large communal rooms, where multitudes of inmates sleep together. We walk down the hallway to shelves and she asks me what size I wear.

"Size 2," I answer.

She becomes annoyed by my answer and throws at me a red XS shirt and pants, "Here." They are thick and feel stiff. "What size shoe?"

"Size 5," I say.

"The smallest size we have is size 8," she responds and then tosses me two size 8 shoes, which I slip on. They are nude, flesh colored, rubber; not flip flops but open in the back. My feet swim in them. I try to walk, but struggle. Every step I take causes me to trip, lose a shoe, then turn back to retrieve it.

I am escorted to a small one-person bathroom.

"I need you to change into your reds. You can leave your t-shirt on under your reds, but I need the white pants back."

"Ok," I say and wait for her to leave. We stand and stare at each other awkwardly. I wait... she waits.

"I have to strip search you." she looks at me tired, as though I should have known.

"I was already strip searched?" I ask stunned.

"I have to do it again," she says annoyed.

"You do?" ...Seriously? My heart begins to beat hard.

"Take your clothes off, one at a time, and put them here." She points to a white plastic chair sitting across from the toilet. The bathroom is too small to fit us both, so she stands holding the door open, which leaves me exposed to the hallway. I feel as though I am going to faint. I was so geared up for the last search, and thought that my humiliation was now over. I was wrong. I start the process; one by one I remove my clothes. I feel the tears welling up in my eyes. My breathing is short and panicked. I stand and look at her once every item is off, all dignity gone.

"Turn around." I feel sick. The room is small and it smells of sewer.

I turn with my back to her, the hair on my neck stands from a feeling that at any second people in the hallway behind me will walk by. This building houses both male and female inmates, and was just littered with male inmates and guards lined up against the walls minutes ago.

"Bend over." she says.

"What?" I ask.

"Bend over." she says again.

My heart stands still, frozen. The blood leaves my head and I feel all warmth depart.

"Bend over and touch your toes." Her voice is raised as she adds the emphasis on each consonant for impact.

"No, no, no, no. Please God, NO! ...Please? ....God?" I plead under my breath.

I slowly, bend over and touch my toes. My stomach becomes queasy and the feeling of nausea overtakes me. Blood rushes back to my head. The door is open, who else is going to be part of this show? My head and neck are pulsing, as my heart beats rapidly, its drum pounds in my ears.

"Take your hands and spread your cheeks." she says in a sharp voice.

What? I can't... "Please? God? Please?" Once again I pray in vain.

My cries bounce off heaven's floor. God has been silent, how foolish to ask Him to rescue me now.

I hesitate. My body trembles with such force that my hands feel as though asleep... but I do as I am told.

My head is almost touching the foul bathroom floor, my face inches from the toilet; frightened by the busy hallway behind me as she stands with the door propped open; yet I remain in this position frozen, degraded. Could life be any lower? I hear a click, then the spot from a flashlight's target circle around on the bathroom floor near my face, up my legs and eventually to and on my genitals. My face tingles with the intensity of my mortification. My throat and chest burn with shame. Why? What did I ever do to deserve this type of disgrace?

"Put your reds on." she says as she clicks off the flashlight.

I have nothing left, my spirit has fallen into a great abyss of shame. This woman enjoyed herself. She found pleasure in my disgrace. I have been demoralized, forced naked, sexually exposed, against my will; humiliated before eyes that ridicule and condescend. I am not angry, I am devastated. I am without spirit, numb, and truly just want to die as I put on my jail issued clothes.

With my head low, body slumped, I follow her out of the bathroom, back into the hallway. I am led and told to enter a small closet. Once again, the door closes behind me and locks. It is not a closet, it is a cellar, a dungeon, with one 3"X5" window on the door that is covered by a curtain on the outside. I am encased by four block walls, cement floor with only one white plastic chair that sits in its center. There is no water or toilet, just a black cellar with an outdoor plastic chair of which I collapse into. Light sneaks in and out, as the window's small curtain is pulled back periodically for onlookers to see their spectacle. I feel this is a test to catch me... waiting for me to scream, stand up, start punching walls, call out; a way to claim that I am under the influence, or mentally disturbed. However, I have nothing in my soul, my spirit, or my body to even move from this chair. They are watching me, I can't see them, but the change in light from each pull of the curtain lets me know their eyes are there. I sit...

and sit as time drags by. I am sure most, at some point, need to use the bathroom; adding to the fun for those behind the curtain to see each squirm and finally resort to having to defecate on themselves; but I am able to shut everything down, my soul has left my body in its despair. If only I could find a hole to lie in and die. Why should I continue? I am as low and as defiled as I can be. Here I sit in a tiny dark cell, humiliated, and without hope, with a husband who loves me not and my body made to strip and spread. I do wish I could just perish, be taken out of my misery, removed from this reality by sleep that offers no wake.

"Have you turned from me, God?" I say softly, no longer worried about the curtain that continues to be moved aside. "Are You angry with me?" I call louder, looking toward the ceiling as if He were there. "I have loved You, served You, worshipped You. I followed Your commands and You arrested me, You have thrown me in jail. What have I ever done to deserve Your wrath? Is this where You would have me sit? Please Jesus, help me."

My heart crumbles, as silence and loneliness surrounds me. I wish for my life to be done… All I want is to curl up and give my spirit and soul back to my Maker; a bitter end to a beautiful start. "Just take me Jesus…" I whisper.

My heart touches my sorrow and reveals to my mind the beautiful faces of my children. In truth, I do have so much; I have two precious children that are worth living for. I think of their smell, my son's eyes, my daughter's round face. I am broken and humbled, yet have a greater cause that is beyond myself… I have them. I clear my head and sit up straight, summoning the will to pull myself out of despair, because I must. I will not be broken and am determined to remain the kind, loving mother, wife and friend I have always been, no matter what I face today. Life has its thorns, but this is not going to break or ruin me, because I won't let it.

CUBA, 1961

My father's best friend, Paul, married a young woman and had two beautiful children. When my father, Abram and Anna left Cuba, Paul took over the church as their "adopted" son, continuing their work and its message of compassion. Immediately his life became a living testament of the power of God's grace.

Paul stood at the altar proclaiming to all the same beautiful redemptive message that turned him from a prostitute to minister, yet this message was interrupted by an army of Castro's secret police who invaded the church, machine guns in hand. Paul and all who were assembled in the service were arrested at gun point. They released the attendees, but Paul was charged with being an informant to American spies (my grandparents) and sentenced to 20 years in the Cuban prison. His only meals were that brought by his young wife and her family.

As my grandfather carried my mother home to their little house in Cuba, she still didn't know if she would ever be able to walk again. Her lower body was encased in casts with feet too shattered to hold any weight. She was tormented that she could not help her dear friend, Paul, who sat in a Cuban jail, but was facing her own nightmare. Tragedy didn't end for her. Sam and Naomi's home underwent continual and consistent attacks. Having become traumatized by the sound of firearms, my mom now was reminded of that tragic night, and her life once again at death's door, by the same source that took her feet only months prior.

The military would fly over civilians' homes and fire at and into the Cuban peoples' homes randomly. My mother's home experienced this often. She was frozen, unable to move because of her fragmented feet, as aircrafts closed in. She would lie defenseless while her house was barraged. Bullets ricocheted off appliances, and pots. She laid motionless, eyes pressed closed, heart pounding, as they targeted her home, again deafened by the ringing of metal as each bullet hit. It was a high pitch song as the slugs whizzed by, paralyzing her heart, causing the blood in her veins to freeze still.

Sam would run over, pick her up, carry her in his arms and place her under their concrete kitchen sink, while bullets penetrated their home and whistled by their ears. Many times, Sam didn't have enough time, fearing they both would be shot before he was able to reach safety, so Sam would throw himself on top of her, using his body as her shield. She was scared and cried out, "Daddy, NO!" He ignored her protests. "Please, Daddy, find somewhere safe, please!" she cried again. He turned his head to her ear, "I love you."

Chapter 6

"For he was a good man, full of the Holy Spirit and of faith. And a great many people were added to the Lord."
Acts 11:24

CUBA, 1961

My mother recovered, slowly. The bones of her feet had been pieced back together and healed. The precision of the Cuban doctor was skilled and she learned to walk normally once again. Her feet were horribly scarred and even a bit deformed, but she was so grateful she could walk, wear shoes and go back to her life as she knew, yet her heart still belonged to Daniel and his family. My father had learned of the shooting, and of Deborah's injury. His love for her overwhelmed him, as well as the reality that her life was almost snuffed away. He could not imagine life without her and realized that it was her he couldn't live without. Anna prompted her son to send for her, propose the moment she arrived and have a wedding before she left; because, she warned, it wouldn't be long before Deborah was swept away by another. He heeded my grandmother's warnings and immediately wrote to her and asked her and her parent's to come to Florida to see the family and him. When she arrived he immediately asked her to marry him, she accepted.

My father had been given a youth pastoring position in a small church in the Florida Keys. The little chapel where my father worked was ready for the impromptu wedding. My mother bought a $10 wedding dress. It was short, white, just below her knee, with a full skirt and tight waist. It was a simple gown, yet beautiful... she was beautiful. Her allure could have rivaled a Hollywood movie star. She could have married anyone, but loved him. They married and lived in a small trailer and had one plan, to save enough money to go back to the "mission field", which is exactly what they did.

They worked until they were able to purchase a small, one cabin boat. Abram joined them for many of their missionary voyages out to sea. They sailed from the Keys to the Bahaman Islands and onto Bimini, preaching wherever they beached. Anna stayed home in the States with their three small children.

I have pictures of my mother washing her hair on a dock, pouring a bucket of fresh water over her head to rinse, while locals stood around to watch, staring at the beautiful girl who walked and washed among them. They set off once again, this time adding Abram's friend Simeon, a local black man, on the tiny ship.

That evening, on their way back to Bimini, the boat's motor gave out. There was no sail and no radio on the little vessel, which was weighed down with its four passengers. The ocean had full control and it pulled them deeper and deeper out to sea and into the Bermuda Triangle. Each passing minute took them further away from any hope of finding help. They sat helpless as the boat continued to be swept into the channel and further from land. My grandfather and Simeon decided to take the boat's dingy to find help, which they did. The two men in a small dingy were alone in the ocean. My mother and father remained on the boat, while huge waves rocked them violently. Moving further and further from civilization, they held on and prayed that Abram and Simeon would find help and they all would live to see another day.

Hours and hours passed. My mother dropped to her knees and cried out for their life and for the life of Abram and Simeon. In the distance she heard a rumble of a plane. She called to my dad and he heard it too. He took a flashlight, and began to click Morse code, SOS. Then they saw a faint light of a boat in the distance. Feverishly, my father continued clicking the SOS sequence. They yelled and did all they could to be noticed. The plane's lights grew closer and closer and just as soon as it appeared to be overhead, it quickly passed and became small once again. They waved, called, cried, and pleaded for God to let that plane see them, yet it was gone. A quiet, hopeless whimper erupted and tears began to fall down my mother's cheeks. Their hope lost, until they heard, once again, the rumble of a distant plane. It returned! It did see them and came back. The plane circled above them and the light from the ship became brighter. Other ships appeared and also closed in. As each became more visible, the letters written on the side revealed that the Coast Guard was their rescuer. One pulled up beside the little boat. The first thing my mother saw next was an outstretched hand. When they docked back in Bimini and placed their feet upon dry land, they were immediately embraced and kissed by Abram, who was tired, yet relieved. Without Simeon's ability to read the stars to guide them to their final destination, none of them would have survived. Simeon's navigation skills along with my Grandfather's determination to save the life of his son and daughter-in-law, enabled them to overcome the seas, its current, the darkness, and gave the alert and location to the Coast Guard.

It was that moment that my parents decided that their calling was no longer at sea, but land. Mexico was where they moved, lived and served, together with Abram and Anna. The two couples built churches throughout Sinaloa that today still stand and continue to thrive. My parents had one daughter. When she turned five, they stopped in Tucson, Arizona, to apply to adopt. They had been trying for several years, but were unable to carry another child to full term.

During their stay in Tucson, my father began working at an aluminum plant and on his days off, he worked at a used car lot. His diligence and relentless work ethic quickly promoted him to management in the plant. My parents were blessed through adoption with a beautiful baby boy, who they named Michael. They were overjoyed. Since the adoption process required them to wait in Tucson, both my father and mother took the time to enjoy their expanded family and search themselves to hear from God for their future. Although my father was working two jobs, he and my mother couldn't avoid speaking the Gospel to those who would listen. They began a Bible study in their home for a few college students.

In just a few months of starting, the Bible study grew in numbers and the home could no longer contain the crowd, forcing them to meet in city parks under a lamp post. Young adults congregated to hear this message of compassion and grace, numbering 150 to 200 at every meeting.

My father led them to salvation, then brought them to local churches, in efforts for each to continue their faith's development. Because these kids had long beards, blue jeans and beads, the churches asked the youth and my father to leave. My father was grieved, realizing these young people were hungry for the Word, yet had no place that would receive them. He wasn't going to give up.

There was a multiple church youth rally in the center of town and my father brought 150 young people to hear the message, worship and find a church home. Although it was these 150 that ran to the altar, crying out with tears, the Pastors overseeing the event were offended by their dress and notified my dad that they were not welcome and that he and those he brought could no longer attend future events.

Grieved again… In prayer my father called out to God. His spirit revealed to him that he was to build a church in Tucson.

This was a blow to his missionary dreams. He wanted and felt he was called to go preach the Gospel where no one had preached before. My mother and he had been well prepared for missions, they had experienced being lost at sea, shot, lived on pennies and were ready for more. They believed that all these experiences were the preparation they needed for even greater adventures to come. To stop and stay and build a church in the desert of Arizona didn't have the romance he and my mother had imagined.

Although they loved and were proud of their titles as missionaries, my parents knew that this prompting was not their own, but from God. Realizing that lamp posts and parks were not the appropriate place to build a church, and homes were just too small to hold the current crowds, my mother and father bought a small church building in 1969 and with it brought in all the young people he had been leading. Parents of the youth joined their kids and the church was immediately a healthy-sized congregation. Within just one year, the leaders in the church asked my father to become a full-time pastor, since he was still working long hours with the local plant. The church was strong in numbers, so my father agreed.

Not long after this, my father joined forces with another man who had a specific ministry to older youth called "street people", or hippies.

Their open hearts and the church's casual feel appealed to the street people and soon my dad's church was attracting hippies from all over the state and country. Wanderers who slept by camp fires and sang of love, peace and not war, found their way to the little church. The word spread fast and soon the hippie movement had invaded, causing a tremendous upheaval among the congregation. A man in a suit next to a boy in bell bottom jeans had become an uncomfortable situation. At the altar were girls who came to church in bikinis, with long hair and open hearts. Even my father struggled within himself at the very look and image of these kids, having little patience for their ideas and feeling that they were just rebellious young adults.

Yet, his spirit was quickened and he knew that the church was to be God's, its image not what he or others think it should look like, but what God wanted it to. He searched his heart and asked if God was sending them, how could he not show them welcome.

Once my parents realized that it was God who was bringing these misfits, their hearts were opened to understand their mindset, their spiritual search and rejection of society's ideals and values. Unfortunately, the church as a whole was responding to this movement and its people with coldness and impatience.

As my parent's cleansed their own hearts, they were filled with compassion rather than judgment. They lost many members as a result of their welcome and soon became known as the "Hippie Church". Other ministers began to patronize them and claimed they were a place for drug addicts. Yet my parents knew it was God who was bringing each person and as a result, their little church grew daily.

They purchased an old Tucson guest ranch far outside the main flow of town and let many of the hippies live there; offering Bible studies and allowing each to work as maintenance and janitors for their board.

The church continued to grow and the little building could no longer contain the crowds, so they began meeting in junior high and high school auditoriums.

My father's depth of the Scripture and its history became an immediate draw. Unlike the typical preacher, my father had no legitimate speaking skills. He was not personable, but quiet, even shy. He preached information, with little to no personal story. He pulled together verse, after verse, and every message was a look into the Bible as a whole. He included recordings from Josephus and other historians from Christ's time. His quiet, honest nature appealed to both young and old, rich and poor; but it was the Message, the same Message of compassion, grace and hope combined with acceptance into the Kingdom, without rejection from the religious, that moved and changed lives. People wanted to learn and hear more and soon he and my mother needed to find a facility to hold a church that could accommodate the large group that congregated. It was time to build. They began construction on a building that would be able to hold a congregation of 500 people on the guest ranch property, but before the completion of the new building, the expanding congregation had already outgrown the new facility. This began another construction project for a building that could hold thousands.

By 1984, fifteen years after its incorporation and nine years after the large building's dedication and opening, stood a beautiful church, which held thousands of people, every pew filled at each of its multiple services. It came with a school, a thriving, joyous Christian elementary, which taught foundational Biblical truths that prospered in its reputation as a leading elementary school in the city. Where once stood a guest ranch alone in the desert, far removed from the hustle of the city; now it marked the center of town. Tucson had grown and spread, encircling its location, making the property central to the very city it belonged.

In spite of my parent's reluctance to the change in their life's calling, they were in awe as the congregation continued to multiply. They knew it was God alone and rejoiced as they watched each life become touched and changed. People were healed, ministries were inspired to serve and reach those who were suffering. Those very "hippie" youth, rejected by the religious leaders of the day, are now our city's leaders, council, business men and woman, as well as a good majority became ministers themselves, reaching throughout our state and country with large and thriving churches of their own. Their message the same loving, compassionate message of Jesus Christ that impacted their own hearts in 1969.

My father's church thrived over thirty years, until his forced retirement....

JAIL: DAY ONE, TEN HOURS

The same female guard is back; her silhouette as the darkness meets light personifies what has brought me to my desperate state. She tells me to stand up and follow her. I am given my paperwork, which "I am to keep on me at all times." She leads me to a room just off the cement block hallway, I follow, still tripping on my shoes. She opens a door. Immediately, my body recoils and my skin begins to crawl from an overpowering shriek. I shiver from its power and want to cover my ears and run back to the lonely cell I had just left. In front of me standing, yelling, is a black lady in her deputy/guard attire. She continues without pause to scream with a high pitched deafening wail. Her hair is short and spiked, standing up and curled at the ends. She has a strong swollen brow line, which symbolizes her misery, as it folds across her face and makes a neanderthal appearance of irritability. I breathe deep as I look at my new home. It's beyond any horrible dream leading up to this day that kept me up at night. I had envisioned a small cell, with one or two other inmates, an exposed toilet and a television; I realize now, that perplexing image was actually more luxurious than what was in fact to come. I stand at a guard desk that overlooks a large open gymnasium-type room. My spirit deflates and my body quivers as I grasp the depths of my incarceration. My nightmares were better than my reality.

Inmates are piled in together resembling in structure that of a concentration camp. Beyond the guard's desk are bunk beds, one after the other. They line the concrete walls and back up against each other making a row where heads meet feet. In the center is a glass room fill with more bunks. The glass room looks like an aquarium. It is either designated for those in trouble, or for the privileged, but clearly separated from the rest. In front of the myriad of bunks is an open space for eating and leisure. Sofa-type sectional cushions are piled one on top of the other and tucked into a corner. One very small television screen is propped up on the half wall that divides the bunk space from the rec- reational space but facing away from the bunks and toward the guard's desk. There are long tables set up that dominate ninety percent of the leisure space, chairs are stacked by a small half wall. There is one drink- ing fountain, several vending machines and a short three-tiered book- case of books and Bibles. The bookcase is leaning up against a glass window to the outside, which looks out onto an intimidating blocked-in yard; high walls encase the space that stretch fifteen feet high for effect, with one small basketball hoop and a long six foot table underneath to show its deliberate lack of use. A wire fence-like ceiling spreads across the outdoor space from block wall to block wall, making a mesh en- closure to ensure no one escapes. Concrete meets block wall, meets chain roof. The outdoor area is extremely small and seems impossible for the amount of incarcerated women to all fit at one time. The black guard continues to holler, military style, at the inmates. The object of her screaming are the female detainees who are mopping, cleaning toilets, sinks, tables, and emptying garbage. The inmates are disconcert- ingly quiet, with only the guard's screeching voice to be heard, a gnaw- ing sound that echoes throughout, bouncing off the concrete floors and walls. She continually barks, without pause, until she looks at me.

"Sit down!" she shrills in an unnecessary aggressive pitch, "and don't speak."

She pulls out a chair from a stack by her desk. Her shouting begins once again. Inmates keep cleaning, through her ranting, which never stops; a continuous, relentless yell.

Her attention comes back to me.

"You seem to be the quiet type, so you may be ok. My rules are: I don't like noise…"

"Make sure your bed is made and your area is clean. I hate beds that are not smooth."

"Go into the GRD ('grid') and get two sheets, a towel and if for some reason you find a blanket, fine."

"You are bed 43-1."

"Go straight to your bunk and don't talk to anyone."

I proceed to the glass room… I am hoping, praying, that this room was the "GRD" based only on the fact that she slightly gestured to the area when mentioning the sheets. I wasn't about to ask her to clarify. I walk past inmates in their beds. They have not joined the others as they clean. I approach a big laundry bin and find two folded sheets, a towel, yet no blanket. I keep searching, but to no avail. I give up the quest, leave the glass room and go to the area she had also elusively motioned toward to find 43-1. It is a bottom bunk. When I unfold my sheets, I see they are torn, shredded and balled. The bare mattress is vinyl, one inch thick with large gashes. There is no pillow, I look around and realize nor does anyone else. A pillow… something so basic but beyond my worth or trust. I make my bed with the guard still yelling, keeping an ear tuned to ensure she is not shrieking at me. I take off my rubber shoes and lay down. Under my bed are two drawers, one with the number 43-1, the other with the number 43-2. 43-1 is where I will place all my items once my plastic bag arrives. I am relieved to be able to lie down… kind of. The steel board under my mattress bangs and pops from my weight. It is loud, like a car crash. Frightened, I look at the guard afraid I have just given her a reason to direct her ranting toward me. She only hears herself, so I lay my head down. She claims she likes it quiet, but her volume and voice is all that destroys any peace. The rest of the inmates are still cleaning. I feel guilty not to help, but have been instructed not to move, so I lay still.

I look up to the board above me. The inmate before me scratched in her dates and crossed each day out as a countdown to her going home. This panics me; the idea that this was but my first of many was overwhelming. In truth, I don't see how I am going to make it. My emotions are raw now, and I feel broken from the humiliation of the strip searches and demeaned by the lonely dungeon I sat for hours. The conditions are ridiculous, the oppression so intimidating, this is no way to rehabilitate anyone. In my heart and mind I know I don't belong here, it's a horrible mistake, a tragic injustice I say to myself. I am a stranger getting a look into a world I do not fit. I close my eyes and pray I fall asleep, drowning out the sound of the guard's incessant shouting that knows no end.

Chapter 7

"Hear, O LORD, and have mercy on me; LORD, be my helper."
Psalm 30:10

CHAD: JUNE, 1995

My first date with Chad was nothing overly exotic. He picked me up in his red Acura. I was wearing a sundress, my hair down and straight; he in shorts and Polo. He took me to a little restaurant in downtown Tucson. He played the Pulp Fiction soundtrack on his cassette player as we drove; a movie recently released. I liked that he chose this soundtrack; unlike the other boys who would try to win my affection with Christian music. The restaurant was small, candle lit, and unique. Downtown Tucson was a historical place, where buildings over one hundred years still stood. At the time, downtown was no longer much of a draw. The area had become run down. The courthouse and law offices were really all that flourished. I ordered an ice tea and he a beer. I liked that he wasn't trying to be something he was not, yet was entirely too handsome, and made me nervous. I was not used to caring this much on a date and quickly became more uncomfortable with my own condition.

"What do you do for fun?" he asked.

"I really don't do a lot outside the church. I work out at the gym." We both laughed, then I continued, "I hike a lot, mostly by myself."

"All alone? Where?" he questioned, looking interested.

Still nervous, I answered him while I unconsciously threw my hair to one side, "I like to go to Sabino Canyon's Seven Falls. I love to sit on the rock and feel the spray of the massive falls. It's like a soft shower even if I sit several feet away. I carry a knife though… I have had some close and uncomfortable encounters at the Falls."

"I've been to the Seven Falls. It's beautiful, but quite the party spot," he said with a peculiar smile. Yes, I am sure he knows the party scene well, I thought to myself.

"A lot of young college partying happens at the Falls, but I am long gone by the time they arrive," I said to set him straight on the type of girl he was with.

"Why do you carry a knife? Is it for safety from animals, snakes?" he looked at me confused.

"No, a few weeks ago, I was on the part of the trail that is narrow, one side is a rock wall, and the other side a cliff." I realized I was using my hands too much as I described the trail and quickly set them down on my lap.

"I know that area, it's the last stretch before you get to the actual fall," he answered. I did not sense he was nervous at all. He knew he was good looking.

Becoming suspicious and unsure of his intentions, I continued, "While I took that path, a man came walking toward me, wearing a backpack and tennis shoes, nothing else. I decided that I needed to have some protection after that."

"So he was naked? That is Tucson for you. What did you do, did he pass you?" he leaned in closer.

I continued, "He took full advantage of the narrow trail and obviously enjoyed catching me in an inescapable spot. Let me just say, he clearly found the moment exciting... I, on the other hand, found the moment extremely disgusting and quite frightening."

"Did he do anything?" he probed, his voice a bit lower.

"No, I leaned up against the rock wall to let him pass, which he did without a word, walked right past me. It would have been so easy for me to take my foot and push him right over when he passed... I let him know I had the upper hand when he reached me. I pressed by back up against the rock wall and lifted my foot to let him know, with one tap, I could easily shorten his hike. With the terrain against my back, he had nothing but a cliff, he stopped and then decided to keep walking by."

We both chuckled, even though it wasn't that funny.

"So, I carry a knife, not to use, but to show I am not to be messed with," I explained. Thinking this story might help him understand that I was not as fragile as I looked. His good looks wouldn't be enough to charm me and he would soon know I was not one that would be taken advantage of, ever.

"You are in real estate?" I asked.

"Yes, but since my father's recent marriage, I have been stepping into his business more. I swore to my Dad that I would never work there, but I can tell he wants to just enjoy being newly married and focus on his new life. I know the business well, I grew up around it," he explained with complexity in his voice.

"I am sure he couldn't trust anyone more than you," I responded.

"Yeah, well, I am not certain he is sure I am his best option, nor am I sure this is what I want," he answered. His face sincere, but still holding a sexy smile while he talked. I didn't like it… it made me uneasy.

"Well, you know Ruth's son, Josh?" I asked hesitantly. Ruth was his new stepmother.

"Yes, it's funny, but we were buddies since we were kids. We lived down the street from each other and stayed friends through high school, my dad and Ruth never met, just she and my mom; crazy how my dad and Ruth then met at your dad's church after all these years and marry," he said cheerfully.

"It is. I really love Ruth. So…" I cleared my throat, "Josh was my first date! I guess he's your stepbrother now."

"You dated my stepbrother!?" he said, with eyes big as he leaned back in his chair.

"Yes! …I was fifteen, he was eighteen, and my parents knew him and Ruth well, so they said I could go out with him, in spite of my age. He took me to Golf N'Stuff."

We both laughed, but I could tell he was uncomfortable.

"How long did you date?" he asked. His eyes still wide.

"That was really it. He tried to teach me how to drive a stick shift once after our date, but didn't go out again after that."

It became awkward; we both looked around and took a sip of our drinks. He seemed more at ease that the relationship I had with his stepbrother never became more, yet I was embarrassed.

"He really is a great guy and my father really loves him," I remarked and then felt my face get even redder.

"Yes. He is a good man…" he said with a bit of irritation.

The awkwardness intensified. I changed the subject, but by doing so only worsened the discomfort.

"Where are you in your faith?" I asked.

"Wow! That's a loaded question!!" he laughed.

"I don't know you. I don't normally date people that I do not know what they believe, or how committed they are to Christ; however, I am interested and want to know where you are in yours."

"You are too serious. I need to loosen you up and show you how to have some fun," he said with a big smile, leaning in closer once again.

"Interesting… What do you have in mind?" I said suspiciously. Was he a total player and misread the type of person I was? I stiffened and began to prickle.

"I want to take you water skiing. I have a boat, we can go for a day. Join me?" he asked.

"I have never been water skiing," I said apprehensively and turned off.

"I'll teach you." His smile broadened.

"I will think about it," shutting him down, intentionally.

He chuckled. His smile was far too sexy. I looked at him and questioned my emotions. Thinking now he was with the wrong girl. I was not going to have a common romance with him so that he may first test the waters to see if I was worthy for him to move forward. There were a ton of girls he could choose from, far more beautiful than me, that would gladly indulge in a typical affair if that was what he wanted.

His eyes looked at me more pensive and his smile disappeared. "Truthfully, my father has been instrumental in my faith. My mother passed when I was a teenager."

"I am so sorry." I said, warming to him, seeing sincerity in his eyes.

"My dad was a good father, a Godly man. We were not avid church attendees, but his faith and his strength have been a constant in my life. I have known and believed in God in a personal way since a child and through and because of my father's devotion. I have watched you in church, sitting next to your dad…" he said with a slight grin, "…and see the way you respond to the sermon and the worship. You are genuine in your worship. I feel so connected to you, because the way you respond to God is how I feel in my heart."

"I love that." I did love it. This was no player.

"I told Ruth and my dad I was taking Pastor Daniel's daughter out. They both assumed I was taking Esther out. When I told them it was you, my dad told me I wasn't your type and should probably consider Esther instead."

I laughed, "I am thinking your Dad might be wrong about you not being my type." I smiled.

He smiled back. We stayed at that tiny restaurant and talked for hours.

When he drove me home and walked me to the door I could feel the tension, excitement and awkwardness of the moment for us both.

"So, can I show you a little fun and take you skiing?" he asked again.

"Yes, I will give it a try."

"Great. Goodnight," he smiled.

"Good night." I turned and opened the front door and walked inside. I looked back one last time before I shut the door. He turned back as he walked to his car, sensing me. We looked at each other, and smiled again.

Once the door was shut, I fell back against it and closed my eyes. His blue eyes and sexy smile was imprinted in my mind; I was taken.

That Saturday, Chad picked me up. We met up with a couple of his college buddies, making me the only female. We drove for three hours to a manmade lake called Roosevelt. The landscape was dry and ugly where weeds had grown and died. The water was murky and dark; however, the day was warm and beautiful. Chad had a ski boat and his buddies were excited for a day of play. One of them brought a jet ski. They piled the beer onto the boat, I brought my Diet Coke, and off we went. I was wearing a one piece black bathing suit. It was conservative, but showed my figure. I recognized one of Chad's buddies, who was also his roommate. He had asked me out a few weeks prior! He worked at a Mexican food restaurant that my girlfriend and I stopped to have dinner prior to attending the symphony. We were quite overdressed for the restaurant. Chad's roommate seated us, but kept coming back to our table to chat. Later, I declined his offer to go to some bar when he got off work and after our concert had concluded. He was good looking, thick curly hair, tan skin, attractive. He just wasn't anything or anyone that I would be interested in. I was nervous and embarrassed, fearing he might recognize me when Chad introduced us. He didn't recognize me, or pretended not to. I was relieved.

I wore my hair down and wavy. I wrapped a short sarong around my hips and sat back enjoying the wind in my hair and fresh air. Chad handed me a life jacket to put on. "Let's teach you how to ski!"

I jumped in the water, listened to Chad's instructions, put the skis on and then the boat started to roar and pull. I partly stood up and fell. He brought the boat around. "Lean back, let the boat pull you up."

Back to ready position with ski tips up, holding the rope handle tightly, I leaned back, the boat gunned and up I stood. The guys all cheered! I was up. I saw Chad looking back smiling, his blond hair blowing. I lost my focus and leaned too far back. My skis were in front of me, my back was being dragged in the water and I was too stubborn to let go, determined I could pull myself back up, until I felt an intense pain. I released the handle, and moaned. The boat stopped and I heard one of Chad's buddies yell out, "LAKE ENEMA!" and they all laughed. The boat came around, no one was laughing anymore, everyone was looking at me. I groaned.

"You alright?" Chad asked.

"… Ouch!" I said whimpering, then laughed.

"You want to keep going?"

"Let's keep going," I said regaining my vigor, and pain now leaving.

This time, when the boat pulled me up, I stayed up. The speed was intense, I felt like I was running on water. It was exhilarating. Chad was right, it was time I had a little fun, laughed, stopped taking myself so seriously. In spite of my novice, I was exuberant, enjoying myself, living.

I climbed back in the boat. Chad grabbed me, put his hands on my hips and kissed me on my cheek. We both laughed and shouted as his friends skied after me, it was invigorating! I loved it.

"Your turn, Chad!" shouted one of the guys who threw Chad a life jacket. Chad smiled, grabbed his jacket and began to take off his shirt, I watched… his hand grabbed the end of his shirt and he began to pull it up exposing his abdomen. It was cut and chiseled, his skin tanned. I tried to look away but my curiosity brought me back as I watched him pull his shirt off over his chest. He had a small amount of blond hair that sprayed just slightly over his large pectoral muscles, swollen and young; his shirt was now off as he pulled it over his head, showing his shoulders, round and muscular, biceps, cut and strong. He looked at me and smiled. I felt my entire body become warm, my legs lost feeling. I looked away as though I hadn't notice, but my head was dizzy and I felt as though I looked flushed and melted.

He took a sip of his beer and jumped in the water. "Ready," he told his buddy who hit the gas extra hard attempting to make him trip in front of his date. He didn't, but pulled up. He was on one ski, slalom style. He weaved in and out of the wake, jumping off its wave and back to the other side. His muscles flexed with each maneuver. He was wearing a tie-dye blue swimsuit that I thought was the most obnoxious thing I had ever seen. It was light blue and worn. The pattern could have been on the cover of a baby's book with a moon for a sleepy bedtime story; it was truly hideous. Seriously, with a body like that, what was he doing in those ridiculous shorts? I chuckled to myself knowing that he thought he was so hot, but then scanned down and saw his tight and bulging leg muscles shining in the sun, with the backdrop of the water glistening all around him. I was warm again, swooning at the very sight of him. I caught myself and realized that I could not let him see that I was incredibly infatuated. He needed to work for me, not know that my tongue was hanging out and wishing he would kiss me, touch me, something….

We end the day and he drove me home, tired and worn from an enjoyable and thrilling adventure.

"When can I see you again?" he asked.

"I leave tomorrow for Phoenix with my sister. She is in the Miss Arizona Pageant. Come see the banner I made for her and poster for her dressing room," I said as I gestured for him to follow me.

We walked inside the house and I pulled out the poster and banner. It had several signatures and quotations from family and friends giving Esther their support. This was the first pageant that Esther had told us she was in and invited us to attend. She had always stayed so private, so now that she was including me, I had every intention of thoroughly embarrassing her.

"Can I sign the poster?" Chad asked.

"Absolutely!" I handed him a pen and he began to sign his name.

"When do you get back?" he questioned while he signed.

"Sunday, late Sunday afternoon, then I have to go to the six o'clock service. Will you be coming to church Sunday night?"

He set down the pen and looked at me with a smile, "I will… to see you."

"Ok, I will see you Sunday night," I responded, smiling back at him.

I walked him to the door, and waved as he walked to his car. He waved back.

I looked down at the poster and saw his name, which gave me butterflies. "Check out who signed your poster," I said as I handed it to Esther.

"Wow, Chad Smith! Andrea, you are acting like a school girl with a crush! Seriously??"

"I know…" I said to her as I set down the poster embarrassed.

"Keep it in check." she laughed. I laughed too, nervously. I did need to keep myself in check, yet could feel my heart going and fast.

Chapter 8

"My God, My God, why have You forsaken Me?
Why are You so far from helping Me,
And from the words of My groaning?" Psalm 22: 1

JUNE, 1995

Esther was magnificent. I was so proud of her, and made every effort to be the loudest audience member at the Miss Arizona pageant; which she thoroughly noticed and was clearly unwelcomed. The other contestants' talents were unmatched to her natural, deep sultry voice. They were performers, playing to the pageant judges biddings. Esther, unlike the others, was a natural vocalist without the drama or the theatrics; she just stood and sang brilliantly, beautifully. I would have given anything to sound like that. Esther rarely sang though; I was not sure why she didn't sing constantly, everywhere. With the church and our father as the minister, she had the platform to be on stage and sing whenever she wanted, as well parents who were constantly encouraging her to, yet she refused the many requests. I was always urging her, and making it clear that if I had a voice like hers, I would grab the microphone and sing away without end.

It was no surprise that Esther was one of the finalists, even though this was her first time in a state pageant. Many pageant agents saw her potential and were quick to offer their services to her, to help her in her pageant career. Esther was not interested in pursuing more crowns. She got what she wanted, a scholarship.

As Esther and I pulled into our driveway after a long event, we noticed a note and a single red rose sitting at the front door. Positive it was for Esther, I hopped out and grabbed it as Esther parked. It wasn't for Esther, but from Chad. "Thinking of you" the note read.

My head began to spin again. Esther rolled her eyes, but at that moment I didn't care, I wanted to enjoy the sensation of feeling like a school girl with a crush. My mom met us in the kitchen surrounded by several arrangements of roses, some for Esther, and a few from my own admirrors. I grabbed a small vase and filled it with water and gave the single rose a prominent place.

"Andrea, there are extraordinary arrangements of beautiful roses all around me, are you really going to make a big deal of this one rose?" my mom questioned.

"Yes, I am." I walked away. I felt the glares and rolling of eyes as I left the two women. Their silence confirmed the sign language I sensed going on behind me.

That night I arrived to church late. Late because I tried on too many outfits and couldn't find one I wanted to wear. When I entered, I spotted him. We smiled at each other from across the building.

"Thank you for the rose, I love it," I said after the service was dismissed.

"I was worried when I didn't see you at the start of service," he said with a question in his tone.

My face now flushed, "I was running late from my sister's pageant. She loved that you signed her poster." The fact that my sister was at the service on time, probably was not overlooked.

"Can I walk you to your car?" he asked.

"Yes, of course." I worked so hard on my outfit only to have a few minutes with him. I was disappointed that it was late and we both had to go to work the next morning.

"I want to see you again," he said as we walked.

"I would like that."

"Come tomorrow night to my house? I can pick up a movie and order pizza?" he asked.

"Okay, that sounds perfect. Tomorrow night it is." He reached down and opened my car door and leaned in and kissed my cheek. He seemed more aggressive tonight, even strong in his approach. My stomach danced as I thought about being alone with him at his home. I became weakened with the image of him, the way he smelled… I cleared my head as he closed my car door and walked away. I shuddered in excitement; thrilled to soon be with him once again.

The next evening, I arrived at his small two bedroom patio home. It is very cute, with a small winding walkway leading to the front door; nothing fancy, but very warm. The entire front was draped with a lush green vine and covered with pretty yellow flowers. It's a vine I recognized, because of its ability to survive in the Tucson climate, and its distinctive name, cat's claw, because it has claw like features that grab ahold of walls and can stretch across ceilings. I loved the drippy look of the vegetation and wondered how a bachelor pad would have such a warm and lush feel.

I rang the doorbell and soon Chad answered the door. Greeted by his flirty smile and gorgeous blue eyes. I also noticed his t-shirt was tighter than normal and once again, I tried not to show how intense he made me feel by looking away. His house had odd furniture, in odd places. The home had a great room, followed by a small bricked-in patio. The furniture was a pastel southwest, ugly and outdated, which included a typical guy's sofa with tons of soft cushions, comfortable enough to sleep on but ugly enough for the city dump. The television was placed in an entertainment piece that was hand-painted with juvenile southwestern patterns. I learned later that it was the artistic master piece of his roommate. There was a galley type kitchen with western details added to its cupboards. His place was cute and had potential to be adorable.

He brought me a soda and I saw pizza on the coffee table. I sat down and he started the movie, "Speed," featuring the box office heavyweight, Keanu Reeves, and costar, a newcomer, Sandra Bullock. I was happy to snuggle up to him for the first time, feel his arms around me, innocently resting my head on his shoulder; at the moment safe, but anticipating, wanting his touch, craving the feeling of his mouth next to mine, longing to be captive to him.

We watched the movie quietly. The moment was awkward and although the movie was full of action, my mind was scattered. I sat next to him pretending to be watching but wondering if he was going to kiss me. I wanted him to, worried he might expect more… yet nowhere else

I would rather be. I started to get too nervous and decided to clear my head and go to the bathroom. I stood at the mirror and noticed in his shower was a small Batman figure hanging from a little string and suction cup that the figure had attached. I thought how cute, a twenty-five year old man, still channeling his superhero self every morning.

I returned to the sofa, where he was waiting. He looked at me and smiled. I loved his mouth, his smile. I felt warm again and trembled a bit. He took his fingers and brushed them against my neck, then my lips, which caused sparks to run down my spine. He sensed my body melt from his touch and leaned toward me, his lips, warm and moist, tenderly caressed my neck, his fingers still softly stroking my lips. He moved his lips toward mine and I felt his breath against my mouth. I swallowed nervously. His lips touched mine, softly he kissed me tenderly. I was helpless in his embrace, without fight, hypnotized by his touch, by his kiss.

JAIL: DAY ONE, ELEVEN HOURS

There is a shift in guards. The black guard has left. She is Deputy Cain; I learned this overhearing other inmates whispering of their hatred for her. Having her gone was a relief to my nerves. With her incessant screaming, my body and emotions became tense and frantic. The yelling was so constant my mind was able to move her grading sound into the background and became accustomed to its vibrato, her words drowned by its persistence, yet it still drained me physically.

The new guard looks to be younger than her alternate and of Latin American decent. Her face is long, oily and unattractive. Something is wrong with her mouth. Her jaw remains clenched tightly at all times, which looks uncomfortable. Her skin has no warmth with a grey-green hue. Blemishes encircle her strange pursed lips. Her small eyes are pulled and deformed by the tight bun her black hair has been forced into. The entire time I have been in this block, the lights over the bunk, eating, and leisure areas have been off. The only light was over the guard's desk. After the inmates had completed their cleaning duties, they went back to their bunks, no one talked, or else they were yelled at and threatened to get written up by Cain. The new guard didn't yell, but leaned up against the desk and watched us with clenched jaw and scowling eyes.

My bunk is against the wall with the bathroom on the other side. Mirrors, like those you see at convenience stores, are propped up in corners of the ceiling where bunks lay, as well as the leisure area to give the guard at the desk a view of all. Video cameras are also throughout. On the guard's desk is a computer with the video images of each camera's live feed. The bathroom is long and narrow. Sinks and mirrors line up at entry, toilets are at one side and showers on the other. The showers are separated by groups, four heads to one shower stall. Each toilet has a short dividing wall between, with no doors. The same convenience-store security mirrors are set up above the stalls and showers so that no person has any privacy.

A rolling cart of food trays enter and two inmates get up from their bunks and start unwrapping and preparing the trays. The smell inspires the other inmates to start moving and wrestling in their bunks. The guard turns on lights over the leisure area. Then she calls out "SSBlock SOne, get your sstray and ssfind a sseat." the guard yells with her teeth clenched, so it is hard to understand her. Each word is muffled. Everyone in my area gets up. I follow their lead. They stand in line and grab a tray and a stacked chair, then go to a nearby table. I am hungry; I checked in at 8 a.m. without breakfast and sat in the pit for more than five hours, followed by an extended stay in that empty cell. It is now past seven and this my first and only meal for the day. I follow the other inmates, praying I don't make a wrong move, not knowing the jail procedures. The guard continues to sneer orders, but I can't process what she is saying due to her impaired speech. I figure she is agitated from any inmate that walks outside the painted lines in the eating area, or that come too close to her desk as they set up their chairs. I walk up with my tray of food to a table full of inmates and feel uncomfortable to sit with them. They look at me, a stranger, and say nothing. I am afraid there is a pecking order that I am not a part of and could be setting my tray and chair in someone else's designated spot, as seen in the movies, so I set my chair and tray at a table that is empty.

"SSGet your sstray and seat and ssput it next to the ssperson in front of you in ssline!" she yells.

She quickly moves toward me and is now standing over me. My heart sinks, my hands are tingling. I have read the inmate booklet to prepare myself for any rules. It doesn't even mention trays or that I will be eating in the same room as I sleep. The booklet gives rules for the cafeteria and nothing about having to sit following the person in line. I am panicked and in shock. I get up, trying not to touch her since she is within inches of my face, and quickly move my tray and chair. She follows me and proceeds to yell, her oily skin and clenched teeth are the only thing I can see.

"SSI'm sssgoing to sswrite you ssup! Do you sssknow what that ssmeans?"

"I am sorry, I didn't know the rules." I say softly with my head down, not moving.

"SSThey are my sssrules, you ssneed to sfollow my ssrules."

She has spit that bubbles between her clenched teeth when she talks. I sit and look down, a strategy I see all the other inmates seem to have adopted. I do the same. She stands over me silent. I keep my head down. She stays there, breathing heavy, seething and vexed. I am the object of her anger. She then sees another inmate who she decides warrants her fury and moves away from me. I sit rattled and stare at my food. It has been a long day, my emotions are getting the better of me and all I want to do is curl in a ball, lay in my bunk and cry. My eyes are burning, but I hold back the tears. "I can't be weak, I can't be weak." I say to myself. I look around the table; each woman a stranger; each is an intimidating exile. They look at me enigmatically, which frightens me. My tray has an enormous piece of meatloaf soaked in a thick brown gravy, a large cup-size portion of mashed potatoes, two slices of white bread, a large piece of cake with Koolaide to drink. I try to take a bite of the meatloaf: the gravy is a thick jelly. I can't eat. Tears are starting to well and I just need to find a place to hide. I see other inmates take their trays and scrape the remnants of their dinner in the trash, then stack the tray back on the cart and return to their bunk. I start to get up and take my tray to unload its contents in the trash, but the inmate across from me grabs my tray. I stop and look at her. Her eyes are black and narrow, she says nothing, her face has strong features, hair black and straight; she looks the criminal, harsh and cold. She doesn't say anything, nor does her face show any emotion or humanity; she points to my food. I sit down and point to the mash potatoes; she nods and takes her spoon and sweeps it up onto her tray. The other inmates around me take her lead and spoon the uneaten food from my tray, grabbing the cake, meatloaf and bread. My tray is now clear. I get up and scrape the crumbs in the trash, stack my tray on the cart and walk back to 43-1. My eyes are burning and my chest begins to heave.

"I don't think I can do this. I'm not going to make it, I just can't make it…" I say under my breath as I approach my bunk.

"Jesus… I have nothing left but the fragments of what was once my soul. Help me?" It is so instinctive for me to pray, but foolish.

"God, I really think this is too much for me. I don't think I can make it through this… I really can't!" I say under my breath.

Inmates are trickling in around me returning to their bunks. An older inmate with dark curly hair walks close to my bunk on her way to hers, and discreetly and undercover puts her hand on my head and whispers, "It's ok, we have all been where you are. You will get through this." She then walks to her bunk which is four down from mine.

Her kindness breaks my strength, a dam I needed, but now broken, making my tears begin to flow uncontrollably. They gush down my face hot, burning as they run. I make no sound, but my face is wet. I drop my head low, so my hair covers my cheeks in a hopeless effort to keep others from seeing my weakness, but this attempt fails, which makes them pour even more uncontrollably. Those around me are quiet, and provide me some dignity by awarding me privacy. Next to me, a woman in her mid-thirties sits at her bunk. Our bottom bunks are about four feet away from each other; I can sense she is facing me. I lay my head on my mattress and try to recover. She lays her head down on hers, but turns her body facing me; I can feel her presence leaning in from her bunk toward me. I slowly turn my face toward her, embarrassed that someone is seeing me, but know she is trying to get my attention. When I look toward her my heart gasps and bleeds once again, I feel a river of emotion at her beautiful gesture, because what I see is that she has reached out her hand toward me, holding it in place, in the open air, waiting for mine to embrace hers. I begin to weep without cover and reach out my hand to her. Our hands clasp. I look into her eyes. They are warm, round, dark brown, a pretty face, offering me her comfort and consolation. Her hair is brown, long, spilling to one side as she reaches out to reassure me. We hold hands touching between bunks. It feels like a warm hug, and I am soothed. We are not allowed to touch each other, this is something written in the jail check-in brochure, so this act is a great risk to her and to me... but her tenderness was felt and needed. We let go and I smile, through my wet and broken face.

"Thank you." I mouth. She mouths back the words, "You will be ok."

I lay back and look up again at the scratched calendar. I deeply want to be home, next to my husband, in spite of his iciness, with my children sleeping sweetly in their beds. I think of their precious little heads resting soundly on their pillows. To lie in my own bed and have them all so near seemed so common place once, yet now an unobtainable view of heaven.

Chapter 9

"A righteous man regards the life of his animal,
But the tender mercies of the wicked are cruel." Proverbs 12:10

JAIL: DAY ONE, TWELVE HOURS

The remaining lights are turned on. This seems to be some type of cue and the inmates leave their bunks and file into the same space we just ate. They pull out chairs and sit at tables. A few pull down pieces of the sectionals and turn on the small television.

"SSKeep the ssvolume ssdown," the guard yells.

The television is already barely audible. There are subtitles at the bottom of the small screen, two inmates move in close with faces almost to the screen to hear and/or read the subtitles. The screen is far too small and the volume so low, which explains why only two inmates attempt to watch. I walk to the book shelves. My tears have dried, yet I feel so embarrassed by my lack of ability to hold in my emotions. I keep my head down in shame, but hope to find a book that will help me escape. There is an entire section of Bibles, no other religious material exists. I find it prejudicial to not offer other religious material; in fact, I find it to be offensive that this jail would even attempt to show any persuasion toward Christianity, where there is nothing Christ-like about its methodology or practices. That being said, I am glad there is a Bible, it's been a long time since I opened the Bible, a long time since I have regularly gone to church even. My faith has yet to change and my devotion to God still foundational, but my life and its many trials has made me disgusted by the infrastructure of the 'church' and even hard to pray to a God who I feel has turned His back to me. A God who seems to continually cut me down, punished me and physically shut me off. In truth, I am angry, sad, and feel betrayed by the One I adore.

I look for a book to read in addition to the Bible I now have in hand. The entire shelf is packed with mystery and sleazy romance novels. Strange choices of literature offered to the incarcerated: violence, criminal activity or sex is their reading options. I look for an author and see Sidney Sheldon, who I am familiar and know I will enjoy. I grab the crime/mystery novel and go back to my bunk, hoping to get through the night as preoccupied as possible. I am grateful for the book and immediately get engrossed in its world. Lights are out again and all inmates return to their bunks. I look at the clock and see the leisure time lasted only fifteen minutes. Once again, it is quiet and no one is talking. I can still read, even though the lights are off, because there is a small glow coming from the guard's desk that provides little but some illumination. The bed is miserably uncomfortable. It is strange lying down without a pillow. The sound of crashing and banging as inmates turn in their bunks from the warped metal boards under their mattresses becomes customary. I lie to my side and go back to my Sidney Sheldon, until I am able to dose off.

JUNE, 1995

"My parents want to have you over for dinner. Unfortunately, my oldest sister, Korah, her husband and baby have just moved in with them. So if you are able to come, you would be having dinner with my parents, and my sister's family... I know it's a lot, but it would mean so much to me if my parents had a chance to meet you," I said nervously.

"Of course," Chad answered.

My oldest sister and husband had left the church they were pastoring in Orange County. They just adopted their little boy, Luke; a beautiful baby whom my sister ended up leaving with me a lot, surprising for someone who just became a new mom. His first few days were in my arms while she went shopping. I enjoyed him thoroughly. He was so very tiny; African-American, Caucasian and partly American-Indian, a racial combination that resulted in a beautiful infant. My sister's husband, Jack, was ten years her senior, but you wouldn't know he was any bit her elder with his youthful gregarious way. He also was incredibly handsome. Jack was easy going and enjoyable to be around. Korah had changed her name recently from her given name. This was the third time she had changed her name, so for the moment… this moment… she was Korah… She was painfully complicated and I really was not excited she or Jack would be there when Chad was coming to officially meet my parents.

At fourteen, I had visited Korah and Jack's new rental home in California with my parents. When we arrived, I looked out her window which revealed a little backyard, lush with a bright green grassy lawn. In the center of the yard erected a white trellis boasting rose bushes in full bloom at its base. The trellis was also adorned with a striking vine of climbing roses; each rose, pink and red, open and vibrant. I couldn't help but escape the family greetings and idle conversation and step out to enjoy the fragrant smell that the roses were sure to bring. I took my sandals off to feel the grass beneath my feet, something the desert didn't provide without great sacrifice and cost. The feel of it was soft and warm and the sensation of the sun on my face enveloped me. With each step toward the roses, their fragrant aroma became more profound.

When I reached the base of the trellis my heart stopped; repulsed. A dead animal laid at the arch and I immediately was overcome with nausea. I began to retreat from the morbid scene but stopped when the animal twitched… It was alive. I looked closer. It was tiny with white and grey hair that only covered its frame in patches; fleas had overcome its every inch, viciously consuming what little life that remained. Using the end of my sandal, I touched its side to roll the unfortunate animal over, to learn its kind. It rolled without fight and revealed itself to be a small cat; a Himalayan Persian, beautiful once, but now a ghastly site of death and neglect. I gulped, concerned that someone's pet must have wandered into my sister's yard. I picked it up and curled it into my arms and ran back into the house.

"Korah, this little cat was in your yard. It looks so sick." I called out.

"Don't bring that cat in here…" my sister scolded me.

"It's dying, we need to help it. Do you know who it belongs to?" I cried.

"It's my cat..." she barked.

My mother had already come to my side and was touching the little life and caressing its head.

"It's dying?!" I wailed in protest.

"I can't have it in my house, it is infested with fleas." Korah demanded.

"Daniel, go to the nearest pet store and get a flea comb, collar and shampoo. Andrea, take it to the kitchen sink and run the water to a lukewarm. We may not be able to help it...but we can at least soothe it," My mom then whispered in my ear, "It probably won't make it even with our help... I think it is just too far gone."

I ran to the sink with the little cat lying limp in my arms. Its tiny body was hot from the beating sun. I held it under the warm water and gently rubbed its fur, as the fleas jumped to its head, while others were flushed down the sinks drain. My mom came over to help, holding a dish towel as we both wrapped the dying animal. It opened its blue eyes and made the most pathetic cry. My heart became consumed with sympathy for the little life. Korah was now angry and turned on the vacuum as if I, and the wretched cat, had contaminated her home. I looked at my mom and she looked back, we said nothing but communicated our reproach. A strong hot liquid penetrated through the towel and touched my arms. I looked to see a black brown fluid had soaked the towel.

"Oh no! The poor little thing!! It's so sick." my mom cried, as she turned the water on again, touching its stream to ensure it was the right temperature. She then unwrapped the towel soaked in brown, so I could once again wash the little cat of its own defecation.

By the time my father arrived with the medicated items, the little cat was clean and towel dry. I took the flea comb and brushed its patchy hair as it lay lifeless, but breathing on my lap. I slept on the floor next to it that night.

The next day, my mother and I took the cat to the local veterinary. Korah had explained that the cat had fallen down the balcony and hadn't been well since. We explained the fall to the vet, who pulled open the cats eyes. Its big blue eyes swung back and forth from side to side as though dizzy and spinning. I had noticed that it held its little tongue out and thought it was just the sign of its impending death; an indication it had lost all control of it organs. The vet looked at my mother and said that the cat's tongue hung as a result of having lost all its front teeth and why it had no ability to hold it in. Her eyes, as well, were not the result of its starvation or fleas, but from great head trauma, not consistent with a fall.

The animal was malnourished, flea anemic and had suffered some type of major physical injury. It was so tiny, no more than five pounds at its healthy weight. How could anyone hurt such a little and sweet animal. The vet gave us medication, yet did not recommend any other treatment as he felt that she wouldn't live through the week, most likely to find its fate that very night.

When we returned to the house, it was awkward. I held the fragile little cat in my arms, vehemently protecting it as though a bear with her cub.

"Korah, Jack, we should go. It was great seeing you. I think it is best that Andrea take the cat home with her. She will care for it..." my mother advised.

My mom looked at me to see if I agreed. I nodded with great assurance.

Jack walked over to me and stroked the cat, as I looked at him confused. Jack and Korah were estranged in their actions. She seemed frustrated and angry.

"Her name is Tiffany." Jack told me with a fractured voice. His lips were compressed tight and white from emotion. He looked sad.

"Andrea, can I talk to you?" Korah asked.

"Yes."

"Privately?" Korah said sharply.

"OK." I looked at my mom and handed her the cat.

We walked to her bedroom and sat on her bed.

"Andrea, I need to tell you something that is hard..." she began.

"Korah, please, you can tell me..." I said expectantly.

"I have always resented you," she said pungently.

I looked at her confused. My emotions as a young girl at the site of the dying little animal were already mounting, so her words cut deep, and instantly the tears began to flow.

"I don't understand, why?" I could hear my voice break as I spoke.

"…Because I had to raise you. I have never felt it was fair that I lost my childhood to have to parent you and Esther." Her words pierced me.

"Korah, I don't have any memories of you ever taking care of me. I don't remember you ever being alone with me? I do have memories of Michael helping Mom and he taking care of Esther and me, but not you. Esther and I talk about how we always had Mom around our whole childhood… we can't even remember even having a babysitter," I protested.

"You didn't have a babysitter, you had me," she refuted.

"But I don't remember you babysitting? I have one memory of Mom going on a women's retreat and I was crying by the window feeling like it was the first time she had ever left. Dad got mad at me for acting up and said I was fine because he was there. When did you ever have to parent me or Esther?" I asked.

"It started when you were born."

I paused because I knew what she was implying… "You were only ten when I was born, Korah."

"I was ten, a child, and when Mom saw you… realized how you were… well you know, she was sad and became extremely depressed and wouldn't get out of bed. She wouldn't care for you; she gave up on life and didn't want to be a mother anymore."

The muscles in my face lost their form and the blood drained from my head and extremities. All ability to hold my posture was now gone and my body slumped in shame.

She continued, "At ten years old I had to be a mother. I had to change you, care for you. I have never forgiven you for that."

I couldn't talk. The pain was too great, it strained and squeezed my throat making anything I tried to say stifled. "I have memories in the hospital. I remember the hospital room, my bed. I remember mom sleeping next to me every night. I remember her holding my hand and stroking my hair. I remember her changing my bandage and coating me with ointment. I remember Dad and Michael visiting me, and helping

Mom. I don't remember you. I don't remember you there, ever?"

"I wasn't there then. I stayed home and cared for Michael and Esther while Mom cared for you at the hospital. You had surgery a lot, your major surgeries were at four years old and six years old," she said to me as if sharing information I didn't know.

"I know when I had my surgeries Korah. My memories at four years old are sketchy, but I have vivid memories at the hospital at five and six. You are not part of them," I asserted.

"Before that, Mom would have nothing to do with you. She detested you. I was the only one who made sure you were clean and fed while you were a baby. Then when you went to the hospital, I had to take care of Esther and Michael while Mom watched you in the hospital." Her voice was cold and harsh. She wanted to hurt me.

"I didn't know…" I said deflated.

"Well I think you should know. Mom hated life, became depressed and wouldn't get out of bed. You would lay in your crib and cry and Mom would just put her pillow over her head and pretend you didn't exist. You should know that at ten, I had to be a mother, your mother. It wasn't fair to me and I blamed you. I realize now that it was not your fault. I want you to understand why it's been hard for me in my relationship with you. I want to start fresh, ok?" she said with no kindness in her tone.

I couldn't breathe, I couldn't talk; I never saw this coming nor knew of my mother's detachment toward me. I tried to speak, but the words and my mouth had lost their ability. I already struggled with the realization of my ugliness as a young teen. I struggled deeply with my birth and wrestled with self-hatred… something I did not want to face or revisit at that moment.

"Ok." I answered.

I walked out of the room and down the stairs. My body was faint and my mind disoriented as my parents looked over at me. I said nothing.

We drove home from California to Tucson, a six hour drive. Tiffany laid on my lap and became sick a few times before we reached home. I was able to drape towels and change clothes on the side of the road each time. None of us protested in disgust, but in horror and sadness, hoping the little life will either survive or find peace, but in the comfort of my arms and free of fleas. The doctor gave me a syringe to feed Tiffany twice a day, which seemed to only make her sicker, yet each day she still breathed, confirming to me she wanted to live.

Tiffany survived. Her eyes were never able to focus nor her tongue contained, but her hair filled in and her bones disappeared from her skin. She lived under my bed, but the moment I came through my bedroom door she jumped up to greet me, and only me. If I brushed her, she would lay with her belly up and purr, soaking in my care. She slept touching me and was my comfort through many teen tears; a little broken life that had been thrown away became a treasure to me. She was to me my consolation, my friend, my tenderness.

After my conversation with my sister I casually asked my aunt, my mother's sister, if my mom had suffered from depression after my birth and if Korah had to step in.

"Korah never took care of you!?" my aunt said with fervor. "That is ridiculous! Korah has never cared for anything in her life but herself," she laughed. "The moment you were born, your mother never put you down. She held you, loved you and gave her every breath for your health. She has loved every one of her kids and that has never changed," my aunt declared with passion.

I wanted to believe my aunt. She could have had reason to lie to protect my heart, but my mother had truly laid her life down for her children. I found it impossible to imagine her not the mother I saw throughout my life, yet my insecurities had already taken over my soul. The words that my sister left in my heart made a lasting image of my family's recoil toward me at my birth. The dagger she intended was effective and only augmented my lack of self-worth at fourteen.

To have my sister present the night Chad was to meet my parents was more than stressful. I did not know what she was going to do, or say, nor did I have any faith she would be kind to me in front of him. Since leaving their church in Orange County, Korah had become severely depressed, not leaving her house or her bed for several months. Her plea was that they move back to Tucson and work for my dad.

I had no way to ask Korah and Jack to leave the house for the night. Korah was there so my mother could help care for her and bring her back to emotional health once again.

I heard the doorbell ring and realized Chad was at the door. My stomach filled with knots as I greeted him. My mom had cooked her Cuban-style dinner, so my house smelled of meat and rice. My father welcomed Chad as I brought him into the living room.

"Hi Chad. So it appears you have taken an interest in my daughter?" So awkward, seriously Dad?

"Yes I have," Chad said with a small chuckle. "Thank you for inviting me over," he continued with a big smile.

I am sure my father was worried that this guy was far too good looking to have any sincere intentions.

"I have a collection I want to show you." My heart dropped, knowing exactly what my dad intended to show Chad.

"Great," he naïvely responded.

My father put his hands on Chad's shoulder, "Come into my home office."

Poor Chad, he probably thought he was going to be seeing a collection of Bibles, but instead I knew far too well exactly what my dad intended to reveal. I was embarrassed and anticipated, soon, that Chad would be trying to find a way to run out the door; which was clearly my father's objective. Exasperated, I went into the kitchen to see what I could do to help my mother. Jack was sitting in the kitchen talking with my mom as she prepared the meal. She and my brother-in-law were very close. My mom was strong, loving, and affectionate. She was safe to me, my dearest friend. I couldn't imagine more reassurance, more comfort, nor could I respect another woman more than I did her. Jack was drawn to her spice and warmth as well; he respected her and leaned on her. I loved that about him.

"Dad is showing Chad his knife collection," I groaned.

"Oh my, how unfortunate for Chad," Jack chuckled.

Jack smiled at me, he was holding Luke in his arms. His baby head and soft curls rested peacefully on Jack's shoulder.

Chad and my dad entered the kitchen. I looked at Chad and he gave me the wide eyed look of, "Are you kidding me?" I shook my head and mouthed, "I'm sorry!"

"Hi Chad, so great to meet you." My mom grabbed Chad and gave him a hug.

My family was open and affectionate; it was the Abram and Anna way. I could tell Chad was not used to all the hugs.

"Chad, this is my brother-in-law, Jack, and my nephew, Luke," introducing the two men and baby.

"It's great to meet you," Chad said and reached out his hand to my brother-in-law.

"Dinner is ready, will you all join me in the dining room?" my mother called out.

All the men headed to the dining room, while I helped my mom bring in her serving dishes. My mother directed everyone where they were to sit and we each took our places at the table.

"Should I go get Korah?" Jack asked after putting his little guy back in his carrier, which was propped up on a chair.

"Oh, there she is," Jack said in surprise.

I choked and almost spit the water I was attempting to swallow onto the table. In walked my older sister, Korah, wearing a tight, short dress, her short bleached white hair was curled and over-styled; sporting new and enormous breasts, while walking with her chest visibly forward, shoulders back, looking gauche. I looked over at my mom and her jaw was dropped. My sister looked ridiculous! What was she doing?? I felt my face flush and I became instantly unnerved. Korah, without whatever she had on, was actually a small A cup. This had been such an issue of discontent for her. Tonight, she had grown remarkably, and dramatically, for what seemed to be the benefit of Chad. She walked slowly, conscious, seductively, with her lips slightly puckered. I started to laugh, nervously; my mom joined me. Jack acted as though he hadn't noticed, my Dad put his head to his plate as though staring at his reflection on its white surface, while Chad looked at my mom and me, and shifted in his seat uncomfortably. She sat down in the available chair in a slow and deliberate way. Tossed her hair and looked back at us all, her lips now even more puckered as though posing for a porn magazine.

Seriously, this could not have been a more painful night.

Chapter 10

"But You, O Lord, do not be far from Me;
O My Strength, hasten to help Me!" Psalm 22:19

JAIL: DAY TWO, 3 A.M.

I wake, wishing I could go back to my dreams, but instead I am pulled back to the current and back to jail. There was a male guard at the desk earlier, but now there is a woman who is on duty. She is very tiny, her hair is pulled back into a bouncy ponytail; she seems so little in her uniform, especially considering that she has a bullet proof vest on underneath. I sit up and muster the courage to walk to the half wall and wait. Once I do, she waves me over.

"I have been waiting for my things, it's been well over eight hours since I have been at my bunk. I would like to have something to sleep in, toothbrush and hair brush. Can you help me?"

"Let me find it," she says.

"Thank you," I answer, hoping she is more productive than the guard who slobbers. I had asked prior, but only got a slurred groan and no results.

No less than fifteen minutes later my bag is in my hands.

I am so happy to see these small items. It is dark and everyone is asleep. I want to take advantage of the quiet and decide this is the best time to go to the bathroom, brush my teeth, wash my face and feel human while the other inmates rest. I sort my items, which now have become valued treasures, place them in my steel drawer under my bed and go to the bathroom with a hair brush, toothpaste and toothbrush. The toothbrush is two inches long, awkward, but so appreciated. I begin brushing my teeth, which feels like such a luxury.

The guard walks over to me, "You are new here so I won't yell at you. If the lights are off, you cannot use the bathrooms and have to stay on your bunk quiet… no talking. If the lights above the common area are on, but not the bunk area, you can wait until your group is called to get your food, then need to go back to your bunk once you have eaten. When all the lights are on, you can use the toilets, sinks, shower, talk and hang out in the common area. Take your toothbrush and personal items back to your bunk and wait until you see all the lights on."

How do these women control when they need use the restroom? There are so many secret, unwritten rules.

I return to my bunk grateful that I made this mistake under the petite guard's watch.

JUNE 1995

With my face red and flushed, I looked into Chad's eyes, "I am so sorry about my family… and about the knives…"

"I got the message." he smiled.

We had left the family dinner and went back to Chad's patio home. His roommate was home with a date, so Chad suggested we walk to the pool to give them some privacy.

He led me down a little walkway to a small community pool. We both took off our shoes and dipped our feet at its edge. Chad looked so handsome in the moonlight's gentle haze. I hadn't felt this type of heat with anyone and was afraid of myself with him. I had such control and restraint without issue. With Chad, I was weak, and became immediately submissive, wanting more of him.

"I need to talk to you about something that I am a little nervous to bring up." I said to him.

"Ok." he looked at me apprehensively.

"Jack's brother and I have gone out a few times, nothing serious. He lives in California and works for Universal Studios. He has asked me to go with him to a premier of a movie he worked in… I haven't answered him. How do you feel about me going? We have never discussed being exclusive and I wouldn't want to hurt you by accepting."

"Do you want to go?" he looked at me with probing eyes.

Not sure how to answer, I paused, then tried to formulate my thoughts, "I think it sounds fun, but would rather be right here with you… if you don't want me to go."

"I don't want you to go. I don't want you to date anyone else," his voice matter of fact.

I was happy, surprised and attempted to act nonchalant. "So… Umm… does that mean we are not going to see anyone else?"

"Yes. I want to be exclusive… as you say," he said and smiled.

"I am good with that." I smiled back and placed my hand on his thigh above his knee. He gently touched my neck, pulling me toward him. I was powerless to his touch, his kiss. My mind became absent and lightheaded while his arms pulled me into him tightly, kissing me.

I heard a door open from one of the surrounding patio homes, which made me jump. Taken back at how enraptured and lost I became in his touch. My head cleared and I looked into his deep blue eyes.

"I am sorry about tonight… and my family." I swallowed hard, hoping he could look past the night's theatrics and see the loving family I knew and adored.

"They are fine. Will your brother-in-law, Jack, be upset about his brother?" Chad looked at me with a bit of concern.

"No. It wasn't serious. No one will be heartbroken," I responded and saw he was content.

I took a deep breath and brought up the obvious, "My sister… Umm… I don't know what to say… I am just so embarrassed."

"I didn't grow up with any siblings, so I can't relate," he said as he put his hand on my knee.

"Well, I don't think anyone can relate to Verna… excuse me, Korah." I said, rolling my eyes, accidently calling her by her given name… hoping I did not have to explain her name change.

"Yes, she seems complex," Chad responded softly, but I could tell he was holding back.

My face heated up from embarrassment. I reached down and put both hands in the water, then patted my face and neck to cool it from its burn.

"So it was just you and your dad for a while?" I tried to change the subject.

"Yes, it had been eight years after my mother died, until he married Ruth," he said and looked over at me. His eyes were soft and his touch tender.

"Was it hard to see him get married again?" I continued.

"No, I am so happy for him. My mom and dad did not have a peaceful marriage," he said as he looked down and put one of his hands in the water making it ripple softly.

"How did your mom die?"

He didn't answer, but continued to instead play with the water. I panicked, feeling that my question was too personal. Then Chad looked at me, deeply. I felt paralyzed by his expression, "She killed herself." I gasped in my heart, but hoped he didn't see my shock.

"Oh Chad, I am so sorry! I didn't know. I can't imagine your heartache." I said as my spirit sank.

He was silent again. I stared at him, not knowing what to say. Chad hesitated and then continued. "By the time she actually took her life, it was almost a relief, which is hard, because I really loved her." His head remained down and he continued to toy with the water, gazing deeply at each ripple.

"How long did she struggle?" I said and grabbed his hand.

This caused him to now look at me, "She struggled for a long time. As a small boy, some of my earliest memories are sitting at the window, watching my mom drive away. She would tell me she wasn't coming back... because she was going to take her life. I would sit at the window and wait to see her headlights return, praying she would come home. She would be gone for days throughout my life, then return. I loved her, but after time, I kind of pulled away and went on with life. She never seemed happy. She even moved out and got an apartment, wanting me to come live with her. I wouldn't, which hurt her, but I needed to stay with my father, he was safe... stable. On the outside we looked like a normal family, but at home we had secrets."

I moved his hand up and pressed it against my cheek. I could see inside that little boy, who I wanted to just hold and comfort.

"I am sure she loved you." I responded. I swallowed hard as I thought of the unanswered prayers of that little boy, and the agony of his dad who couldn't fix his son's pain, or that of his wife's.

"I know she loved me, but she had her own internal battles. She and my dad got married young, she came from an extremely rigid and religious home. She just seemed to be searching. She wasn't sure what her faith was and that was the real reason we never went to church," he said as his voice deepened.

Chad's eyes were soft, sincere, yet he had no tears, no strain in his voice, as though he was telling someone else's story.

He stopped, and looked up at me, into my eyes as if searching, "I don't know why I am telling you all this…"

I was moved by his openness. "Chad, how was it with your dad? It had to be hard for him too?"

"My dad loved her, but she put him through a lot. She wasn't faithful… I had caught her when I was twelve." he said without any deviation in his voice.

I stared at him, trying not to show my stun. "I am so sorry. Your father never left her after the affair?" I asked.

"No. She got an apartment to figure things out. My father paid for it, which didn't last long, because she came back home after she found out that she was pregnant and the apartment left vacant."

"Was the baby from the affair?"

"Yes…" he paused, took a breath and then continued.

"My father had been building a new home, the construction was complete and we moved into it, but our old home hadn't sold yet. She picked me up from school with a bottle of vodka in the front seat and drove me back to our old house. The one I lived when I was younger. She got out of the car and walked into the house with her bottle and locked the door. I banged and banged for her to let me in, she wouldn't answer. Finally, I went to the neighbors to call my dad. When she came home, that is when she told me she was pregnant."

My heart pulsed from grief, "What did your dad do when he found out about the baby?"

"I just remember my dad asked me to walk with him; our new house was on three acres with views of the Catalina Mountains. It was there he talked to me, man to man, and not to the boy I was. He explained to me that he loved her and will always love her, because she was my mother. He told me that the baby she carried will be loved and nurtured by him in the same capacity he loved me, even though not his. He wanted me to know that he would commit to embracing the baby as his very own. I wasn't so forgiving. I warned my mother that she couldn't put another child through what she had me. Not long after, she aborted the baby. I think that was her final heartbreak and she never recovered after the abortion."

He paused again. His voice even deeper, speaking slowly. "Honestly, I have felt responsible for the abortion… after what I said to her."

"You were not responsible, Chad! Please don't carry that."

"From the day she aborted the baby, my mother was emotionally gone, and would mourn the baby's expected birthday, every year. She struggled before, but never pulled out of her depression after that; the baby's life was shut down, but in the end it killed her too. The final act that took her to a new level of self-loathing. When my mom finally took her life, it was hard because a side of me was released from the daily torment of knowing her pain and fearing the day she will act out on her promises… to me it was finally over. I was sad, very sad, but had pre-pared for that day so many times. I sat at her funeral and didn't cry… I couldn't, I had nothing left."

I reached with my other hand and touched his cheek, with no words to say, but loving him more for his openness, and all that he had overcome.

"She rented a hotel room, and shot herself..." he said with an exhale.

I sat motionless, grieving for him; sad for her too. Her torment so severe, with such devastation to her own life and those she held dear. A horrific childhood past, yet he told me everything as if narrating a book he had read; a young man with no tears left to show his true pain.

Consumed by his past, I wrapped myself around him and pressed myself hard against his body, squeezing him tightly. I felt him breathe deeply and exhale long.

"I don't know why I have told you all this," he said softly.

"Chad, thank you for telling me. I am glad you did," I said.

Chapter 11

"Why did I come forth from the womb to see labor and sorrow, that my days should be consumed with shame?" Jeremiah 20:18

JAIL: DAY TWO, 5 A.M.

Violent banging wakes me up from my slumber, my trance. I am stunned and jerk, completely disoriented to where I am and confused by the sound of a car that is colliding, crashing metal against metal, my ears ring and my body feels the vibrations of each bang.

"Andrea Smith!" my name is being called vehemently with each bang. It was Officer Cain, standing at my bunk yelling within inches of my face, her baton gripped in her hand as she whacks it against the metal of my bed's frame, for effect, for fun. I sit up startled, jerked from the faraway place my dreams had taken me. I realize that when Cain had taken her post and started her habitual screaming, the in-mates' boredom to it infuriated her. Each of us had learned to drown her ranting out as background and continue to sleep unstartled. I too had already become accustomed to the sound of her chronic yell. She decided to walk to my bunk, bang her baton on the metal near my head and scream my name within two inches of my face. Inmates around me jumped as well, which pleased her. The room is dark and the actions unnecessary, even obnoxious.

"Smith." she yells, her face next to mine, spitting on my cheek. Her Neanderthal bone structure is my first image as I open my eyes.

"Yes?" I whimper, embarrassed and traumatized, as she wanted.

"Specialist Salome is at the officer's station for you. NOW!"

I threw on my reds as fast as I could, while trying to maneuver around Cain as she hovered, and headed to the guard's desk, where a woman stood. I recognize her. I had met her previously at 'orientation'.

The jail requires you to come to an orientation days prior to check-in, where they play a video explaining jail rules, provide you their booklets that describe additional procedures such as what to do if you are assaulted. The video begins with a cheeky, "We welcome you."

During my first introduction to Specialist Salome, I found her to be kind. "I admit doctors, lawyers and people from all walks of life. You will be fine and safe, I promise," she explained at orientation.

I approached her now, thankful to see someone who I thought would act humanely as she did at our first meeting. I looked quite different from when I was at orientation, per my lawyer's advice. I had shortened my hair that had been long, warmed up its color, gone are the eyelash extensions and makeup. More importantly, I am now dressed in jail-issued reds. I smile at her... she scowls at me in return. I step back, surprised. Her face now hard, her eyes show her disgust. I am shaken. Her personality quite different from orientation, the same face, but uglier. Harshness has consumed her countenance; she is not the same person.

"You put in a request to speak to me," she grunts.

"Yes, I needed to discuss a letter I received from the MVD the day before my required check-in. It states that I have thirty days to go and update my license. In my booklet it describes that any variances from court approved work locations are to be approved by you. Will you give me approval to go to the MVD, or my license will be suspended? I will call the jail recorder as required to notify them of my location."

"Fine." Her look of indignation unveiled. Why am I repulsive today, yet a human being just days prior? She writes a note on my paperwork and signs it.

"Thank you," I say, showing appreciation that is not due.

She grunts again, so I leave and return to my bunk.

The lights are still off. I am looking forward to brushing my teeth. The food tray cart emerges. Cain turns on the lights to the leisure area and leaves the bunk area lights off. Two inmates go to the cart and begin unwrapping and preparing the trays.

"Block One!" Cain yells.

The girls in my area jump out of their bunks and line up. I hesitate,

I don't eat breakfast most of the time, but since I actually didn't eat anything the day prior, I decided to get up and give breakfast a shot. The inmate who reached her hand out to me last night was getting out of her bunk, we make eye contact.

"How are you?" she whispers. "I am ok, thanks... missing coffee!" I say in a low voice. Coffee, it was the first thing I realized was not available. My back ached, my emotions were drained, what I wouldn't give at this moment for a nice hot cup of coffee to soothe my tensions and just give me that beloved treat from home. She nods, walks over to a table near the food trays and picks up a Styrofoam cup that is stacked near an igloo of orange juice. She fills the cup with hot water and returns back to her bunk, pulls out her drawer and a bag of instant coffee and stirs it with a little spoon. I realize she must have bought the instant coffee from a vending machine with her commissary money. Then she hands me the hot cup. My face feels hot from blushing. "I didn't know... thank you... I wasn't asking..." She shakes her head, and brushes the air with a kind smile and walks to the line. I am embarrassed, I didn't realize that there was even an option to have coffee, let alone unintentionally asking her to give me some of her private supply. I did appreciate the coffee, it was hot and smelled like coffee. Although embarrassed, this little cup of instant, was a pleasure I had thought beyond my reach. Once again, this woman, this inmate, has shown me such kindness.

I wait in line and grab my tray with my open hand and walk to a table. Inmates are sitting wherever they want. Cain unaware of the rules the slavering guard implemented the night before. Each seem to be choosing their location to sit down based on friendships, like a school room lunch cafeteria. I find a spot open and look at the inmates who were sitting at the table. I point to the open spot in a gesture to get permission to sit. One inmate slightly nods and I place my tray and coffee down and grab a stacked chair. So many unspoken rules, it almost feels like the jail has a system to sabotage its new inmate's ability to acclimate. I want to be able to serve my sentence without issue, but realize that with these unknown regulations and procedures it is unlikely I will carry out this journey unscathed.

Cain, again, is yelling, but I am not paying attention, nor are the other inmates. She has the company of another guard; he is male and behind the desk with her. It is an awkward time for a male guard to be hanging out in the women's unit. Inmates are waking up and are required to change into their red jumpsuits, if leaving their bunk to get breakfast. They can only do so by their bunks. So he, deliberately, I assume, is getting his intended free show. Seems very calculated. The two guards are talking and laughing, between Cain's bouts of screeching. None of the inmates are speaking, as ordered. I see the younger girls gesturing. They are animated, as they smile and laugh without sound. There are a lot of young girls. The older inmates, my age and up, seem to all keep to themselves. The young girls definitely have a pecking order and they clique in groups, pushing the limits by silently giggling and boisterously gesturing. Cain does not appreciate their level of freedom, yet really she has nothing to be angry about, they are doing as told, "eating without saying a word."

On Cain's desk is a basket of tampons and pads. I guess the women have to check them out when needed, each time. The toilets have mirrors above and no door. The male guards are ever present and not only does one have to ask for each feminine item, every single time it is needed, the women have to do so in the presence of all, including the men. I am not looking forward to the time I will have to endure this portion of my disgrace.

Breakfast consists of two large pancakes, a large pile of oatmeal that is dark brown and sickeningly sweet, with orange juice. I put my fork in the pancakes that are wet and mushy and lift up a piece that includes thick globs of syrup that string from my fork to the plate. I look around and see the young girls devouring the saturated pancakes, as well the oatmeal loaded with sugar and cinnamon. I am disgusted by the food and decide not to eat once again. I point at my plate to see if anyone wants anything before I stand up, there is a nod and immediately my entire plate is cleared of its contents. As required, I go back to my bunk. Lights are still out; I watch the young girls return to their beds and fall back to sleep. I don't know how they are able to eat all that sugar and then sleep. They must be wired. How can any of them eat this breakfast, then be still on their bunks, where they will stay for the entire day.

I pick up my mystery novel and see I have only one chapter left. I am so very sad I was finishing up the book so soon, leaving me nothing to look forward to once complete. Without a book, I will be left to just stare at the top of my bunk. There are no pencils or paper. I had thought I would journal, but not an option in this jail. The television doesn't faces away from the bunks, so no one can watch it. With no other option, I lean back and finish the last chapter of my book.

JULY, 1995

The weekend came and I was back at Chad's place. I knew I was dangerously attracted to him, unable to hold back, wanting to give myself fully. I was excited to be back in his arm and kissed by him once again. He tenderly touched my neck, brushing my hair away and leaned up against the side of my face, his lips and breath against my ear, in a soft whisper, he said, "I love you."

I pulled back, my heart was beating hard, while the blood in my head rapidly fell. I realized that this was the hour of truth and I could no longer continue without revealing my secret. "Chad, I need to show you something." He looked at me surprised. I stood up, took his hand and led him into his bedroom. He appeared completely puzzled and confused, as I directed him to sit down on a chair near his bed. The room was dimly lit; I stood in front of him, turned around to face away, and took off my shirt, and bra. With one arm I covered my breasts. I could hear him catch his breath.

"Chad, this is hard for me. I need to show you something... As a child I had a birthmark that was precancerous. They had to remove it. I was hospitalized in and out from infancy to age six. I am left with scars," my voice cracked.

I slowly, reluctantly, moved my long hair over my shoulder and off my back, wishing with all my soul that what laid beneath was not there. I longed to live a life like the average girl; yet I was not, and it was time for me to reveal my ugly truth. My hair was its cover, now it laid bare. He sat quietly as he looked at me. Before him was a gnarly, disfiguring scar. It started from just below my neck, spread across each shoulder blade, covering me like a sheet down to my waist. The skin was angry, shiny, uneven, discolored and unsightly. It was my shame.

"It looks like a burn," he said.

"Yes. Even doctors who see it for the first time assume it is from a burn. It is not though. It's from surgery for skin cancer, something called skin grafts."

My nerves started to take hold of me, and I began to tremble. I stood half naked, ashamed, and afraid… but also sad. I wanted to be perfect for him, but I was not and never would be. My dad warned me that I needed to be prepared that men would probably reject me because of my scars, being too ugly and disfigured for some to ever overcome. Chad was the first man whose rejection would have mattered.

As a child I was teased, girls would dig their nails into my back when I walked by at school to torment me and to let me know how disgusting I was. Finding clothes that would cover it was hard because it went up and onto my neck. The feeling of someone behind me made me anxious and I learned to always move and stand where my back faced walls, or where people were not in a position they might have access to see if unknowingly unveiled. I lived always aware of its presence. When I hit preadolescence the reality of how deformed I was became overwhelming. I feared not ever being loved, grew to abhor myself and pleaded with God to heal me. Created by Him in my mother's womb, I was born marked, by His hand. I became so depressed, as I watched my body mature, my breast grow, my frame become feminine, yet so did the scar that marred its beauty, symbolizing the unsightly remains of God's scorn. I vowed to stay pure in everything I did. I believed that if I did and was faithful up until my wedding night, maybe God would heal me as my reward, so I could come to my husband in confidence and he could actually want me.

At fourteen, I made a decision. Boys in school knew what lied beneath my clothes and kept their distance, even my own mother checked out once she saw it, or so Korah professed. I decided to just give up and let my insecurities win. I went into the bathroom and found a carton of pills. They were green and yellow capsules, with a prescription for a guest that had stayed at our home. They looked fatal. My mother and Esther were in bed, my father still at church. I held up one pill… afraid, but willed myself to put it in my mouth. Once I swallowed the first, the deal had been made and I grabbed one fist full after another, swallowing without reservation. I sat on the bathroom floor and began to cry. I hated myself… if only I was able to scratch my entire scar off, to demonstrate my hatred of its existence. My tears stopped and I became mad… mad at my body. I hated it, it betrayed me. I wiped my tears and put the bottle back in the medicine cabinet. As I closed the cabinet door, my face reflected in its mirror. I was content, at peace, resolute. Methodically, I walked back to my room and laid in my bed, closed my eyes and enjoyed the dark room, waiting for the ultimate blackness to take me. I began to think of my father at church and my mother in her room. My eyes welled up as I considered their pain and hurt. I wasn't thinking about them. My mind began to consider how selfish my actions were… I did this because I wasn't perfect, because I was scarred and afraid of being rejected. I thought of the memories I had in the hospital, my mother sleeping next to my bed, holding my hand, kissing my head. My scars are there because my parents wanted to save my life. They had no insurance, yet found ways to get me treatment. How could I take my life, when all they have ever tried to do was save it?

"Mom… I have done something… something that is not good." I said reluctantly.

"What honey?" she sat up.

"…I am so sorry…" I began to weep.

"You're scaring me, what is it honey?" she said anxiously.

"Mom… I have taken a bunch of pills."

"What do you mean?!" she looked confused. I didn't know what to say and stared at her in silence. She shook her head and moved to the end of her bed, gathering her thoughts, while the depth of what of my confession absorbed in her mind and heart.

"Oh my gosh, Andrea!" she said as panic set in. "Why? Why would you do this?" She looked at me, still not sure she understood, her voice raised, while unconsciously moaning between each breath.

"I..I.. just want to die, I want to be done! I am so sorry, I wasn't thinking about you and Dad." I said, feeling desperate, foolish.

"Andrea!" Frantic. "What did you take?" She stood up, grabbing my shoulders. "Jesus, help me!" she called out.

"I took the pills that are in the medicine cabinet in Esther's and my bathroom. I am not feeling well, I feel dizzy," I said and sat on the floor.

She rushed into the bathroom, and returned with the bottle. "You took these? You took these, Andrea?!"

"Yes… I am sorry." I said ashamed.

"What are they? I don't know what they are! Esther! Esther! Call your dad at the church. Tell him I am taking Andrea to the hospital… Now! Hurry!" She said crazed, manic.

She grabbed the pills and threw on pants and a shirt. Esther ran to the phone confused, frightened.

"Uh… Yes, this is Esther, Pastor Daniel's daughter, please get my Dad… (pause) Can you interrupt him, please!! … No… I need you to walk up to the podium and put a note on the pulpit… say that my mom is taking my sister, Andrea, to the hospital!" I could hear Esther, her voice strained and stressed. I felt so reckless, what did I do? I should have allowed myself to die and then wouldn't feel this regret or the shame of having to tell my mom.

"Get in the car!" my mom yelled. I walked to the car, feeling weak now. It had been a while, probably close to twenty minutes.

"Esther, get Andrea a change of clothes. I will call when I get there. Have Dad come pick you up."

My mom drove frantically to the hospital and I was immediately brought in. She handed them the bottle of pills. I was given something that made me throw up, while the nurses prepared to begin the process of pumping.

"Why, Andrea, I don't understand why?" My mother looked so confused. Her face showed complete disbelief.

"Mom… I am so sorry I hurt you. I wasn't thinking about you." Tears of regret consumed me.

"But I don't understand?"

"Excuse me Ma'am, can we speak to you?" The doctor who was standing by the curtain motioned for my mom to go where they could talk, away from me.

"Yes." she answered as she left.

I was alone, sick from the stuff they gave me, my throat sore, laying on the bed with a bowl in my hands. A nurse came in. "Hi, just checking in? How are you feeling?" she said kindly.

"Sick." I answered and turned my head to the side, wishing I could disappear.

"Hey… I know you. You're Pastor Daniel's daughter. I go to your church. What are you here for?" she looked at my chart. "Oh…"

"I am sorry, I am going to be sick. Can you come back later?" My heart dropped. I grabbed my bowl and began throwing up again.

"Andrea?" I looked up to see my father's face. He was angry.

"Dad! Dad… I am sorry!" I reached for his hand and grabbed it. He squeezed hard, then pushed my hand away, turned, threw open the curtain and walked out.

I began to sob.

My mom reentered and closed the curtain.

"Andrea… my heart is breaking… I just don't understand? Why would you do this, Honey?" she asked, still not believing.

"I just hate myself, Mom. I just want to die. I am so sorry I hurt you." I began sobbing again.

She grabbed my hand, pulled me up into her chest and we both cried.

"Is Dad mad at me?" I asked.

"No honey… he is just mad. He needs to walk and pray. Listen, we are not mad at you, Baby. We didn't know you were hurting… we just didn't know." Her voice cracked.

I was so ashamed and vowed to God to never take my life out of His hands again. I asked God to be its author once again. After that, I grew my hair long, a cover that I could hide behind. I learned to pretend, smile, act as though I felt beautiful, as though I was beautiful, but was really hiding.

Now I stood before a man that took my very breath, who I longed for, revealing what I hated, revealing to him my truth.

He said nothing. His silence made me tremble. I moved my hair off my shoulder, making it fall back down as a cover once again. I bent down to grab my shirt… he stopped me, placed his hand on my arm, stood up, and moved closer, up against me. With his other hand, he moved my hair off of my back and over my shoulder. I shivered. Then I felt his lips kiss my neck, my shoulder. I froze as he leaned down and kissed the center of my scars. My eyes burned with emotion from the gesture while the air in my chest left. His hand moved down the side of my body, down the sides of my breasts, onto my belly, pressing my body against his. He kissed my neck softly, passionately. I turn with my arm still covering my breasts and kissed his mouth. Then let my arms fall as I pressed myself against him. We embraced. "I love you, Andrea." He said softly in my ear.

I whispered, "Chad, I love you too."

Chapter 12

*"For His anger is but for a moment, His favor is for life;
Weeping may endure for a night, But joy comes in the morning."*
Psalm 30:5

JAIL: DAY TWO, 10 A.M.

My last chapter of the mystery novel has been read and I have been sitting twiddling my thumbs in the dark. I see the Bible I had set down at the end of my bunk. My heart feels a pang as I confess to myself that I was avoiding it. I reach over and grab it. I really do love this Book. It has been my constant and through it He has spoken to me personally... I do miss it, I miss hearing Him. So many times I would read and feel His presence in its Words. I never had a goal to read it daily, or coach myself to make it a chore I must check off. I read it at will, because I loved it. Each time I read it, I would pray that each Word would become true to my spirit, become part of me. He answered that. Each verse stuck, became cherished, became life.

I turn the pages and see the story of the Samaritan Woman at the Well:

Just then his disciples came back. They marveled that he (Jesus) was talking with a woman, but no one said, "What do you seek?" or, "Why are you talking with her?" John 4:27

There is a rabbinical saying, "A man should hold no conversation with a woman in the street, not even with his own wife, still less with any other woman, lest men gossip." As well, Aristotle and most Greeks of that time believed that the male was superior physically and mentally to the female. Compound this with the Greek law that a woman, who being inferior, was to be under the authority of a male throughout her life.

Beyond the fact that the woman at the well was, in fact, a woman, she was also a Samaritan. Jewish and Samaritan religious leaders taught that it was wrong to have any contact with the opposite group, enter each other's territories or even to speak to one another. The relationship between Jews and Samaritans was hostile. Josephus reported numerous violent confrontations between Jews and Samaritans throughout the first half of the first century.

I love that Jesus spoke to her. I wish I could see the disciples' faces as they walked up to their spiritual leader, speaking to a Samaritan woman. They believed Jesus, but also culturally knew this was completely inappropriate. How very perplexed they must have been at such a sight.

What is more puzzling, this woman seeks water at Jacob's well, alone and at midday (the customary time that women gathered to draw water was evening). So why would she decide to go to the well, outside her city at midday?

The woman was surprised that a Jewish man was speaking to her, so she asked:

"How is it that you, a Jew, ask for a drink from me, a woman of Samaria?" (For Jews have no dealings with Samaritans.). John 4:7-9

Jesus answered and said to her, "Whoever drinks of this water will thirst again, but whoever drinks of the water that I shall give him will never thirst. But the water that I shall give him will become in him a fountain of water springing up into everlasting life."

The woman said to Him, "Sir, give me this water, that I may not thirst, nor come here to draw."

Jesus said to her, "Go, call your husband, and come here."

The woman answered and said, "I have no husband."

Jesus said to her, "You have well said, 'I have no husband,' for you have had five husbands, and the one whom you now have is not your husband; in that you spoke truly."
John 4:13-18

So, now we have an understanding why she avoids the other women in the evening by going to the well in the afternoon, and why the living water Jesus speaks of was just what she needed to avoid her own people entirely.

The woman said to Him, "Sir, I perceive that You are a prophet."
John 4:19

Her first revelation: this man is a prophet. Yet He is more than a prophet.

The woman said to Him, "I know that Messiah is coming" (who is called Christ). "When He comes, He will tell us all things."

Jesus said to her, "I who speak to you am He." John 4:25-26

This is the first record of Jesus revealing his true identity as the Messiah. Jesus chose her. He saw her and picked her to be the first person to reveal Himself to, and through her, He would touch a multitude of people that had been rejected and unseen.

This precious Samaritan woman, in this moment, through Jesus, finds triumph over more than just her womanhood. The Messiah reached out... to her... and by doing so, He disregards the gender divide, the cultural divide of a Samaritan with a Jew, the spiritual divide of their religions, as well her disrepute in her own city, a known sinner... an outcast. Her past life soon becomes her strength, not her weakness, and now transformed by Him alone as a credible witness to her people.

"Come, see a Man who told me all things that I ever did. Could this be the Christ?"
John 4:29

So when the Samaritans had come to Him, they urged Him to stay with them; and He stayed there two days. And many more believed because of His own word.

Then they said to the woman, "Now we believe, not because of what you said, for we ourselves have heard Him and we know that this is indeed the Christ, the Savior of the world."
John 4:40-42

Jesus knew that she had been married several times, knew that she was rejected and thrown away by each husband, knew she was now living with a man whom she wasn't married. (By Jewish law, she should be stoned.) Yet, He speaks to her, even though she has sins, and reveals His identity as the Messiah (something He hadn't even revealed to the disciples yet). It was her, an outcast in every way, scorned and rejected by all, who then brings an entire city to meet the Messiah.

I am moved again by this story. Today it touches me in a different way than ever before. It was not about her as the messenger, but the message that transformed her testimony and changed her life. It doesn't matter the oracle, it matters if it comes from Him; His Word can turn ugliness into beauty, painful pasts into hope for others.

If God could do this with her, is there still hope for me? …A convict, sitting in a lowly and depraved place?

My heart and chest begin to feel warm and the heat continues into my belly, like a deep embrace, and somehow, I feel peace. I look around, sitting in a bunk, in jail, with block walls and Cain yelling as my habitat, surrounded by strangers… convicts. I am in no place to feel peace or God's presence, but I do. With the Bible open, I press its pages against my chest, to my heart and close my eyes and ask God if He is speaking to me.

I am not innocent like Paul or the Apostles were, who were imprisoned and finally killed as a result of their testimony of Jesus Christ, and because of their faith. I am here from my own doing. I am here because I failed; as much as I try to reject my conviction, I am no martyr. Yet, I feel these Words are telling me to not lose faith, to not lose heart, to not be destroyed. In this Book I find hope once again.

I squeeze my eyes shut, wanting to focus on my spirit as it fills with assurance and faith. Although I sit in the lowest of places, I feel Him here with me.

The Bible is pressed against my chest and suddenly I am aware of myself and imagine how I must look hugging this Book to all those who are near me.

I look around, embarrassed, just as Cain turns up all the lights. Inmates pile into the bathrooms. I grab my short little toothbrush and half inch tube of toothpaste, excited to clean myself. I was given packets, like ketchup packets, for deodorant. To use, I squeeze the packet to ooze out the cream, so that I can smear it under my arms.

There are a lot of women in the bathroom at the same time, so to find a sink requires elbowing through, spitting quickly, before I am pushed away by another inmate to get their chance at a sink. Others are sitting at tables in the leisure area, trying to watch tv, with the volume down so low the actual sound is like a quiet hiss. I see a couple of ladies, my age, walking in circles following the walls of the outdoor space. One woman is using the table, under the basketball hoop, as an exercise bar, attempting diagonal pushups.

"Hey, get off that table, no exercising!" Cain yells. I watch this interaction confused. I have seen movies and documentaries of jails and prisons; they all show big yards with exercise equipment. In contrast, this jail has no yard, no exercise equipment and inmates are not allowed to improvise with what is provided; while being fed large quantities of straight sugar, then made to sit in the dark, confined to their bunks all day. None of this makes sense. Are they trying to make these women crazy?

I decide to wait to brush my teeth and instead go back to the book shelf to see if I can find another book written by Sidney Sheldon. I quickly find one and return to my bunk excited to start something new. Before I do, I acknowledge that I should use the bathroom since it is almost empty, before the lights are turned off. I grab my things and walk to an open sink, brush my teeth and wash my face, attempting to pull myself back to the world around me and out of my internal Spiritual place I just escaped. Another inmate is at one of the other sinks, I recognize her; she sleeps on the top bunk across from me. She is there with two other young inmates. The young girls have a clear social structure, like High School in jail; with popular girls, loners, etc. I find it sad that this is their only world, where they create drama, friendships, develop and grow as women. She sees me and walks up to me at the sink.

Since all lights are on at the moment, she speaks freely, "I like your hair style." she says to me, with her posse of girls right behind her.

"Thanks." I say, as I smile at each girl.

She moves a step closer as I grab my towel and wipe my face. "How do you get your teeth so white?"

"Not naturally," I chuckle. The girls giggle too, but I don't know if they understood my response.

One of her friends steps up. "You look so innocent, like you don't belong here."

Such a strange statement from someone so young, to a woman who is almost forty.

"Do any of us really belong here?" I ask them all.

"Yes!" she laughs and the other girls laugh with her.

Their laughter catches me off guard and my heart feels the sting of their acceptance of this place. The original ring leader speaks up again, "I am in the bunk across from you, on top."

"Yes I recognize you," I say with a smile.

"I am Dinah," she says and smiles back.

"Dinah, I am Andrea. It is nice to meet you." It is awkward for me to introduce myself without reaching out my hand to shake hers. I wave instead and then grab my small items and walk back to my bunk to tuck them into my drawer and start my new novel.

When I reach my bunk, in all its splendor, I find it comforting in some way. I realize this small space is my own, my only refuge and all I have that is mine, with its balled sheets, and metal bunk rails that define each corner. This tiny open space is a place of solitude for me, yet in truth offers no real privacy at all. I grab the new mystery novel I had pulled. Laying down, I open its first page, but am quickly interrupted.

"You have a great figure. Do you work out a lot?" It's Dinah again, she is sitting on her bunk across from me, her feet dangling. She is a dirty blonde and appears so very young. Her face is round and sweet. She is wearing decorative Hello Kitty socks. Colorful or decorative socks are worn by the young girls and must be provided to inmates from family outside. The girls seem to wear them as though a great new pair of shoes. They stand around and adore each other's patterns and colors. It seems to make them feel unique, special, something that the others will admire and help them feel set apart from everyone else. Sadly it is the only item that they feel pretty in. I absorb that her socks give her a sense of distinction among the sea of matching polyester jumpsuits and rubber shoes.

"Thank you. I don't really work out very much, but I do watch what I eat," I whisper. Then check to see if Cain is looking, afraid our conversation will ignite her fury.

"Oh… It's ok to talk, if we whisper… but only when the lights are on." Then she continues, "Everyone gets fat when they are here. The girl who was with me at the sink, she was tiny like you when she got here. She has been here two months and already fat," Dinah says with her hands spread out.

I am not surprised. "I am sure it is hard, since they serve sugar and starch and do not allow any way to burn it off?"

"I am trying to just eat the stuff that doesn't have all the sugar," she says resolute.

I smile and put down my book, realizing she wants to talk and has no intention of ending the discussion.

"When I get out, I want to get a boob job," she declares.

She looks as if she was only sixteen, but I assume she must be at least eighteen to be in an adult jail. It is hard to see any type of figure under the thick jail suit, but from what I could see, her breasts are small, but not lacking.

"Well, I don't think you need one; however, I think if anyone does get surgery such as a breast augmentation, each should make sure they are doing it for themselves and not for anyone else. If it will help make you feel more confident, then I support it, if it is for some guy, I would not. You should really consider if this is what you want and if it is for you, or for someone else," I say as if her mother.

"Do you have children?" she asks, as her mind jumps from subject to subject with no connectivity.

"I do; a boy and a girl. I miss them," I say with a lump in my throat.

"I miss my family too, especially my mom. I am adopted, so I have two moms… but I miss my adoptive mom the most," she says openly.

I look at her inquisitively. "You have contact with your biological mom?"

"Yes, I lived with her until I was eight. She is a total drug addict… I guess I am too…" She stops and I feel the dagger that her own comment had on her heart. She quickly moves on and continues with her thought. "CPS took me away and put me in foster homes. Then I got adopted when I turned ten. My adoptive mom said when she saw me, she knew I was her daughter. She said she had already seen me in her dreams and when we met for the first time she cried with joy because she recognized me as hers."

"That is so precious!" I whisper.

Dinah continues without reaction, "I love my adoptive mom. She is so good to me. I love my biological mom too, but she is the one who introduced me to drugs. She gave me drugs when I would go and stay with her to visit. She wanted me to party with her. So, I started drugs when I was fourteen."

"Oh, Dinah, I am so sorry. You were far too young and innocent to have been introduced to something so destructive," I say in a gasp.

Seeing my response, she begins to explain, "I know, but I still love her. I know my adoptive mom is so sad I am here, but drugs are just so hard. I feel like I am better here." She looks around.

I swallow air once again and feel my own emotions build with the thought of her life and acceptance of where she is. "It breaks my heart that you would say that. God Himself looked down from heaven, showed you to your adoptive mother before she met you, to give you a new destiny, new identity, and a new life. Your biology is part of your story, but it is not a forecast of your future."

I breathe in hard, but feel I must continue, as if she were my own daughter. "Dinah, I want you to know that I feel that God showed your precious face to your adoptive mom before her earthly eyes ever looked upon you, because you are special. Don't let this place steal from you what God gave you. Don't go back to the destruction He pulled you from, or not accept the new life and destiny that is now yours to take."

I persist, "I know it is hard to hear this, when everything around us tells us that we are lowly and forgotten, but I know that there is more to you than this. I, too, am certain that your adoptive mother believes that there is more to you than your past. It hurts me to see you, and all the young girls, who have learned to accept the psychological belittling that is rampant here. Don't believe it, please don't believe it. These guards are small and get pleasure in mistreating and lessening the individuals they oversee. I fear that you have accepted that this place is who you are, yet it is not. You are so valuable, so much so that God looked at you and separated you to a family who will love and care for you and give you opportunity that equals your potential. I am happy you love your biological mother, but that is not the image of your future, but only what you overcame. You have been given a new future."

"Please, remember this and believe that you are beautiful, you have great worth, you have people who love you and believe in you. Do everything you can to get help with the drug addiction. It is unfair that you were introduced as a small child. To me it looks like your whole life has been attacked and targeted. The scriptures say, 'Satan comes to steal, kill and destroy.' Make no mistake, Satan only goes after what he is afraid of, what he knows is valuable. No thief steals that which is worthless, but goes for what has the greatest value. If you were worthless, Satan wouldn't care. Let that be evidence of how much influence you have and the potential inside you. If you look at these guards, this is as good as it gets for them… Their joy in life is to get off on yelling, tormenting, making others feel lowly, when in truth, they demean you to make themselves feel better. You have such opportunity for greatness.

If you can come from addiction, and then this hell, and rise above and beyond it, and become well, nothing would be too great for you. People who know and love you will be in awe and you will have no limits."

Dinah is crying, her are eyes red and cheeks wet. She jumps off of her bunk, "I'm sorry… I am going to be sick!" she says in a distorted and belabored voice. She lunges toward the small garbage can that sits between our two bunks and picks it up and holds it as she heaves into it. We are not allowed to touch each other, so I sit and watch, but want to rub her back and hold her hair as a mother. Her sickness surprises me, she was fine and suddenly became ill, but I feel it was her beaten spirit that became sick. The message of value and her worth I spoke over her, was in direct contrast from anything she believed or told herself. She stood up and over the small trash can. Her face now sweaty and wet.

"Are you ok?" I ask softly.

"Yes… I don't know what came over me. Thank you for what you said; I am sorry. I need to clean this before Officer Cain gets upset," she says in a strained voice.

"Five minutes everyone," Cain warns.

Dinah grabs the bag inside the can and ties it up and takes it to the larger trash in the bathroom.

"What do you think you are doing?" yells Cain as she sees Dinah with a bag heading to the bathroom. Lights are still on, but she doesn't understand what Dinah has in her hand.

"Officer Cain, I threw up in the trash can, I am just changing out the bag," she says in a stuttered voice.

Content, Cain gives her final warning, "Make it quick. Lights out in five."

"I will." Dinah answers as she runs to the large trash.

She returns to her bunk as the lights go out. In the darkness, I see Dinah look over at me as she tucks herself under her sheet. I can see her wipe her face, and realize she is beginning to cry again. I lay my head down on the thin mattress and smile at her. She rests her head down and smiles back, then close her eyes.

"Please, Lord, touch her heart so that she may hear You while she dreams," I pray silently.

Chapter 13

*"Now may the God of hope fill you with all joy and peace in believing,
that you may abound in hope by the power of the Holy Spirit."*
Romans 15:13

SEPTEMBER 1995

"Andrea, what if Chad proposes to you? You know Chad's dad proposed
to Ruth on their first date. These Smith boys seem to be in a hurry."
My mom said with concern. Chad and I had been dating for only two
months, but my parents could see our connection was deep and our
love real. I was sitting on the end of her bed, a place she and I were
often while we solved and discussed the world's problems.

My father hurriedly entered, having been in ear shot to my mother's
question, "I too would like to know what you would do if Chad proposed to you, Andrea?" he asked poignantly.

I hesitated, then answered, "I would say 'yes'!"

"Andrea, you barely know this kid!" my mother gasped.

"I feel like I do know him… and I am not letting this one go. If he
asks to marry me, I would say yes," I said determinedly. This was not the
answer that they had hoped for.

I left their room awkwardly and went back to my own to change,
thinking how fast things had progressed with Chad. It had been a
whirlwind, but I could honestly say that I was truly falling in love
with him. It was scary, but I decided to let my heart go to him without
restraint. If it ended, it would end fast and I would have no regrets.
I could tell my parents were nervous; they hadn't seen me so taken.
I heard the doorbell, which interrupted my thoughts, and caused me
to race to the door before Esther or my parents, excited to see Chad
when opened.

"Ready?" he said, with his hand reaching for mine.

"Ready." I said with a smile.

We had spent every day together, on weekends and after work. Tonight we were on our way to dinner. As he drove, I took his free hand and cradled it in my mine. His hands were strong and handsome. As I looked at him and back at his hand, I realized I loved him. I wasn't falling, but was sincerely in love. He was the one, I told myself. I opened his hand and kissed the center of his palm.

"Chad, I.. I.. um.. I am waiting… for marriage. Do you know what I mean?" I said timidly, feeling uncomfortable.

He glanced over at me and smiled, and squeezed my hand tightly. "I know."

I smiled, glad I didn't have to continue with that portion of the conversation, but my anxiety still present for what I still felt I needed to say.

"Um.. I haven't been with anyone, but.. I.. I know things are different for you." I felt my air trapped in my lungs, making my voice sound peculiar and labored.

His face changed and he turned to me to talk.

I interrupted him before he could say anything, "Best to not talk to me about any of it… ok? I would like to keep things like this, just about us, no one else."

He looked over at me again, his face serious. He was quiet for a while, then responded, "Ok."

I lifted his hand to my lips and kissed it again.

I was entirely, and incredibly insecure. Having no history with anyone sexually, and with the scars I carried, I knew that whatever and whoever he was involved with in the past would tear me up. It was truly best for me to enjoy the ignorance of what I did not know and focus only on our love for each other.

JAIL: DAY TWO, NOON

The cart of trays are back. It is lunchtime. Cain had turned off the lights, and we all sat in our bunks in the dark, quiet for hours.

Cain yells, "Block One!"

I am in Block One, on the other side of the glass room is Block Two, who will be called next to get in line to eat; it's like a pecking order I suppose. The girls in the glass room are in the GRD, or "grid." They eat at their bunks, unable to leave that space, even when lights are on. They are called last for mealtime. Dinah waves at me to sit with her and her friends. I smile and sit down, but feel out of place to be sitting at a table with a bunch of young girls. I can tell they can be full of drama, with levels of popularity which seems an integral part of their daily interactions.

Lunch is a bologna sandwich on white bread, banana, and grape juice. I can't remember the last time I have had a bologna sandwich. I eat this time, although it was quite unpleasant. I do need to eat at some point, so I make myself eat this. Instead of grape juice I ask for permission to go to the water fountain to fill my Styrofoam cup. There is a water fountain, but accessible only if permission is granted.

"This is Andrea, she is nice to me, and I like her," Dinah whispers to her friends.

"I like your hair. Where do you get it done?" one of the girls ask.

"Shhh, I am not going to let you get her in trouble. You are here for another nine months, there is no way you will remember her hair place." Dinah whispers while looking back at Cain, making sure she is not looking in our direction.

We all sit quietly, saying nothing after Dinah scolded her friend. They all seem to follow her lead. I am happy with the silence. I appreciate her gesture of friendship, but do not belong at this table. I offer my banana to those around me and go back to my book. The few lights are turned off and we are forced to the confinement of our bunks for the rest of the day, in darkness.

AUGUST, 1995

I was running late. I felt panicked and wished I hadn't told Chad that I would come by his house before our church's Thursday night service. I didn't want to see my father's stern look of disappointment as I shuffled into the pew after the service had started. Chad's roommate was out front talking to a neighbor. He waved at me. I waved back as I walked to the door. It was locked, so I rang the doorbell. There was no answer. I turned back around to call to Chad's roommate. "Why is the door locked?" I asked. He waved his hands up in the air gesturing that he didn't know. I rang the door again and knocked. Silence. "Chad, are you there?" I yelled. "I'm going to be late for church! Will you please open the door?" Now frustrated, and rattled by my tardiness that extended with each second.

"Chad, are you there?" I yelled.

Finally he opened the door.

With my hands on my hips, "where were you? I have to go." I said sternly.

He smiled and reached both of his hands out for mine, "calm down, just a minute. I have something for you."

I heard music. It was Bryan Adams, *Have you ever loved a woman?* With both my hands in his, he walked backwards and led me to his small patio. There were candles lit everywhere and in the center the candles spelled out "I love you."

Roses were lying down where we were standing.

"This is for me? This is so sweet!!!" My face flushed with a sting of guilt for having been frustrated.

"Andrea." I looked at him, his face serious at first and then his sexy smile. I laughed. "…Andrea." He said again.

I smiled back, "Yes?" confused, trying to focus while I looked around at all the candles and roses.

We had just gone to see the movie, Don Juan Demarco with Johnny Depp. Chad told me the theme song from the movie was his to me. He must have bought the soundtrack, I thought to myself. The words are so sweet.

"When did you get this soundtrack?" I asked, touched, excited.

"Andrea." He said strongly, forcing my thoughts and attention to now be on him. Still holding my hands in his, he lowered himself onto one knee. I gasped.

I stood paralyzed as he pulled out a little black box out of his pocket and opened it. Inside a beautiful engagement ring with a one-carat diamond center stone. My head spun, my heart leaped.

"Will you marry me?" he asked.

Since meeting at the gym, it had only been three months. Here he was on one knee asking for my hand. I had no secrets from him, yet he loved me.

I choked, and cleared my throat as I made him stand. Then I threw my arms around his neck and before I kissed his mouth I answered, "you know I will, yes!!"

JAIL: DAY TWO, 7 PM

I look up at the scratched calendar above me. It taunts me, reminding me of how long the road is ahead.

Sleep is another tormenter. The days and nights are hard, not only due to the thin mattress and the ache of my back from its warped board, but also from the heat. There is a small standing fan in the center of the bunks, but the fan doesn't lower the intensity of this humid heat. Its only benefit is its sound that drowns out some of Cain's ranting when on duty. I struggle to sleep, because my body hasn't adapted to being down all day and all night like the other inmates. I do find some consolation in the mystery novel and the Bible to get through the long hot hours of this, my second day.

Dinner trays are being set up by two inmates. My current life revolves around food. When I see them, I know I can soon stand. When I do, my joints ache. The partial lighting over the common area is uplifting to me, which is pathetic. I am excited that it is dinner time, but not because of the food, or that I am hungry, but eager to be released from my bunk. I am but a caged animal, excited that my only activity is to be able to grab a chair and sit under a bit of light. This is the only highlight of my day and the extent of liberty's leash, which I so quickly seem to conform to. Again, how very pathetic.

Dinner is served under the watchful eye of Officer Santanas. She is the deputy with the slurred speech, who again perches at her post with clinched teeth and bad skin. This time, I sit alone with enigmatic strangers. Today, Officer Santanas doesn't seem to mind people sitting where they choose. The guards and their rules are a mystery, changing at whim, yet severe consequences to those that become their casualty.

Once done eating, we all file back to our bunks and the lights turn off over the common area. Darkness greets me once again. One fifteen minute break earlier that morning, then hour after hour in one spot. I realize that all day these ladies have learned to sleep. They sleep through the night and the day. It doesn't seem possible to condition yourself to sleep this much, but they have. Lights are off all but thirty minutes the entire day; they eat, then sleep. We sit in darkness, cannot talk, or move about. Even a dog in the pound can move around at whim in his confinement, he can drink, go the bathroom as needed, a luxury prohibited here. How low have I sunk to envy a dog in the pound? This thought makes me close my eyes and try to sleep so I may find escape from my reality once again.

NOVEMBER, 1995

Chad and my wedding had over one thousand attendees. It was total chaos with generally members from my father's church of whom Chad and I did not know personally; however, it was so important to me that I married Chad in the church. I wanted to stand at the altar and vow to love him, forsaking all others until death before God. Our reception was crazy too. There were too many people, requiring tables to be added in hallways and near bathrooms, and eventually running out of food. I was so happy to leave the whole event and start my life with the one I loved.

Chad carried me into our hotel room; I was still in my wedding dress. He had to help me get out of it and untangle my hair from the veil. I was wearing a corset, stockings and garter underneath. I believe those items woke Chad up from being tired and worn out from a long night. After he helped me step out of the dress, I went to the bathroom to put on the silk white nightgown I had set out and planned to wear that night, our first night… my first night.

I stood looking at myself in the mirror, scared, but excited. I had waited for him, I had waited for this moment. "Please God, give me confidence to feel beautiful." I prayed. I didn't though. "Please God?" my last and final plea-a prayer that I had prayed since childhood, yet still unanswered. I turned around in the mirror and saw what I had hoped would be gone. I was still disfigured, still marred.

My eyes had tears that wanted to be released, but I held them back, willed them away, took a breath and reached for the handle, knowing he was waiting for me on the other side of the door. I opened slowly and then saw Chad; he was beautiful and smiling at me. His shirt was off, but tuxedo pants still on. I smiled at him. I loved him so much and I knew he loved me too… I just wished that I could be beautiful for him... He reached his hands out to me and I met them with mine. He pulled me into him and caressed my face, my neck, then kissed my mouth. I turned and reached to turn off the lights, but he put his hand on mine and stopped me, "let's leave the lights on," he said with a smile. I shivered as he pulled me close again and began to kiss my shoulder. He looked back at me and softly pulled the straps of my nightie off my shoulder, one at a time, letting the nightie fall to my feet, leaving me standing naked. He picked me up and carried me to the bed and laid me down. He undressed himself from his remaining clothes. We were naked. I was scared, but completely dizzy from the sight of him. I wanted him, I was helpless. He came back to me and crawled onto the bed, and over me. Our naked bodies touched. He brushed his lips against mine, softly, a tease, not even a real touch. I could feel his breath on my face and I trembled with excitement, from nerves. Then he gently kissed me, tenderly. I melted. His kiss became more passionate. Enveloped by him, I returned his passion. He let his body rest on mine, I felt him, all of him against me. I wrapped my arms and legs around him. Now warm, burning. I returned his kisses, pressing my hands tightly around him. I wanted him, I wanted all of him. He began to kiss my neck, my shoulders and my breasts. I felt heat go to my face, now yearning and longing for him. His touch made me feel crazy. "I can't believe I am doing this." I say delirious, feeling guilty for letting myself go to this gorgeous, man, to my husband... my husband. I felt myself soar, my body enraptured, burning, but gratified. I thought this would hurt, being my first time; it didn't. I was spiraling in this crazy intimacy, shared between two people, between Chad and me, enjoying each other, wanting each other, loving each other.

I laid next to him, dizzy from his tenderness, his passion. He leaned in and kissed my lips and then my shoulder. I smiled, but laid still. He reached over and turned out the lights. My first time, our first time, a beautiful night over. I didn't move and soon could hear him fall asleep. I waited until I was sure. Then quietly grabbed a blanket and tiptoed to the balcony of our room. It overlooked the city, lights were twinkling. I sat and stared, as my emotions hit me with strength, rising from deep within. I breathed hard to control myself, but tears began to fall. I knew I was just a child, but deep in my heart, I thought that God would uphold my bargain, that He would heal me, so that I would not be scarred when I presented myself to my husband. I knew down deep it was a foolish hope, but I truly wanted to feel beautiful to him. I wanted to be as beautiful to him, as he was to me. I never will be. I sat on the balcony with my heart broken, disappointed, betrayed.

"Andrea, are you ok?" I hear Chad's voice behind me.

I turned and there he stood, still naked, still perfect. "I didn't mean to wake you, I thought I was quiet," I said as he reached out and touched my cheek.

"I didn't hear you, I reached for you and you were not next to me," he said and looked at me closer realizing my face was wet with tears. "What's wrong? Did I hurt you?" he said confused.

"No! You were tender. I loved being with you." I cleared my throat and wiped my face. "Chad, I just don't understand, our wedding was so chaotic, I worry that God hasn't blessed our marriage." I was lying. I didn't want him to know how ugly I felt. I didn't want him to know why I wept.

He exhaled hard and scooped me up into his arms. "It is fine. We are married. I love you, you love me. God is going to bless us. Come with me."

He led me to the bed and I wrapped around him. I did love him so; I just wished I could be the beautiful wife he deserved.

Chapter 14

"The heart is deceitful above all things, And desperately wicked; Who can know it?" Jeremiah 17:9

DECEMBER, 1997

My little home smelled of pine from the tiny tree Chad and I had decorated in the corner of our living room. It was Christmas Eve, I was hastily wrapping last minute gifts for my family and my husband of two years. Life was good, I was so happy and excited about the holiday season. Chad and I lived very small, but thought we were rich, and even felt guilty for what we believed to be a luxuriant life. Together we dolled up his little home, tiled the entire house with our own hands. I planted flowers in the patio where we enjoyed many evening meals, accompanied by music, laughter, and love-making, in the very spot he proposed to me. I was so happy, so in love. My love for Chad intensified each day, growing deeper and stronger with time. Yet I still struggled tremendously with my scars. They became Chad's and my secret. He protected me, I hid them. I was ashamed. Chad understood this and sheltered me, holding my truth safe and to himself.

Spread out on the floor, with wrapping paper and Christmas gifts piled all around, I eagerly worked on each with ribbons and bows. I enjoyed this time of year, especially the little ones, who made the holidays bright and exciting. I had been off birth control for one year, wanting to one day hold in my arms a little one of our own, excited to start a family together.

My phone rang and surprisingly the call was from my sister, Korah. I was surprised to hear from her, since she and I were not really speaking to each other.

"Korah?" I answered with a question in my tone.

"Andrea, can I come over? I have something urgent to talk to you about," she said as if out of breath.

I was silent, confused, "Umm... ok?" I said reluctantly.

My stomach felt sick. She was the last person I wanted to see. The sound of her urgency and secrecy in her behavior had me on guard.

Korah lived only minutes away, so I shoved the stacks of gifts in the closet and looked toward the kitchen cabinet questioning if I should take a shot of something strong, as I contemplated what 'important' issue she may have. What could my sister need from me?

My doorbell rang... I sighed and gathered that it was now too late for a strong gulp of spirit. Reluctantly, I opened the door and ushered my sister into my home and into my living room.

"Do you want a cup of coffee?" I asked.

"Yes, please." She was wearing sweats. I never knew what personality to prepare for each time I saw her, but her clothes did give me an indication of her emotional state. I brought her a cup as she curled up on the sofa and pulled a nearby blanket up to her chin.

"Andrea" she said as she swept back her hair, while clearing her throat, "I'm leaving Jack."

The blood dropped from my head. I stared at her in disbelief as she held her glare, waiting for my response. Now it was my turn to clear my throat. Whatever our past, she was my sister. This would not be easy for her or for my parent's church. I touched her hand and told her I would be by her side; she would not walk this alone.

As a preacher's daughter, the debauchery that I witnessed in my father's church, and many other churches that I had contact with, was without end. Many and continual affairs were caught between our youth pastor and our music director, youth pastor's wife with college students, janitor with the church lady, Sunday school teacher with the usher, the list goes on and on, yet somehow all was neatly swept under the rug, tightly tucked away with little damage to the daily functions of the services. If our church walls could talk, there would be a lot of licentious behavior to be told in what was supposed to be God's house. However, in spite of all the sinfulness and immorality, the church and its services never missed a beat and the people kept coming, turning a blind eye to the many dramas that ensued.

Beyond the typical affairs, when and where it seemed the Bible was preached, crazy people flocked. The extreme insane were a part of my life and frequently so. One Sunday we had people with 666 written on their foreheads picketing out front of our church doors. Another Sunday, bomb-detecting dogs rushed in with cops after a threatening call was made to the police department promising to blow the congregation up. Another memorable crazy moment was when a man, a complete stranger to our congregation, ran down the aisle during a service toward my father, who was preaching at the pulpit, with an axe, waving it, determined to end my dad right there and then in a bloody exhibition. The man, wild and crazed, with axe in head, ran and reached the altar, but suddenly turned to see my grandfather, Abram, sitting in the front pew (known and beloved as "Dad"). He stopped and decided that before he murdered my father, he would first spit on Abram, which he did. As my grandfather softly wiped the spit from his face, several men in the congregation ran and tackled the demented fellow at the altar steps, holding him while the police were called. My dad only stopped for a moment, thanked those who intervened, and without much pause, continued his message.

It's hard to imagine such terrible things happen, even in the Lord's own house. Yet the church, because it consists of people, is not immune to the wicked and depraved. Our worst discovery was that one of our ushers had been molesting children in the counting room during service. Children coming to learn about Jesus, assaulted by its leaders. At times I felt angry with God for allowing these things to happen, but then read the Scripture, *"Jesus wept."* John 11:35. This is the shortest Scripture in the Bible, but so powerful. How many times has God wept over the actions not just of the world, but of His own people? A burden I became aware of in my youth, my God weeps.

In spite of all the crazy threats, fanatical minded people and adulterous love affairs, my father's church seemed impenetrable. Its masses continued until it met its demise in Korah's divorce. The congregation could look the other way during scandals, infidelity and the bizarre, but divorce ripped it apart.

The church split in two: those who stood by and believed Korah's many allegations, and those who didn't. Jack was beloved by many. His heart and kindness was known and trusted. This faction took its toll on attendance as well as the church's financial support.

As a family, we publicly, without show of waiver, stood by Korah. She needed us. Chad worked with her tirelessly to help her recover her personal finances. He gave of his time and effort to help her get her affairs in order, so that she could stand on her own.

My parents also stood by Korah, without question. They supported, backed and defended her without fail or hesitation. Not only did they take Korah in to live with them, they became her kids' caregivers, financial custodians and Korah's promoters.

The church's private Christian school had to close, due to the inability to support it. The school was a leading private Christian elementary school in our city, serving the community for over twenty years. It was a personal love and vision of my father's and the principal who started the school. Unfortunately, the school was never self-sufficient and relied heavily on the church to finance it to stay afloat. With the loss in members and immediate drop in financial backing, the church could no longer support it.

In addition to working with my sister, Chad began to come in to our church office, after his work hours, to review the financials and see how he could help remedy the severe condition the church was in.

The facility had grown over the years to accommodate its once larger numbers, stretching an entire city block. Now its enormity had become a burden, due to the recent mass exodus. We needed answers.

Esther, in efforts to help the financial and school crisis, wrote a charter and submitted it the Arizona Department of Education. It was written as a "family values" charter. Its concept was teaching moral values, implementing high standards, focusing on excellence in education, while offering many sports programs that encouraged team building. It was approved and she presented, to the church board, the idea of opening a state-and federally-funded elementary charter school. Esther then hired the private school's staff back, and many of its students also chose to enroll in the new charter. The school and its concept was extremely successful, with student waiting lists for every class. Now the expensive property was once again filled with children and a school that was not a drain financially on the church, but a benefit. With the church now receiving rent every month for the property usage, things were starting to look up again.

Esther also was able to relieve even more of the church's financial emergency by purchasing the desks, chairs, books and chalk boards from the church. Her efforts were a huge aid and gave my father the ability to focus back on his writing and sermons and be released from the pressures that the financial crisis had taken on the ministry. Yet, the church had lost many of its members and many who stayed were close to leaving. The divorce not only divided the church, its finances and its ministry, my parent's health was quickly failing too, and there was nothing I could do to help.

JAIL: DAY THREE

Today I will be released from jail on work release! I work for my sister, Esther. She has seven elementary charter schools throughout Arizona which includes six hundred employees. I am her chief of operations, overseeing budgets, human resources and facilities. Esther had sent a letter to the judge requesting that I be allowed to be on work release from nine a.m. to nine p.m. during the work week and after my first forty eight hours. The judge agreed to these terms and signed judgment orders for the jail to release me during such times, permitted only to go to my home office and to the corporate office to work.

I now sit on my bunk in the dark while I wait for the clock to hit 9 a.m. My bed is made. I can't wait to feel human again, and be released from this cage and able join the outside world, if only for a short time. Most of the girls in Block One seem to be either on work release, or work furlough, which means they, with a group of other inmates, go out and pick up trash on the side of the road, or sweep parks. The entire room is dark. Most of the inmates are sleeping. I have been watching for two days what other inmates do when they check out. Without any instructions, I fear I will make a mistake, but have learned it is better not to ask the guards for help. I am nervous, and excited.

I can only imagine how ridiculous I look as I sit on the side of my bed watching the large round clock that sits above the guard's desk tick. It teases those captive to it, making time screech to a painful pace once behind these bars. I have wished for time to pause since the day I held my son in my arms, wanting each phase of his and my daughter's life to be preserved so that I may savor each moment longer. Time rushes by in the world beyond these walls, yet here it freezes, without motion. We sit in the dark, minute after minute, hour after hour, day after day. Each time the clock ticks, it does so with insult, yet time is our entire existence; while the rest of the world tries to catch up to its unyielding race, we watch its sluggish pulse, aware of each thrust, each second, every minute. It is the symbol of our hostage state, our deserving hell… because the decisions we have made has cost us our lives, our time. My eyes focus on the minute hand, my mind can hear each second's pound, an ever so quiet click in my ear, but a loud bang in my mind.

As soon as the minute hand hits the twelve, I jump up and walk to the guard's desk. Another inmate is ahead of me. She too was watching the clock and nine o'clock was her freedom hour. She fills out the form that sits available. I follow her lead. Then she leaves her work release paperwork on the desk. I follow suit and step back against the wall next to her. Cain acts as though she doesn't see us and doesn't care that we are waiting, as she sits watching the monitor of inmates sleeping. Finally she turns, without looking at us, and grabs our papers. She rolls her chair to the back of her desk and pulls our cards from an alphabetical system. This seems daunting to her, and she takes her time to figure out where our alphabetical letters would be in the shelves. She pulls my card and slams it on the desk with my paperwork in an exasperated huff. On the card is my picture, my mug shot. I want to laugh because it's hideous. I embody the image of a true criminal. My face is surrounded by the grey blanket they draped on my neck. I am not smiling and the pose I held was not captured. I look angry, villainous. I find it comedic, and stare at it with a chuckle under my breath. I look up at Cain and quickly stop myself; none of this is funny, in truth, it is very tragic. I look at myself again; I am disgusting, an offender. Before me is my face, my record, my reality. Cain never looks in our direction, but turns her head so we see only the back of hers and lifts her arms to wave us on.

The inmate next to me quickly takes that as a signal and pushes the door to the block open. I shadow her out to the jail hallway. She, with a skip to her walk, turns left and proceeds down the hallway to a locked door among the many. She doesn't do anything but stands in front of a camera and waits. She is older than me with shoulder length hair. She looks like she is in her late forties, maybe early fifties. I would have been completely lost, not knowing which way to turn in the hallway, which door to go through or what to do once I walked out of the block. I was so grateful that she was there with me and I was able to follow her lead and learn.

"Let's hope it's not Samil. He will take his time to open the door. He is a total jackass," she says freely.

"I am following your every move. I don't know what the procedures are, and am really appreciating that your time out is the same as mine," I say softly to her, letting her know if she has any direction to give me, I will take it.

"So, FYI, Samil and all the front desk people are really awful. They will yell at you, just to yell. They won't help you or explain any procedures for work release. Here is the 411, sign the form on the desk and put your badge on the desk, next to the form, then walk and stand by your locker. Do you remember what number your car keys are under?" She is talking fast, so that once the door opens the conversation will be complete.

"Yes." I answer short for time purposes.

"When you sign the form, ask for your keys and tell him the number," she says and moves her head slightly toward me, but makes no obvious motions to signal that we are having a conversation.

I exhale, feeling a bit more at ease now that I know what to expect. "Thanks. Really, I could only imagine how bad this would have gone for me if I didn't have your help."

She nods slowly. "They are really into writing people up for not following these procedures."

"I am shocked at how hostile they are," I say, giving my two cents.

"I so agree." The other inmate answers strongly and even looks at me as a formal acknowledgment.

The door buzzer sounds and the inmate pushes it, entering the jail waiting room. The front desk is on right and lockers on the left. I fill out the form and leave my badge on the desk, then call out "my car is parked on number seven." And walk to my locker… and wait.

Samil was at the front desk. He is an ugly little Caucasian man, with deformed ears, little beady eyes and a grossly oversized bottom lip, which hangs open and never shuts… a bitter small man. He slams the door that holds the locker keys, marches toward me. "How many days do you have?" he thunders. His demeanor is severe and insolent. "Twenty," I say quickly.

He glares and then hisses, "Well then you need to get your own lock. This is the last time I will open it for you. Put some money in the commissary and get yourself a jail-issued lock of your own."

With that he storms over to the other inmate's locker and beats it too. Then dramatically throws the locker keys back in the drawer. I chuckle as a result of how obnoxious he acts. I have never seen anyone so ridiculous.

I grab my purse and trade out the rubber size 8 to my own pretty sandals from my locker; a pitiful sight to have such lovely familiar things in such a lowly place. Then I freeze and realize Samil forgot to get my car keys. My stomach rolls as I muster up the strength to ask him again.

I walk to the desk, clear my throat, "Sir, my car keys… number seven," I stutter.

"I opened your locker." he says with such force that spray from his spit erupts from his long horse-like teeth and hits my face.

"My car keys?" I say again.

"…Fuck," he says and glares at me with such loathing I cringe.

He smashes the drawer he was placing our badges in. With fists clinched, he bangs his hands on the desk in crazed anger and walks to a small cabinet.

"What kind of keys are they?" he rages.

"I am parked on lot seven." I answer, feeling that was what he needed to know.

"I heard you! What… kind… of… car… do… you… have?" he says slowly, deliberately delaying each consonant so that his words are overly emphasized.

My face flushes and I answer, embarrassed… "Mercedes…"

He grabs the keys from the cabinet and then pounds them on the counter as he stares me down. His hostility even more escalated by the price tag he assumed belonged to those keys.

I take them and walk out the front door. The other inmate is behind me. The sun is shining, it is bright and beautiful.

"Oh my gosh! That was ridiculous." I blurt.

"I know. I have never seen anyone act like that, but unfortunately he is consistent," she says. Our relief to be out shows in our boisterous body language.

"It feels like a joke. Could he really be that rotten and bitter? To actually act like that everyday has to take its toll on his health," I say in disbelief.

"Crazy. It is all just crazy," she says. She doesn't look like a criminal or someone who belongs in jail. She has a soft face, stands with poise. Her hair is a dark blond with grey that curls under at the ends. I want to hug her, but I don't… but I want to.

"He must be getting off on it. A small insignificant man feeling important, I guess." I say while walking with her to the parking lot.

"Unfortunately, the others are not better," she says as she leans in close as if this was a secret.

"Well, I will pray that I don't have to have any more encounters with Samil."

"Good luck on that!" she says as she presses the button on her car key making her car chirp.

We both wave and go our own ways. My car is black, with shiny chrome custom wheels. It looks very out of place in this parking lot. Before I start my car, I pull the phone from my purse and see that there are many texts and email messages from my friends, my parents, Esther and my brother; comforting words, prayers, encouragement. I told all of them not to call or text, I told them I wanted to be left alone... they didn't listen. I didn't know how much I would need and cherish each word. I feel so beaten, so ugly, yet they remind me that I am loved, needed and there is more to me than this place.

My emotions are all over the place; I am horrified with what I have been through, terrified to return, excited to be released, saddened that with all the texts and voice messages, there is not one from my husband; this makes me weep hard... this time no one is there to see, so I let my tears fall as I drive to my home.

The route from the Pima County Jail to my home is like driving from one country to another. The jail is on the side of town where the highway and train tracks break through its outskirts. Houses along the way boast tin and pressboard additions erected from their sides. These type of structures anywhere else in this city would be quickly assessed, fined and permits required; however, when it comes to southwest Tucson, the government employees, or county assessor, seem to stare with blind eyes. City politicians love to throw money at south Tucson, but shrug when there is no actual benefit from its funding; a lot of talk about how they help the south side, without actually setting foot to assess its progress. Old sofas and chain-link fences abound on each porch and yard. Streets do not flaunt medians, curbs or landscaping. It is a sad, neglected part of the city. Being near the airport and highway, this is all most visitors see of our city. I am sure many wonder what could possibly bring anyone to Tucson, Arizona; a dirty city riddled with poverty and dilapidated buildings, where dogs and kids run loose and parents of school children plead for security.

In less than thirty minutes of my route home, Tucson becomes clean, landscaped, with restaurants, thriving commerce, houses on acres, SUV's and family sedans. My neighborhood is an old country club with estates that stretch out with manicured lawns and grand entrances; built in the fifties and sixties, the homes spread wide, flaunting yards of green grass and tall shading trees. In the center of the neighborhood is its old boys' club, boasting a golf course, tennis, pool and even a men's only grill. Women are guests, not members. The neighborhood is filled with both young families and the elderly.

Tucson terrain makes for crazy streets that turn, drop, and curve, yet the country club has wide open streets that allow children to ride bikes, play in the grass and climb trees. Other neighborhoods are filled with cactus, deep canyons and cliffs; this is a small oasis in the middle of the desert, with reclaimed water, which allows green grass to grow in one hundred and fourteen degree weather. Driving through, it feels like visiting the neighborhood of Beaver Cleaver; stay-at-home mothers watch children play together in front yards, drinking coffee and chatting about the day's plans. The elderly walk their dogs, wave and stop to talk to those who are out.

The club is known for its bubble, not much happens that isn't tomorrow morning's gossip. Its reputation for a wonderful place to raise children is muddled by the never-ending dramas that keep the stay-at-home moms meeting for coffee, and the older folks walking their dogs, getting their fill of the latest chatter, and motivated by tales and updates on who has checked into rehab, who was caught cheating, and who is late on their country club dues. Two houses down from me, a wife was out with her lover, while her husband, unaware, was at home with their two children. Everyone's phone was buzzing with pictures of the two lovers deeply embraced in an adulterous kiss while at a nearby bar. The husband responds to the images by grabbing every Gucci shoe and Chanel purse, as fuel for his newly built community size bonfire ablaze in his front yard. In one year, one husband leaves for a secretary, a business man was caught with his wife's best friend, and let's not forget the expected tennis pros accused of affairs with the members' wives. All this happens while men and woman drink in the club's bar until closing, shuffling home in a haze at the end of the day, only to start it all over again the next morning.

My arrest was outside my home at nine p.m. Before I had a chance the next morning to contact a friend down the street, she had already been duly informed of my state and circumstances by those who watched it all unfold from their windows.

As I drive through its streets, neighbors stop their conversations and watch me pass, offering an uncomfortable wave or just a blank stare.

The awkwardness only confirms their knowledge of where I have been and where I am to return... there really are no secrets here.

When I enter my house, it is dark and quiet; I am alone, greeted by no one. I make a cup of coffee and savor each sip, a pleasure I never knew its value until now. As I walk to my bedroom, I see the pictures that hang on the wall of Chad and me holding our infant son. Our faces show pure joy. I was so blissful, so grateful to God for that precious baby in my arms. I hurt now to think that my son has a convict for a mother, and my husband an inmate for a wife.

I set my coffee down by my sink and strip the sweat shorts and approved t-shirt off, walk into the shower and stand in its hot stream. The water runs down my face, stinging as it clears away the tears, hits my breasts and runs down my waist and legs. My body is beautiful. I have never felt as attractive as I do now. The insecurities of my youth have gone, and now, a woman, I see my shape, its curves as striking.

I turn the shower off, grab a soft white towel and walk to the mirror. With my hand, I remove the steam fogging the mirror and gaze at my reflection. It is still me. The same girl who I have always been, the same wife and mother; loving and sincere. I cover myself with fragrant lotion and feel refreshed and human again. After blowing out my hair, freshening up my face, I walk into my closet and grab a dress for work- black, straight, sleeveless, with a pair of high heels. Dressed, I feel like the Andrea Smith everyone else knows, quite the change from the red jumpsuit I changed out of just moments ago. I head back to my sedan and begin backing out of my garage, when my cell phone rings and my car screen lights up: "Chad Incoming". My heart sinks, it has been well over an hour since I have been released, and two days since we have seen each other. Feeling like he is only playing the part, yet really not concerned, I hesitate to answer... I consider not answering at all, requiring that he tell family and friends the truth, the truth that he hasn't talked to me... revealing our divide. Publically he is right by my side, but behind closed doors, he has sentenced me too.

I answer the call because I need him, I need his warmth, yet brace myself for the antithesis of love.

"Hi Chad," I say monotone.

"Hey… so how was it?" he says inappropriately cheerful and deliberately nonchalant. My spirit deflates, my anger gone, my fragile state flaunts my brokenness. I do wish he asked if I was ok, inquired if he could do anything for me, told me he loved me; or better yet, had waited for me at the house to greet me and hold me when I came home….

"It was tough…" I begin.

"I'm sure…" he says interrupting as if he knew.

Silence.

"Is that all?" he asks.

"Are you asking?" I say while trying to hold back the emotions that are building.

He pauses, then answers, "I guess."

"Then, yes, that is all." I answer deflated.

"Ok," he says flippantly.

"I am at work now, I should head in," I say, to end the call and regain whatever composure I could muster.

"Fine… Bye," Chad says and hangs up.

"Bye," I say to myself.

Chapter 15

"While we do not look at the things which are seen, but at the things which are not seen. For the things which are seen are temporary, but the things which are not seen are eternal." 2 Corinthians 4:17-18

WORK RELEASE: DAY THREE

Driving up to my work's parking lot was strange, like everything was back to normal and my reality of the last two nights, and where I will be returning not real. By all appearances, life is great for me… but it is not. I came from the sewer… of which I shall return. I look in my rearview mirror, rub my red eyes, and smooth my skirt as I leave my car; doing all I can to suppress my all-consuming darkness and put life aside to focus on my job. I do love my job. I believe in what I do, and because of its mission, I am able to leave my current circumstances and embrace its role and vision. Education in the United States requires teachers to have such a high level of education, certification and skill, while the State and Federal pay scales and their budgets require such minimal salaries. In spite of this, I have seen that each employee is dedicated, clearly following their life's mission; it is a choice, even a sacrifice to be a teacher. They work tirelessly to improve, grow and instruct the life of each child that enters their doors. I have so much respect for them all.

Those at work know where I have been and why I am arriving later than usual. I felt I needed to be honest with them, understanding that for a time, I'll be working from the corporate office and home only and cannot visit schools; as well, at times areas will need to be covered for me on days where I cannot come in or be accessible. Their love, support and understanding is remarkable. They all surround me when I enter and offer me prospective on my existence outside the hell I will be checking back into.

The day moves quickly and before I know it I must leave the office and settle back into the sweat shorts and t-shirt that await my return. I pull back into my garage and my heart leaps to see my kids are waiting for me. As I close my car door, they rush to me and I am immediately squeezed by four precious arms. For the moment I feel heaven again, as my heart and emotions melt in their embrace.

"Mommy, we missed you!" my son says, as I lean down and press my cheek against the top of his head, feeling his soft hair on my face.

"I missed you too," I respond.

"Do you have to go back?" the question from my son feels like a dagger through my heart.

"Yes... I have to go back. I will be back tomorrow night and can kiss and hug you again, but Daddy will get you ready and take you to school tomorrow morning, ok?" I say to comfort, and hope they don't hear the torment I feel.

"Ok..." he answers. I feel his disappointment. I am so sorry, my precious little man... I say in my heart.

"Put on your pajamas. I want to hold you before I leave and think of you all ready for bed when I lay down," I ask.

The two run off to change into their pajamas.

"Hey." Chad walks over to the kitchen.

"Hey." I return the greeting, if you can call it that.

"Are you going to tell me anything?" he asks, but I sense no true interest.

I look at him directly in his eyes, "Do you even care?" I ask.

"Of course I care." he answers but won't return my eye contact.

I continue to look at him directly, searching. "It sure doesn't feel like you care."

With a raised voice Chad roars, "I don't know what you want from me." This time I get eye contact which unveils a deep anger and resentment

"Don't act like your coldness is not deliberate. None of our distance is my doing. It is clearly what you want, and where you are working at taking us," I say bitterly.

"So that's it? You really are not going to tell me anything?" His eyes narrow and become as though ice, glaring through me. Those beautiful blue eyes have frozen over. In them I see that I am a failure, a disappointment, and all the expectations he had thought I would be, the wife that he believed I was, shattered.

In truth, I stood before him completely broken, spiritually beaten. I was walking on the strength that didn't exist in my heart or soul. His voice, his demeanor now took what little physical strength remained and enabled me to stand. I wanted to fall to the floor and lay dead, but determined to hold myself as though strong.

"It was terrible. I get strip-searched with flash lights. I am frightened, dreading what's to come. The deputies yell and scream and treat me and the other inmates like dogs… I feel like scum… and you, my husband, have been very good at re-enforcing that I am."

I stop when I hear small feet running toward us from the hallway.

I see my two children coming and force myself to regain the inner strength I need. They will always help me fight for the strength to continue. I could never give up, they need me and I will not fail them. "Anna, it's time for bed. Why don't you pick out two books and I will be there soon to tuck you in," I say to my little girl all cute and snuggly in her pink Hello Kitty pajamas.

I leave Chad in the kitchen to change into clean sweat shorts and a white t-shirt then head to my daughter's room, who is now waiting with her books in her hand, sitting sweetly on her bed. I am grateful that I am able to tuck my daughter into bed for the night. Sad I have to leave before my son's bedtime, which means instead he has to watch me drive away.

"Gabriel, you know I love you so much." I say, on my knees, looking into his eyes, before I drive off.

"Yes," he says with his head pressed against my cheek.

"When you came, my heart left my body and is now in you. So wherever you are, that is where my heart is also," I say as I kiss the top of his head.

"I need to go, but will see you tomorrow night, ok?" I say softly, stroking the top of his head, and enjoying the soft highlights that his hair reveals with each.

"Ok, Mom… bye." he says. The word bye is more cruel and cutting than my heart can bear. I feel my face heat up with pain, but smile softly at Gabriel as I take a deep breath and grab my keys.

"Bye Big Boy! …Bye Chad." I say giving my son one last kiss on the head, turning and waving at Chad who is back on the sofa.

"Bye." Chad replies with a wave, via the back of his hand. A farewell not valued enough to turn his head.

I leave and take the wretched drive back to jail. I drove this route the night before, fearful for what was to come, what I didn't know… now I am petrified by what I do.

"What is your parking number?" grunts a woman at the front desk. She has Christian worship songs playing on a small box next to her. She rocks back and forth on her chair to squeeze from the arm rests that hold her captive and lunges forward once she is freed, using the momentum to be able to stand, which is a very strenuous task. She is Caucasian, extremely obese, wearing a muumuu. Her face is fat, but there is no merry in her round cheeks. Her mouth folds down, with thin lips that form into a severe frown. She looks in her fifties, wearing her light brown hair short to her head, like a crew cut. She clearly takes no pride in her appearance.

Her walk consists of rocking her weight to one side to allow one leg to swing in front, then she rocks to the other side to repeat the process. Pounding her hands on top of my keys, she is noticeably upset because I have required her to undergo this exhaustive task. I stand still and silent by my locker. She moves to the cabinet and bangs the keys into their hanging slot. This fury is sure to cause an indention on my chrome smart key. I close my eyes as I hear her grunt and rock toward me, moving back to make room for her, due to the enormity of her size and the limitation of space between lockers.

"Which one!" she roars. I quickly point to my locker. She takes her keys and opens the locker and rocks away. I exhale and then tuck away my purse and flip flops, replacing my shoes with flesh colored size eight rubber sandals. She has put my tag with my mug shot on the counter on top of my paperwork. I grab it and sit on the waiting room's bench. I am there for over two hours. The idea of going back to my block is ominous, so her lack of energy to process me is appreciated.

Another female inmate arrives and gets the same welcome treatment from the obese lady. The other inmate is young, with long artificial maroon colored hair pulled up on top of her head into a messy bun. She wears glasses that are edgy yet quite scholarly. Her skin is grey white, but attractive. By her appearances she is a bookworm, who shows off her sense of style and edge in her hair color. After she endures the front desk woman's rage, she sits down next to me.

"Hi!" she says and smiles.

"Hi!!" I return the greeting.

I look over at the obese lady, worried our interaction will incite a plethora of insults and threats, but am relieved when I see she doesn't react or seem to care.

"I am really not looking forward to the strip search today," the young woman states.

"I am dreading it too," I respond.

"Yes, but I am especially nervous because…" she clears her throat, "…its that time of the month!" she says with a groan. "I don't know what we are supposed do during the search. Do you?" she says as she rubs both her hands together, unconsciously washing them.

"Oh, my! No, but I have wondered myself and have personally been fearing my own start date. I am so sorry." I say as she continues to fidget, nervously. I feel her pain.

She clenches her hands into a fist in a nervous reaction and says, "I am kind of starting to freak out about it… Do you know which guard is on duty today?" her fear and panic of her upcoming degradation is evident in her tone.

"No. I have only seen the front desk lady so far." I say in a whisper, just in case the same rules of remaining silent apply to the waiting room.

A young man walks in and tries to check in. He sets down his paperwork and then proceeds to the men's area of lockers. Once again, the receptionist rocks out of her chair, while her Jesus worship plays, then walks to the counter. She stands at the counter for a while, looking through a drawer where I assume the inmate tags are placed.

"Your tag is not in here," she barks.

"It has to be. I can't go in without my tag, can you look again." he says respectfully as he returns to the desk.

"I told you it is not in here," she hollers in such a loud voice the windows behind me vibrate.

They stand there, she sneering in a stubborn stance, the male inmate hopeless and unsure what to do.

"I handed it to the person at the desk when I checked out. Can you please look again?" he says with a soft pleading voice.

"It is not there!" she says slowly, through grinding teeth.

With unprovoked anger, she looks back in her drawer, abusing it as she swings it open. She ruffles through it frustrated and then with greater force slams it closed... because somehow miraculously the tag was found. She seeths at the sight of the tag and with all her strength throws the tag at the inmate; it bounces off the chest of the surprised and unsuspecting man, then drops to the floor by his feet. He takes a deep self-preserving breath and leans down, picks up his tag and quietly goes to a seat in the designated male waiting area.

The audacity of these employees to be so violent when unwarranted and needless; they are vicious because they can be vicious. I thought to myself, as her Christian music played, if Jesus were visible, whom would He be standing with, whom would He be speaking to? Which of us would He be touching; the male inmate as he holds his frustration together on that bench, the girl next to me as she fidgets and clinches her fist in terror of what's to come, me as I sit and watch those around me, while inside wanting to curl into a ball and disappear from the life I have created, or that woman behind that desk, feeling justifiably imperious, as she plays her worship songs?

As I ponder this thought, a young guard appears from the secured jail doors and walks up to the other female inmate and me. She gestures with scorn to follow her. The guard is somewhat pretty, small boned, with light brown hair and blonde highlights. After we walk through a metal detector, she leads us to a bathroom that is near the jail's main entrance. It has a long counter in the front and a half wall that separates it from the toilet. The guard instructs us to put our paperwork on the counter and stand with our backs against the wall. She then tells the inmate with maroon hair to go over to the toilet area behind the half wall.

"Ugh, here I go…" she says to me in a quiet whisper, humiliation already evident on her face.

She walks to the toilet area while the guard stands in front of her.

"Umm… it is that time of the month," the inmate says in a soft voice.

"Take it out," the guard barks.

I watch the guard stand and watch the inmate. She has a very pleased look, smirking as she watches.

"You done?" the guard yells.

"Yes…" says the inmate.

"Stand here and turn around facing the wall…" I can see the guard pointing to a wall next to the toilet.

"Bend over…" she sneers as she pulls out a flashlight. "Spread your cheeks…" I press my eyes closed, and focus on each inhale and exhale. Again, I inhale and exhale. My eyes stay shut, I want to stay in this mental place, where it is dark and focus only on breathing. It is peaceful… to just breathe.

"Put your clothes on." I hear the guard snap.

"Ummm… I need to replace my tampon… I am not allowed to bring anything in with me." The inmate's voice is broken and small.

The guard walks over to the counter and grabs a basket of sanitary supplies that were tucked away in a drawer, then holds the basket in front of the inmate. The guard continues to watch the young woman. I begin to tremble. It's a nervous response I seem to have developed and now experience frequently. I feel terrible for the girl behind the half-wall and am petrified of my own body's natural schedule… it won't be long until it is my turn.

The inmate appears from behind the wall, now dressed, and takes her original position next to me. Her face is visibly red and her eyes are fixed to the floor. My heart wants to reach out to her and put my hand on hers, but I know that this is against the rules.

"You're up." the guard beckons me.

I walk over to the other side of the wall. There is a white plastic table next to a toilet.

"Take off your clothes and put them there," she snarls as I place each item on a small plastic table that stands next to the toilet.

"That tattoo is huge. Why would you do that to your body?" she grimaces.

"...Because I like it." I say simply.

"I think tattoos are disgusting and don't understand people who get them. I would never do that... ever." she says in a superior tone, yet her comments sound immature and show her age.

"I had skin cancer, it is covering my scar," I say to defend myself.

She laughs, rolls her eyes. "I don't care, I just don't get it and would never do that..." she hisses.

"To each his own." I respond and laugh.

"Get dressed." she sneers and walks away. For some reason, I do not need to be watched as I get dressed like the other inmate.

Returning to my original position with my back to the wall, I look over at the inmate. "I don't know why I told her that; I don't tell anyone about having skin cancer," I whispered.

"You were nervous. Seriously, it's really hard to not have nerves get the better of you in here," she says to me softly, under her breath so the guard cannot hear.

"Why would I share something so personal with someone so heartless?" I admonish myself, upset for sharing a part of my life to the small-minded and cruel.

I had been in and out of the hospital for procedures to treat my back from infancy until my last and final surgery at age six. One of my earliest memories was walking down the hospital hallway to check in for my first of two major surgeries, skipping and singing, while holding my mother's hand. "Don't worry Mommy, Jesus will heal me, Jesus will heal me," I said. My childhood faith strong and unwavering, yet soon to be unfulfilled.

After many procedures that were not effective, I was still left with the precancerous mark that covered me. The only option that remained was to completely remove the birthmark and the skin surrounding, to ensure my health and extend my life expectancy. The next memory I have is when I came out of surgery, a nurse calling my name, pulling me from the deep slumber of anesthesia. All the layers of skin from my back had been removed. In addition, they took the skin from my stomach and remaining untouched torso for graphs to cover the deeper open flesh.

I was not placed in restraints, yet the hospital staff had them by my railed bed, for easy access in expectation of their requirement. They laid next to me, threatening me, a little girl now frozen still by their presence. I was told to lay stationary and not to move; I obeyed. I stayed in one position, lying on my stomach, motionless, a child as young as four, completely still for weeks at a time, naked, without skin and in utter and complete agony. Instead of a bed that was suspended to keep all open wounds untouched, used today for such procedures, I was in a regular hospital bed, on my skinless stomach, which bled and scabbed into the sheets. I would lay with my cheek to the mattress, watching the hospital door, terrified of the nurses who each day brought clean sheets with sponges in their hands. I would begin to scream the moment they appeared. My mother would leave the room in tears, helpless, as the nurses lifted me up by my arms and legs suspending me and my sheet, which was stuck to my body, in the air. With one strong swift movement they would rip the sheet off of my stomach like a bandaid stuck to hair, tearing the formed scabs that covered my torso and adhered and comingled to the fabric where I laid. I would feel the overpowering sting of the scabs pulled off, but quickly and immediately soothed by a warm ooze of fresh blood that would cover my torso, coating it once again and easing the pain. One nurse would replace the mattress with a fresh clean white sheet. They would then place me back onto my bed, relieved it was over, tired from screaming, weak from the pain. Then the sponge became my next villain. It touched each part of my tender body, cleaning what was open and raw. Once done, my body would sense a warm hug and caress from the blood that slowly began to cover my back, and pool under my stomach. Comforting me like a blanket, soon to dry, harden and attach to the sheet where I laid once again.

The scars were all that remained from my childhood and now those scars covered by a tattoo, beautiful art over a tragic wound. The imp of a human who now scolds me is not worthy to comment on its value.

"Come on ladies," the guard says in a cruel tone.

With that we are led back to our block and to our iron bunks. I laid my head down on the mattress, praying for rest, longing to be home, wishing I were instead in the arms of my husband who once loved me.

Chapter 16

"And her rival also provoked her severely, to make her miserable, because the LORD had closed her womb." 1 Samuel 1:6

JAIL: DAY FIVE

The lights were still off in the block as I checked out for work release. Unfortunately, Samil was at his perch when I walked to my locker. His small head, droopy bottom lip, large and deformed ears are a direct reflection of the ugliness he embodies inside. He relishes his post and haughtily waits for the next victim he can make small, his moment to feel important, if just for a minute, in his pathetic and nasty life. I endure his threats and screeching. I purchased an expensive lock from the jail's vending machine as ordered.

Once I am able to walk away and feel the bright sun, I take a deep breath and let its rays penetrate my face and skin hard, while I listen to the buzz and hiss of the cicadas, now grateful to hear their greeting. I feel like kissing the sun and singing with the bugs. I drive away from total oppression and back home to shower and change into the woman I prefer to be. Once again, the house is dark, no sign of Chad and no call or text to see if I am ok.

"Mom, I am out right now, and on my way to work," I say as I drive in my car.

"Oh, honey, thanks for calling. How are you?" the sound of her voice comforts me.

"I am ok. It is tough, but I'm adapting to life in jail," I say and chuckle. The statement sounds so peculiar, so wrong and outside of what should be. My mother remains silent, finding nothing funny about my words. I clear my throat and continue, "I am most afraid of the guards, they are quite cruel and aggressive… but I am ok. Surprisingly, the inmates are gentle and sympathetic. In the middle of a dark room, dark cell, and all the oppression that surrounds me, I have been touched. This may sound strange, but through them I feel like I have been reassured... and comforted... by God."

"Andrea, you make me want to weep. I am so glad you have found peace in God, in spite of all that surrounds you. Dad and I pray for you every day, sometimes on the hour. I love you so much," she says with emotion.

"Mom, how is Dad?" I ask softly and broken.

"He is ok. It's hard, but today he is ok." she answers with a lower voice.

I take a deep breath and begin to rattle my thoughts, "I so am sorry that I can't be there with you. You know I would if I could."

"Yes, sweetheart, you have never left our side. You get through this and when it is over, come back to us. We need you." she says with conviction.

My voice cracks again, "Of course, you know I will be. I want to be there... I am sorry I am not today."

"Can we come and visit you at the house when you get off work? We would like to see you and hug you," she asks.

"I would love that, Mom, but I don't think it would be wise. The material given to me states that undercover deputies, or civilian employees, are assigned to work release inmates to verify their whereabouts and to monitor locations to ensure that inmates are following procedures. Part of the handbook states not to use work release to visit with family. I want, actually need, to see you, but I must stay in accordance and exactly as the rules are written. It's just not worth risking. I miss you though. Thank you for offering. It's hard coming home to an empty house and not having you or Dad to hold me. I feel so broken and your love would be so healing."

"Then can we visit you in jail?"

"Oh Mom, I would fall apart to think of you seeing me like that. It would break me. I never want that image in yours or Dad's heart." I say and begin to cry.

"Oh honey, I understand." I hear that she is crying too. I hate this,

I hate that she cries for me and carries so much worry and hurt for me. She interrupts my thoughts, "I love you, more than you will ever know. We will come if you need us, just know that. Ok?"

"Ok Mom. Thank you. Please tell Dad I love him so very much and hug his neck for me. I'll call you later, ok?"

"Alright. Thank you for calling. We will wait for the next," she answers softly.

My heart now feels like a rag that was squeezed and drained. I want to hold on to her words of love, but my heart sinks back into the depth of reality and shame. I put away my despair and head to work, a distraction that I savor.

That evening, after holding my children and changing into my approved sweats, I brace myself for the indignity that awaits me.

"At some point, we should talk," Chad says to me before I leave.

"At some point, we should," I say to him without turning my head or giving him any farewell. I am capable of facing each of my life's tragedies alone. I don't need him today and don't need him tomorrow. Do I even want him? …My heart collapses: yes! I want him desperately.

It is not long before I am sitting in the jail waiting room while the obese lady once again takes hours to process me, her Christian music playing as background and the sound of her bodily reverberations overpower the music and the smell of the room; I am amused at her complete lack of shame when she belches with great force three times consecutively. She gives Christianity such a lovely personification, both in her spirit toward those that need hope, as well her physical conduct exemplifying a Biblical virtuous woman. How very sad.

There are two vending machines in the waiting room, where I sit. One of the male deputies, who by appearance holds high rank in this very pathetic place, walks passed me to purchase a snack. "How are you?' he says with a smile; a friendly face in an unfriendly environment. I am taken back by the unexpected kindness and the question.

"Well, I am here, so not good," I answer with an awkward laugh.

"Ah, it's not that bad," he says in a friendly voice.

"I beg to differ. In all honesty, I don't understand how this jail can justify providing only two fifteen minute breaks and forcing the inmates to lay on their bunks for the remaining time of the day in the dark; plus not only do you not provide a way for these women to exercise, but actually stop and prohibit it. These conditions are inhumane and only ensure an unhealthy and chemically dysfunctional inmate, by giving large amounts of sugar at every meal without a way to burn any of it off." I blurt, condemning him and this place.

My body begins to feverishly tremble. It reveals how afraid I am of the consequences to my boldness. This trembling has to stop, my emotions are too visible. I am unable, at thirty seven years old, to control it and the more I try to suppress it the stronger its quake.

"Two fifteen minute breaks? That is not true," he says staring at me, as though stopped in his tracks from getting a snack.

I feel my legs and knees join in the procession of shaking. I grab them with my hands in attempts to hide my intensity. "Oh, yes, that is exactly what is happening in the women's block. You should probably look into it. We have a small outdoor space with a basketball hoop, but the deputies have placed the only table under the hoop to prevent its usage. Women are not allowed to use the space to do exercises, push-ups, or stretches. They turn out the lights and will not let us talk or use the bathroom the entire day. Is this the jail policy and appropriate treatment of those under its supervision?"

He stares at me as I profusely tremble unable to hide it. He turns back to the vending machine and puts in his dollar, selecting a snack. The snack falls loudly as we both remain silent. He turns back to me, "Hmm..." is his response. He then walks away, chocolate bar in hand.

After some time of sitting silently, listening to worship songs and corpulent bodily functions, I am beckoned by a new female guard I hadn't met. She is professional and respectful even though the procedures are humiliating to us. I learn her name is Officer Julius. I am grateful for her.

She leads us to our block once we are searched and to the guard's desk where my timesheet awaits. The other inmates initial theirs as required; but I take note and mention to Santanas immediately that the time posted was incorrect. I was clocked as having arrived at the current time, not when I actually checked in. I was concerned that if I initialed,

I would be agreeing that I had instead arrived several hours tardy.

I try to be respectful knowing this will ignite Santanas, but I am not willing to take this risk. "I am not comfortable initialing this time, since I actually arrived at 9 p.m. not 11 p.m."

"SSSSIt is fine, sssjust initial." Santanas demands in a sloppy growl pounding her middle finger on the timesheet where the incorrect time is printed.

"I am sorry, but this is all a matter of record, which is part of ensuring that I fulfilled my court ordered sentence. Please write 9 p.m. and initial the change so that I can show I actually arrived on time. If you have any concerns, you can check with the front desk lady, or review the video, which is dated and clocked." I had asked this at orientation, wanting to know what recourse, if any, I had to verify the truth, if authority claimed I hadn't arrived in due time. I was told by the Specialist that the video cameras in the waiting room were dated and time listed.

Santanas refused, while breathing heavy, chest heaving which caused a hissing sound that sang from her clinched teeth. Officer Julius, who was still standing next to me, grabs my timesheet, crosses out the punched time, writes 9 pm and initials it, then pushes the timesheet in front of me and leaves. This enflames Santanas.

"Umm… can you fix mine too?" the inmate next to me requests from Santanas.

I quickly initial and leave, knowing this was my time to exit and return to my bunk, escaping Santanas' fury and the new conflict that I clearly just inspired.

Tired, I lay my head down, press my eyes closed and pray that sleep will grace me.

Suddenly, my heart drops and nerves freeze in terror from loud banging, metal on metal. I jolt as Santanas hits her baton on the rails of my bunk. My eyes open and my body quakes. I flitch as I see her face seething over me, eyes glaring. I reckon I have awakened the dragon by asking her to change my timesheet.

"SSsput on your reds!" she orders.

"Do I need to go somewhere?" I ask frightened of her retribution.

"SSYou ssneed to sswear your sssreds at all ssstimes," she slurs.

"In bed… to sleep?" I had stayed in the white t-shirt and sweat shorts I had checked in with.

"SPut on syour ssreds," she sneers.

Other inmates sit up in their beds.

"Officer Santanas," another inmate questions, "are we all having to sleep in our reds now?"

"Sssthe ssrules are that you need to ssswear your reds at all sstimes." Santanas directs this order to me only, snarling and hissing, slober oozing from between her clinched teeth.

There is a pause, I get up and change out of my t-shirt and shorts as she stands hovering over me, breathing heavy and giving me little room to undress. She pants and glares while I take off my clothes. I put on the red double knit jail suit that was in my drawer. The other inmates watch, sitting up confused. With uniform on, I lay back on my bunk and pull up the tattered sheet.

I kept an inmate handbook. I had put it in my plastic garbage bag, hoping it would not be confiscated once I checked in. I pulled it out of my drawer to read the written rules for jail issued clothes. It clearly states that inmates were to wear their jail suit to cafeteria and any area outside their sleeping quarters or bathroom. In addition, inmates could wear modest shorts and t-shirt to sleep, but to remain well covered when going to and from bathroom and shower facilities.

The other inmates watch as Santanas goes back to her post. No one else is wearing their reds and no one else is asked to change. They lay down as they were, knowing this was a special enforcement specific to me and me alone. How silly….

APRIL, 1998

"Andrea, I know you won't talk about it, but you need to come with me when I go to the infertility doctor. Just come with me. I will schedule appointments for us both. You can tell the doctor everything." My girlfriend had cornered me and wouldn't let me sneak away.

"Rachel, I am only twenty-four years old. I don't need a fertility doctor." I say while trying to walk around her.

She shadows my movement, keeping me hostage to her pressings. "Maybe you don't, but it won't hurt to go and talk to the doctor."

I stopped and put my head down. "Let me think about it."

"Seriously, I am taking you. I am calling in the morning, and will let you know the date we are going," she says stubbornly.

The truth was, I had been off birth control for over two years and had never even had a false alarm. Having been married three years, everyone loved to ask when we planned to have kids, which only gave me a sense of panic. I was so young though, so I would tell myself I shouldn't be concerned... yet I was afraid to find out the truth, afraid of the doctor's answer. I didn't talk to anyone about the fact that I was trying; I didn't want to see their all-knowing look confirming my fears that something was wrong. I couldn't talk to my mother or Esther either, by doing so would only make my failure a reality. I told myself to remain calm, the doctor, most likely, would tell me that I was vitamin deficient, or advise me to stop taking hot baths; unfortunately, that first visit turned into six years of relentless visits, surgeries, shots, injections, in-vitro, without ever having one positive pregnancy test result. Rachel, after her first treatment, got pregnant and delivered two beautiful twin boys.

In contrast to me, Chad turned out to be a biological super star, a fertility god! Although I was only twenty-four, my doctor informed me that my insides responded to treatment as though a client in their forties. All shots and hormones had to be doubled, due to my body's sluggish response to any chemical stimulation. Doubling the hormone treatment made me feel crazy, yet my body still didn't perform.

The disappointment and anger that my body was not responding as it should and the pain of knowing that it was my fault, did not come close to the agony of realizing I wasn't going to be able to ever hold a baby. I wanted to give my husband his own. I yearned deeply for the day I could say I was pregnant. This desire became all consuming. Yet a desire that remained unanswered.

The infertility treatments were grueling. Chad, however, was a trooper, kind and supportive; he would inject me three times a day and drop off his cup in a brown bag at the infertility clinic. This became our six year ritual.

Betrayed by God was my body and heart. He was keeping this blessing from me, as though I wasn't worthy. Wasn't the birthmark and its encoded cancer enough? Now He was keeping from me the ability to produce and hold life; something He freely gives to so many, even those who don't even want it. Why not me? Why am I not worth this honor? I followed His commandments to the letter. What more could He be asking of me; am I just unfit to deserve something so common to so many.

My mom and Esther knew I was seeing a doctor, but I could not tell them or anyone what procedures I was going through or discuss dates of significance. My torment too great to endure as it was, to bring myself to discuss any of this with anyone, let alone to the two woman that I loved so deeply. To do so would have unleashed the depths of my pain, of which I had been proficient at hiding from the world. I also vowed that I would never show my emotions to Chad. I did not want him to see or have to endure the waves of guilt, desperation, anger and heartache that I felt with every passing day. I had become skilled at stuffing my emotions into a tight little box, going about my life as though not there; yet the weight of it was constant, never leaving me, gnawing at me without mercy. This was my solitary ocean that I had to swim alone.

Each year family celebrations brought joy as my siblings' families increased and little ones grew and became busy; yet that joy also heightened my own reality of what I lacked and God's rejection more evident no matter how much I prayed, or wept or pleaded. My delight for those whom I loved was real, but my sorrow for the incompleteness of the family Chad and I were being denied was overpowering. There was not one year, or one holiday, in those six years that I did not withdrawal to the bathroom, with the faucet running to hide the sounds of my sobs. My secret kept once I turn the water off and left the room returning to my husband's side with a smile stretched across my face. He was so beautiful, and I was just a baron cancer patient. Each time I would feel my husband's precious hand reach for mine, completely unaware of my own personal loathing, I felt a sting of guilt, fear that he too would reject me as God has, yet so grateful for that moment of his love.

On my eighth year of trying, my sixth year of infertility and final attempt of in-vitro, I prayed on hands, knees, even prostrate, begging God to breathe life into me and to give me my heart's greatest desire. Unlike my sisters, I was not career-oriented. All I really ever wanted was to be a wife and a mother. I decided to give up preparing for a child, to lose the family car and start to pursue my own career. I went to school and got my real estate license. Chad bought me a little black, two seat, Porsche convertible, and I continued my education in real estate, able to achieve high level designations. I joined several social charity organizations, where I felt I could make a difference in our community, as well meet people and increase my sphere of influence in real estate. I found so much success instantly in real estate, selling well over one million dollars before my first year as an agent. In the charity organizations, I became a quick social leader and was asked to chair fundraising efforts raising hundreds of thousands of dollars in one evening, reaching unmatched historical gains at every event. Becoming successful, dressing the part, driving the sports car, going out and making strong and lasting relationships with other women was fun and fulfilling, but each success brought deeper sorrow that this life and its blessings was not what my heart was asking for. Why was I blessed in an arena in which I had no interest, but denied the very longing of my soul?

At my final visit and last in-vitro procedure, my infertility doctor told Chad and me that this needed to be our last attempt. He bluntly predicted a 1% chance that I would ever get pregnant; the one percent would be a freak and unexplainable miracle.

Praying, hoping that this final in-vitro attempt would be the answer to my prayers, I laid in bed, my beautiful husband asleep next to me, unable to sleep. My stomach was cramping intensely, this undeniably the end; each step I took to the bathroom was a step away from hope. When I reached the bathroom, the truth was confirmed: I will never be a mother, I will never know what it is like to hold life in my belly, I have been denied my life's desire and cry. My quest was over, there was nothing left for me. I walked back to bed and to my precious husband, asleep. His beautiful face was resting on his pillow and his arm reached out toward my side of the bed. My heart ached as I watched him breathe softly, all the money we spent to have a child down the drain, my body just flushed all our dreams and thousands of dollars away every month. I watched him, so peaceful, his loving blue eyes that captivated my heart closed and dreaming. I have failed him. As I snuck back into the bed, I softly tried to move Chad's arm, wanting him to stay asleep so that I could absorb my ocean of pain. This movement woke him. His eyes open and stared at me, a face covered in tears. I wipe them away and tried desperately to hide; not ready to tell him. He sat up and touched my cheek, which broke me further.

"It's over Chad. I am not pregnant and never will be." My voice just a strained whisper. "I am so sorry." All sorrow rushing out in those four words.

He grabbed me. "I love you. I don't need a baby, I need you. You are all I need, Andrea, you."

My breath left me and with it came a deep wail. Chad gently pulled me down to rest my head on my pillow and surrounded my body with his, holding me as I wept. "I'm sorry Chad. I just wanted so badly to give you… a little you."

Chapter 17

"For what profit is it to a man if he gains the whole world, and loses his own soul? Or what will a man give in exchange for his soul?"
Matthew 16:26

JANUARY, 2002

My Mom was diagnosed with breast cancer, immediately scheduled to have a double mastectomy. At the same time, Esther and her husband learned that they were expecting twins. The beauty and excitement of one, and the fear and devastation of the other became a part of our every hour.

My father had been having health problems as well. He reached out to his denominational leaders to discuss stepping down.

He chose Korah and her new husband to take the church as his successors. Korah was thrilled. The district agreed that this would be a good choice, and assured my parents that they would continue to be part of the ministry, but in a more limited role; with a place of honor. My father was reassured that he and my mother would be able to remain in the home they were living and would continue to get a modified salary that would allow them to live comfortably without having to dramatically change their current lifestyle. I was happy that my parents would be able to step back after thirty-five years serving the church in Tucson. I hoped and prayed this would allow them to focus on their failing health.

It was not long after Korah held her new desired title that a bill was sent to Esther and her school, doubling its rent. Esther attempted to explain to Korah that she would love to give more rent, but her budget had already been submitted to and approved by the Arizona State Board of Education (of which was consistent with surrounding comparatives), as well the three-year rental contract had already been fully executed. This infuriated Korah.

JAIL: DAY EIGHT

I have returned from work and am back to jail. The anticipation of the long hours in the dark and the continual screeching from the guards has my spirit low and my old pal, depression, is once again taking his familiar place in my soul. As I enter the block, it is not dark as expected but lit up throughout. It was break time and inmates were moving about the area freely. While walking to the confinement of my bed, I realize that Dinah's old bunk now has someone else sitting in it. As I approach my bunk a young woman becomes visible, with dark curly hair and a beautiful warm skin tone lying on the bunk. I smile at her as I sit down on my bunk and lay aside the new novel for my usual sleepless night.

Leaning in toward another inmate's bunk, I whisper, "What happened to Dinah?"

She responds back in a low voice, "The Specialist verified her whereabouts with her employer while she was on work release and he found she was not going to work. I guess, she has been meeting up with her boyfriend instead, so they moved her to the 'fish bowl' and now she is no longer eligible for work release!"

"The 'fish bowl?'" I repeat.

"That glass room, right there" the inmate points to the room in the center of the block. "That's basically lock-down when you are in trouble here. Girls in the fish bowl can only leave the room to go to the bathroom when permitted. They eat on their bunks, with no breaks," she says in a whisper, even though the lights are on.

My heart sank because I wanted a chance to say more to Dinah. I wanted to learn more about her adoptive mother and her other family members who were praying for her. Even if she is released from the 'fish bowl', it would be very unlikely she would be reassigned to the bunk across from me. I just hope my words had some impact and became true in her spirit.

There is a lot of activity around me, since it's break time, but I quickly become engrossed in my reading, unaware of the noise or actions that surround me.

"Are you reading the Bible?" the inmate who sleeps directly above me asks.

I startle, I was alone in my world for that moment.

"Yes." I say surprised.

"I have a copy too, from the shelf. I try to read it but it's hard. I would like to read it though" she says openly.

She is young, with jet black short hair, and a lot of tattoos. Her face is pretty and she appears sincere. I quickly glace over at Deputy Cain, afraid since we are talking and realize that the lights are still on, so I relax a bit from fear of her wrath.

"I will help you read the Bible. What part are you reading now?" I ask.

I realize my copy of the Bible is open and I am pressing it against my chest, hugging it. I feel foolish and let it drop to my lap, but then unconsciously start stroking its pages.

"Well... here..." She shows me that she is at page 1, Genesis 1:1.

"So you are reading the Book of Genesis? Amazing, but a hard first read... I like to start with the Book of John when I begin reading the Bible. Let me mark where that is." I grab her Bible and fold down the corner page of John 1:1. "Can I also mark a story in the Bible that I love?" I ask her, excited to share something that is truly dear to me.

My heart is moved by her. I feel such compassion and love for this young girl. I would love for her to experience His presence as I have. I want her to know the God of the Bible, not the god personified so much in today's organized religion. A God I have loved as a child, and now love even deeper today. I want her to know and believe the sacred romance that God has with us, written and exampled in the Bible from its first page to its last. Unable to sit on each other's bunks due to the jail rules, she instead stands by me as I turn the pages of her Bible. I love her sincerity. She just wants to know Him and is asking for someone to show her where to look.

"Here is where I would start. In addition, I love this story". I turn its pages to the story of the Prodigal Son, Luke 15:11-32. "When you are done, let's talk about it; I would love to give you some background and history on what we are reading," I say delighted.

The Prodigal Son is the beautiful story Jesus told of a father and his unconditional love for his wayward son. In the Parable the son asks for and takes his inheritance, squanders it on entertainment and frivolity. Leaving his father's home, he walks away from all his responsibilities as a son, and seeks out a life of drunken celebrations…. It doesn't take long before he finds himself broke and desperate and working for a farmer without money to eat. Eventually the son begins to eat the food of, and alongside, the swine he now serves. Coming from riches, now living and eating with pigs, he realizes that he would be better off to live as a servant in his father's house than the squalor he now dwells. He prepares for what he will say to his father:

"I will arise and go to my father, and will say to him, 'Father, I have sinned against heaven and before you, and I am no longer worthy to be called your son. Make me like one of your hired servants.'" Luke 15:18-19

As the son approaches, his father sees him in the distance and immediately drops everything and runs to his son, then embraces him with a kiss. The son begins his speech, but before the son could finish, his father interrupts:

"But the father said to his servants, 'Bring out the best robe and put it on him and put a ring on his hand and sandals on his feet. And bring the fatted calf here and kill it, and let us eat and be merry; for this my son was dead and is alive again; he was lost and is found. And they began to be merry." Luke 15:22-24

The beauty of this message is how Jesus described that this father was like our heavenly Father, who runs to us even after we have turned from Him, even if we squandered the inheritance that was given to us, even if we betrayed Him as a son; yet still He runs to greet, hold and kiss us when we return…. All He asks is that we turn back to Him.

From this story, I want this young girl to know, if she will just look toward heaven, God Himself will come running, throw a beautiful robe around her shoulders and place one of His own rings on her hand. All she needs to do is just seek Him. He will see her from afar, and before she can ask, He will embrace her with a kiss….

I know that this message in this Book is real. My life is not the Christian story of perfection, but His Word is true in my heart. I have known and felt God. As a child, He has warmed me and filled my spirit with His tenderness. In truth, I have been in love on earth, yet the love I have experienced from my Savior, nothing can surpass. Some may say I am a fool and conjure these grandiose emotions to comfort my sorry soul. However, I have been in a hospital bed, with my skin removed, in grotesque pain; yet felt my Savior hold me. I have been baron and cried for healing, and he answered me. I have rested my head in darkness, in oppression and shame, on the metal bed of jail, and felt my God comfort me. I groan for those that are skeptics, because they have missed life's greatest gift; they have not experienced God's love.

"What are you reading?" asks the young woman who is now in Dinah's bunk.

"The Bible! She is marking some passages to read," replies the other inmate who stands by my bunk.

"Can you mark mine too? I want to read them. I already have a Bible, see here." She jumps off her bunk and hands me her Bible. I have noticed that so many around me have a Bible on their bunk, but I haven't seen them read it.

"Of course," I respond, excited to meet the new girl, realizing quickly that in my enthusiasm, I was no longer whispering.

I glance at Cain, fearing her wrath for interacting with the other inmates…. I inhale short and shallow as I realize she is looking right at me. I shutter from her stare and instinctively look around to find a place to hide, which of course there is none. Cain smears a wide approving smile across her face. I am sickened. Cain considers her-self a Christian… Of course she does; and she wants me to see her ridiculous and unwanted approval regarding my reading and sharing the Bible. She, of whom clearly has no real understanding of its Words, because her very conduct is a violation of its directives. She exemplifies so many: self-righteous, separated from humanity, intolerant, cruel and calloused. Yet, has she ever actually read the Book?

The new girl is half African-American and half Caucasian, her hair is curly, shoulder length and full. She hands me her Bible so I can turn and mark its pages.

"Are you married?" she asks, with her Bible still open as she looks at the pages I marked.

"Yes." I answer and look up at her. Her eyes are big and brown, open and interested. I feel myself pull toward her.

"How long?" she asks in a low voice as she returns to her bunk.

"Seventeen years," I say. The words sting as I say them.

The wounding that permeated my heart must have shown on my face, "Seventeen years? Wow, that's long. You goin' to last… do you think?" Good question, I think to myself.

"I hope so…" I point around me, "this isn't helping though." Can I really blame this place, or should I really blame the condition of both Chad's and my heart.

"I am sure," she says as though taking a different look at the depths of where we both are. "Do you have kids?" she continues.

"Two, a boy and a girl." I say with a heavy heart.

She leans in, resting her head on the metal side rail of her bed, "They young?"

I smile at her, "Yes, seven and four."

"Cute," she says with sincerity.

"I miss them." I say with a lump in my throat.

She nods, looks down and then back at me. "I have three, all girls. They are living with my mom."

She looks so young, I had assumed she was in her teens… maybe she is.

"That is tough, how long are you here for?" I ask.

"Another six months..." She hesitates, then looks at me intently, "Drugs... I can't shake it. I am better here... it makes me sober."

She is quiet and then finishes, "I am afraid of myself, I am afraid of what I am going to do when I get back out."

"Ladies!" yells Officer Cain. We both stop, paralyzed and quickly pick up our books and pretend to be reading. I gather from the emotional switch, Cain no longer approves.

I have my eyes on the pages, but am not really reading. My spirit is heavy. I close my eyes, and think of her little girls. I am sure they are beautiful, with curly hair and caramel skin like their mother. My heart aches as I think of them... my heart aches for her. Drugs: its grip has taken so much. She believes this hell is a better place than the horrible pit her addiction could take her. I wish there was something more I could do, my Bible verses are not enough. If only I could find a way to help these women become functioning and loving mothers, even wives, and a chance at becoming contributing members of society... an opportunity of hope for them, and for their children. I wish this place could be more than sentences being served, penalties a must, nor should our stay be easy, but there is no benefit to demoralizing, screaming at, and exacerbating their broken souls. I wish I could offer them all a chance at a better life, an opportunity for second chances. Those little girls deserve a healthy mother, she the opportunity to be well, to hold her daughters in her arms as a mom, not just an addict or a convict. Feeling helpless and hopeless, I rest my head down, close my eyes, and pray for her and her girls....

Chapter 18

"But evil men and impostors will grow worse and worse, deceiving and being deceived." 2 Timothy 3:13

FEBRUARY, 2002

My mother's surgery was scheduled within weeks of Esther's due date. Esther's twins turned out to be big babies and her doctor insisted she rest, let the babies grow in utero as long as her body will hold them; making her unable to come to the hospital for my mother's surgery.

I sat with my brother in the hospital waiting room. He had taken off work, left home before the sun and driven down just to touch her and kiss her forehead before she headed into surgery. Together, he and I were alone in the sterile and icy room that smelled of alcohol and latex gloves. My father came out of double doors and asked us to follow him back to my mother's room. As I walked in, I could see her small frame in the distance, under covers, hooked up to an IV and many other contraptions, taped and monitored. She looked so fragile and helpless. A strong feisty woman, now made feeble by cancer. The thought of losing her was too devastating, and where I wouldn't, couldn't, allow my mind to go. She was to me my friend, my mom, my mentor. I kissed the top of her head and grabbed her hand. "I love you, Mom. I will be praying." I said with a bright smile... my best attempt at a good show.

"Thank you, honey," she answered, as monitors blinked and chimed.

A herd of nurses and medical technicians suddenly entered and ushered us out as they began their preoperative procedures with a great flurry of movement. The three of us walked back to the waiting room with our stomachs in knots. I sat next to my father and grabbed his hand; his face was white, his body stiff, he was distant. All we could do was wait. Korah arrived later. She was holding coffee from a coffee shop. "Oh, did I miss her." We all looked at her blankly. Michael responded awkwardly, "Yes, they took her thirty minutes ago…"

My brother a man of few words, but when he did speak, people listen. A father, a husband to one for over twenty years and hard-working. I looked at him, a beautiful man, handsome, thoughtful; yet still my big brother. I adored him as a child and adored him still. He was a caregiver to Esther and me and our protector. As a little girl, I was bullied. Little girls can be mean and were. In fourth grade, one girl brought a Michael Jackson Thriller t-shirt for every girl in the class but me; which they all wore proudly… except for me. I was a Michael Jackson super fan. Everyone knew it. I had the folders, the glove, sunglasses, jacket and my locker filled with images. I held myself together until I saw my mother in the school parking lot and bitterly wept the entire way home. My sweet, sweet brother, only fifteen, rode his bike every day after school to a hamburger chain where he worked and fried patties; then rode his bike home. On this day, he did not go straight home, but on his bike went to the mall and bought me a Michael Jackson t-shirt. I put the t-shirt on the next morning. Their t-shirt was blue, mine black. Their t-shirt had his name printed, mine had Michael's face with Thriller eyes. I wore it over a red collared shirt which I popped and a chain studded belt around my waist. I didn't' get a t-shirt from that girl, I got a t-shirt from my big brother. He loved me and I was worth his fifteen year old hard earned money to ease my heart… and he did. I love that man, I thought to myself as he sat in the hospital waiting room.

Michael was a successful minister in Phoenix. His church was by the University and filled with students. He had found stardom in the ministry and even became a spokesperson in our denomination on how to develop and grow the modern day church. He would train and teach other pastors on what it takes to be relevant in today's world. It was not his coffee shop approach, or his college casual appeal that the denomination was trying to replicate, it was Michael, my brother, who spoke openly, profoundly and lives were changed. His true gift no one could replicate. His daughter, at two years old, almost died from Type1 Diabetes. Since then, he resigned from the church and has worked at UPS, because it provided great insurance benefits. A church filled with students wasn't going to make anyone rich, and the inability to have insurance with an ill child was too much of a risk. I respect him so much and believe he chose to instead set aside everything he had worked for and achieved for a much higher calling, his children.

Korah walked up to my father and leaned in to hug him, then squeezed in beside him and began rubbing my father's back.

"How are you Dad?" she asked.

"Not good," he responded quick and rigid. His lips were tight and white and he looked as though he was about to burst into tears. I looked away, to give him time to compose himself. We all looked away and sat silent, troubled, and anxious.

Korah was fidgety, "I can't sit here, I am too nervous; I need to walk. I am going to go shopping up the street. Want to go with me Andrea?" There was a large mall a few blocks away.

"No, I'll stay here with Dad." I said looking back at him.

When Korah returned from shopping, several hours later, she found the three of us in the cafeteria. She was flustered and informed us that the doctor was in the waiting room asking for my Dad. Immediately, we all scurry up to find the doctor still there.

He touched my father's arm in a sympathetic gesture, "I believe we were able to remove all the tumor," he said with great assurance. "I am quite confident it was cancerous. I will have everything tested by the pathologist to confirm, but by its appearance it seems to be as suspected. The tumor looked like an octopus with tentacles that stretched out. The good news is that I believe it was contained and feel confident we were able to remove everything."

"How is she doing?" my father asked.

"She is fine. She is still asleep. It will be about an hour until you can go see her." The doctor looked back at my dad and leaned in closer to his face, "She will be fine… She's tough."

"Yes she is," my father responded strongly. "Thank you."

With that the doctor left, as we all groaned a sigh of relief. My father learned how to care for my mother, bandage and treat her. Bringing her home brought so much joy to us all, but the vulnerability of her life was still very evident.

Four days after my mother's release, my sister, Esther, called, "They are taking me in now for an emergency C-section! I guess I'm toxic, so today's the day!" she said nervously.

"Oh no, Mom is not well enough to come!" I said to Esther.

"What? Yes I am! There is no way I will miss seeing my grandbabies." My mother sat up in her bed as I talked on the phone. "Daniel, tape these tubes down so I can put on a sweater, you are taking me to the hospital," my mother hollered.

In spite of our urging, my mother would have nothing to do with missing this moment. So off we went to meet the new little lives that were ours to love and hold.

Again, we sat in another hospital waiting room, but this time my mother next to me, tiny and tired, but stubbornly present and excited.

The operating room was separated from the nursery and NICU. We noticed two nurses in scrubs walking briskly toward the nursery holding two tiny little babies, one was screaming.

"That is my Esther... that is just like my little Esther. I know it." my Mom yelled as she dashed toward the nurses to get a better look.

"Mom, stop running!" I scolded her.

"I know those are her babies. I can see it in their faces," she shouted back. One nurse stopped and turned around to give my mother a quick glimpse of a mad little face squished by the blanket that was tight around its head.

"Oh my gosh, Mom, it is a little Esther. It looks just like her!" I shrieked.

"Is it a girl or a boy?" my mom called to the nurse.

The nurse hesitated and then blurted, "It's a girl."

We both squealed like little pigs while trying desperately to stop my mom from dancing in the hallway and sit down.

Esther's husband came out of the operating room, "It's official, I'm a Dad..." he pronounced in his scrubs and hospital hat. "...A boy and a girl, Candace and Caleb!" We all cheered and hugged. Of course, if Esther decided to get pregnant, she would get pregnant in a big way and bring us a baby boy and a girl all in one very happy day.

"How is my sister?" I asked.

"She had a lot of water. They were very worried, but she is fine and babies are healthy and fat: six pounds each."

My eyes welled as I looked at my mom, who was still too excited to sit down. In that moment I thanked God for health and for life.

I wondered where Korah was, sad she missed this joyous moment.

As Esther attempted to settle into life as a new, working mother, and my mother continued her required preoperative cancer treatment; a notice to vacate was delivered to Esther and her school, signed by Korah and her board. The notice cited that the entire school must leave the church facility by the end of the week. It was the middle of the school year, with five hundred students enrolled, as well as employed many teachers and staff. The eviction stated that my father and his church board did not have the authority to sign the school's lease/rental contract without the consent of the denomination; making the lease agreement invalid. Korah was unaware that my father had a written agreement from the denomination's governance giving him the authority to be the signer for any lease agreement for the church without the denomination's involvement.

Esther was stunned and hurt. She was a new mother, with a school to run, a myriad of elementary students, their families, teachers and staff. She cared deeply for them all. None of us knew or saw it coming. Esther, personally, never had any negative interactions with Korah, and was always kind and loving in her responses.

The school was a financial benefit to the church, which Korah had no understanding of, nor knew the lengths that Esther, my husband, and my father went through to get the church in a financially viable place.

As we all absorbed the depths of her actions, my parents got a notification that the newly appointed church board, each selected by Korah, decided that my parents "modified salary" would now need to be reduced to only a hundred dollars a month, due to the new Senior Pastorate's salary changes. In addition, they would no longer be able to provide medical insurance for my parents... for my mom who just had undergone a double mastectomy, and in the depths of cancer therapy.

Korah cut off contact with all of us. My husband attempted to reach out to her, and her new husband, to appeal to them and explain the financial implications the loss of the school would have on their church. Without that income the church would not be able to survive. Korah responded as though possessed and crazed with hatred, and began ranting her spiritual need to cleanse the church of evil. She described the school as being a demonic force that had caused the church to continually suffer through its years. Chad then asked, "then what of your father and mother? Do you consider them evil as well?" For this Korah had no response or concern. It didn't take Chad long to recognize that there was no reasoning or negotiating. Korah was injudicious in her ambition.

My parents and sister were publically, and with great hostility, exiled. This being the very church and grounds that my father started in his living room, and Esther served from the time she was thirteen years old.

At the week's end, after all personal appeals made, yet denied, Esther felt she had only one available option… She filed a lawsuit, signed on the night before the notice's deadline. That morning each student was able to walk to their classrooms. Had Esther not filed, the police would have been waiting to arrest each child, parent and teacher for trespassing if they set foot onto the property, as described in the notice. The lawsuit legally paused the school's banishment.

Korah used the platform of the church to make a public stand against all of us, from the very podium my father handed her. These events were scandalous, the lawsuit salacious and the Christian community ate it up. My parents and Esther now shamed.

My anger was overpowering and those gut forewarnings I felt over the years were now nauseating. My father wouldn't say a word in his own defense, just that God was the only One who vindicates; however, my mother was not well and the banishment, lawsuit, as well as the financial and medical termination took so much more of her remaining strength and even her will to live. She was completely reliant on the cancer treatment and life dependent on health insurance. I watched my mother's heartache, fearing it would take her last breath.

My husband received a call from the denomination's Supervisor, who oversaw Korah and the church. He notified Chad that he was flying into Tucson and requested to meet at Chad's office, to see if together they could bring an end to the lawsuit. Chad, who was on Esther's school board, stated all that needed to be done was to rescind the notice to vacate and uphold the executed contract until the end of the school year. Esther was willing to release the church from all future remaining years.

Korah was now overruled by the authorities of the denomination and her notice was stopped. As promised, Esther withdrew her lawsuit. The denomination never discussed their reasons for their change of heart, but they did provide my father an apology for their lack of faith in his integrity shown in the legal notice by one of their pastors… his daughter.

Esther found investors in bonds and was soon able to purchase land to build on and move the school. Within months she had already broken ground; her facility a block away from the church my father built, and once finished, erected a beautiful, expansive school that made the old facility pale in comparison. This begun Esther's realization and cause to build schools and to educate children throughout Arizona. Esther hired my father immediately, after the church cut him. Using his doctorate, Biblical knowledge, and heart of grace, he was part of its foundation encouraging a focus on good character, integrity, honor, virtue, and moral development. He encouraged administration and faculty to teach the students to become honorable, principled future leaders in our community. He also began parent-training seminars for the school's parents offering strategies to tackle the crucial issues that they faced with their children in today's society. This added an element that has been what has set Esther's schools apart. My father was not only recharged, he was needed and my mother's life saved by the medical insurance his job provided. Now, my father was part of a new calling, of which enabled him to touch families and children inspired by the foundational truths revealed to him by the Word of God he adored.

Korah started a Bible college and made herself the Dean of Students. She believed this was a better opportunity and would fill the empty school's classrooms with young adults seeking to become pastors and church leaders with her as their mentor. It failed and closed before its first semester. The church's school facility, its classrooms and offices were boarded up; the grass field dried and playground became a haven for weeds and thorns that grew and swallowed all life and vitality it once knew. In less than six months, the entire church property that once thrived and touched so many lives became a wasteland, decrepit, as the leadership lost its congregation dwindling down to a small, tiny flock, unable to fill or sustain its size or buildings. Such a beautiful place with a beautiful history, now an eyesore to our city; its level of impact and influence soon forgotten.

Chapter 19

*"The righteous cry out, and the L*ORD *hears,*
And delivers them out of all their troubles." Psalm 34:17

JAIL: DAY TEN

I wake up and am sadly reminded that I do not have work release to-day. As a mother of two, the thought of being able to sleep in, better yet, sleep all day, seems like a dream. Yet I can't sleep. I sit with my legs crossed and pull my chest down to my lap to stretch my back, which aches, its intensity crippling. The lights in the block are turned on throughout a few hours after breakfast is served, as Officer Cain stands at her cherished post. Inmates pile in the bathroom to shower and brush their teeth. I wait, but may not be able to use the bathroom if I wait too long, with only fifteen minutes of light. I need to get my basic hygiene done or will have to wait to do so after dinner.

The drone of Cain's obsessive drills are no longer unfamiliar to me, nor startling. This time I watch Cain as she snarls. Her face now disfig-ured harsh from her expression, causing her forehead to be conquered with deep lines, adding density to that all too present Neanderthal brow line that physically reveals the fury that boils inside. She sees me staring at her and stumbles on her words. I don't release my gaze but look at her in her eyes, searching for a soul beneath. Cain clears her throat and looks away, then continues her rant.

I remind myself that this woman smiled when she saw me share Bible verses. She has to have more to her than this place and some-where in her is a heart that seeks God. Yet here, she justifies her revile, her contempt, and doesn't view those in her care as His; or maybe she has been in the military and found the tactics she experienced and learned by the drill sergeant, of whom she placed her life, beneficial. I continue to watch her and wonder if she feels she is trying to exemplify the very person who helped steer her to a disciplined life. Yet, unfortunately, her emphasis on authority will only result in frustration, resentment, anger, and low self-esteem in those she berates, bringing her in return aggression rather than respect. She walks strongly towards an inmate who is leaving the bathroom with toothbrush and towel. Cain's face an inch from the young girl as she spits her dissatisfaction of some action made. For the first time I felt sad for Cain. She will go home every night, to a family of her own, yet her days are filled with the sound of her own screams, and the knowledge of her vile treatment of others. Her face is snarled and scored, unrepairable. I close my eyes and pray for Cain's heart to be softened. Cain is God's too and He offers her forgiveness, just as He has me.

I rest my head back down on my mattress. I miss home. I relish the day I can rest my head in my own bed, with all this behind me. Mostly, I miss my kids. I miss waking them up, brushing back their hair for a good morning kiss to their brow. I love to walk into their room and see them snuggled in their beds, sheets and comforters pulled up to their chin. I want nothing more than to be able to lean down and kiss the tops of their little heads and say good morning, a great privilege once part of my daily routine but now an honor I can only envy. I miss breakfast time with them and packing up to drive to school. The best conversations with my son happen on the way. This is the time I hear his fears, his worries and his dreams. Anna is young, so she just talks a lot. She narrates everything she sees, sings loudly, and makes each drive to school full of theatrics and fun. She takes more work than most, and tests everything, pushes every boundary. She is a happy vivacious girl. A joyful spirit that cannot be suppressed, nor would I ever want to. Her heart is big, she loves big, feels big, cares and is compassionate to others in a big way. I love her spirit. I love her more than I knew I could love. She is my precious little joy and holds my heart deep in hers.

Gabriel is a quiet little soul. Chad and I have to be so careful in how we discipline him; his heart completely breaks if he thinks we, or a teacher, or a friend, might be disappointed in him. He tries so hard and puts so much pressure on himself... he is so much like me in that.

He is a soft spirit that loves sincerely, is aware of everything, cares about others and feels other's pain. His depth is beyond his young years. He is loyal and careful, observant and cautious. His heart is as deep as his eyes are blue and his kindness and sincerity an unusual trait. He is my heart. Chad and I are truly so blessed with these two little lives. We have devoted ourselves to Gabriel and Anna and dedicate each day to teach them, prepare them and give all we can to ensure that the sky has no limits to their future and their dreams; yet in the end, it is them that teach and give to us so much more just by being their unique and beautiful selves.

There are other small things I miss, like my pillow, something so insignificant, yet so divine. The thought of laying my head down and feeling it fluff around me is a piece of heaven I can only dream about here. ...Nor can I wait to stretch out in my soft bed, pull my magnificent sheets up with our supple down comforter and close my eyes as though royalty. The joy of rest and comfort will be savored; a new realization of the depths of its luxury.

A group of men enter the block, and Officer Cain begins barking orders for all inmates to go outside; outside meaning the blocked-in space with chain link as cover. We all pile into the small area. There is one table under the basketball hoop. That table is the only seating available for the entire block of inmates. I am not sure how many women are in this outdoor pen, possibly 80 or 90 is my guess. We all stand in the middle of this concrete slab with block walls. A few lean against the wall where there is space and the others sit on the ground. Cain takes the men to the bathroom. The sun is directly above us, which gives us no shade; in fact, the concrete block encases the sun, which now beats down, hard and strong.

"What are they doing?" I ask the inmate near me.

"Not sure. They are either working on the bathroom or they are doing a search," she says. Beads of sweat are balling on her nose.

The men, along with Deputy Cain, are in the bathroom area awhile, then after thirty minutes move onto the bunk area called block 1. I decide to follow the other inmates by sitting on the concrete surface. My red jumpsuit insulates the heat making my sweat drip down my brow, under my arms and breasts. I feel thirst begin to grip me and my tongue and throat feel dry and desiccated. We wait, with no shade. The walls bounce the light and chain roof sparkles. I peer once again through the glass and watch the men and Cain direct their attention at each bunk, pulling up bedding and mattresses. They are opening drawers, shuffling through books, leaving items in a heap on the floor. All personal items dislocated and comingled with another's. One inmate opens the door to the inside. Cain's vociferous screams rattle the windows.

"But, I need to use the bathroom," the inmate pleads.

"No!" Cain snaps.

"What should I do? I have to go?" the inmate pushes.

"I already gave you my answer, close that door NOW." Cain snarls with unbridled venom.

There are a few girls that are very pregnant. Being directly in the sun, no water or shade for over one hour, has taken its toll. Their physical condition is visibly deteriorating at a more severe pace than the rest. Time continues to draw out, the sun continues to pound, and my head begins to hurt. A sharp pain begin in my temples traveling the entire top of my cranium, then begins to throb. It feels like we have been placed in a solar oven, directly under the sun, to burn and cook. Other inmates begin to use their hands as a fan for the pregnant girls, yet the sun's power is unremitting. Two look as though they are close to their due date; several woman have surrounded each in effort to help or assist. One appears to be cramping, crouching over and holding her belly. While a few hold their hands up to block the sun from her face. A desperate and kind effort, but futile in its benefit. I feel helpless... I think we all do.

Another hour has passed, Deputy Cain and the men have now moved from block 1 to the "fishbowl". This is concerning, as the last block on their search is the largest with many more bunks than the other areas, which means it is going to be awhile before we are out of the sun and the intensity of its heat. I can't stand by and watch these young women, who are clearly ready to give birth, remain locked out in this solar furnace with no shade or water. At this point, I decide to open the door and call to Cain to take these pregnant women to medical immediately. My heart begins to beat hard, rapid and loud, its drum spreads into my neck as I muster up the courage to call for help. I am worried what the consequences of what I am about to do will have. Will they extend my sentence or withdraw my work release? I am extremely frightened, but I need to act. I stand up to walk to the door, and immediately become dizzy. I try to hold myself straight but feel my body sway from a woozy and disoriented head.

"Oh fuck this!" an older inmate roars as she storms over to a cabinet and leans behind it, pulls out a garden hose and stomps to my location. Behind me was a spigot I hadn't noticed. She screwed the hose to the valve. "Get those pregnant girls over here now!! Fuck Cain! Fuck this place!" she shouts.

The two most pregnant girls are immediately ushered toward the running hose and begin drinking as water hits and splatters onto the concrete floor. The other women are careful to make sure that all the pregnant girls have been able to drink the water first, forcing them to also wet their hair to bring down their body temperature. After the pregnant girls had their fill, the other inmates line up and take their turn. No one was disrespectful to the other. Their own order; each caring for the other... we were all in this together. The heat was intense and I was extremely thirsty, my head was throbbing, but I stayed back to let the other inmates drink; my situation clearly not as desperate as theirs.

Through the glass window, I see Cain storm toward us in an obvious rage. Quickly the hose is turned off; however the evidence is now running all over the pavement. "Sullivan!" Cain calls with much spite. I hear the inmates moan and hiss. Coincidentally, it turns out to be the same older woman who grabbed the hose and turned the water on. She is now being summoned inside to face whatever deed Deputy Cain has uncovered and its punishment. Sullivan straightens her stand, holding her head high, and walks strongly toward Cain. Sullivan appears to be in her mid-forties. Her hair is blonde, curly, short and her skin fair. She wears no makeup, but no one does in here. She is stocky; built like a man with breasts. She walks like a man as well, and has a proud, assertive step. The door closes behind her.

I can tell the others were worried and hurt for Sullivan. I don't know where Sullivan went, because I never saw her again after that day. Clearly she was important to a lot of the other inmates; the moment I saw her take the risk to ease the suffering of others when she pulled out that water hose, explained why they all respected and loved her. I never saw Sullivan drink any water from that hose. Her selflessness cost her.

APRIL, 2005

My sister and brother, Esther and Michael, were both adopted. My only biological sibling was Korah. My mother had Korah and then was unable to carry again. She had one pregnancy, when Korah was two years old, that ended in a miscarriage. After my parents moved to Tucson, they applied to adopt. Before long, my parent's arms were filled with a beautiful baby boy, Michael. Then after four years of being a family of four, my parents were approached to see if they knew of a couple in the church who would be interested in adopting. A young fifteen-year old girl had been living with the family while pregnant. They were friends of her parents and needed to find someone that would adopt her baby. They asked my parents to assist them in finding a family in the church that would be appropriate for the baby girl that was soon to come. My mother's heart leaped immediately, knowing that this baby was to be hers; instantly my father and mother responded that they were indeed that couple. Three months after Esther was home, my mother learned she was pregnant, ten years since giving birth to Korah. After the pregnancy was confirmed by her doctor, my mother sat in her car in the doctor's parking lot, with a tiny little three month old in the car seat behind her, and began to cry. I was born on Esther's first birthday, I decided to come during her birthday party. We now share the same celebration day and are exactly twelve months apart. Sorry Esther… I am a genuine party crasher.

Adoption was a natural and beautiful part of my growing up. In truth, Michael and Esther were my closest family. I loved them deeply and still do. They were my playmates, my arguments, my protectors, my nucleus. As my parents professed, they were our family's greatest gift; of which I completely agreed. They changed us all, gave us a new personality, made us all better. I knew that would be so different, if I didn't have those two siblings in my life to help mold me.

So, for me, adoption was something I wanted. I wanted a little Esther or Michael to love and to bring their precious spirit into Chad's and my home, to give all the opportunities that we could offer, to delight in their unique and precious personalities, to change and shape our family dynamic into a greater and deeper unit.

In such a loving and compassionate gesture, Esther offered to surrogate for me; however, my infertility doctor explained that my issues were not just my lack of being able to carry. I was also not able to produce healthy eggs to donate. I asked Chad to consider donor eggs, along with Esther as a surrogate, but Chad wasn't interested in those extremes.

My ability to carry, create, even help produce a child in any way was obsolete. Yet the longing in my heart for a child was not going to go away and adoption was the only door that I had left, if we were ever to be a family. Chad, as an only child, had no experience with adoption and wasn't comfortable with the notion. He was afraid of himself and wondered if he would feel like he was raising, even babysitting, someone else's child. To me, who God placed in my arms, whether from natural birth or through adoption, was never really mine to claim, but an entrustment from Him. Every child is God's alone. As a parent, whether biological or adoptive, we all will stand before the Lord to be judged on how we cared for such a precious assignment.

With his fear of adoption and my deep longing for a child, I decided to leave the entire matter in God's hands. God, Himself, had closed my womb, God, Himself, needed to change Chad's heart toward adoption if I were ever to have a son or daughter. I needed him to want this baby, I needed Chad to want to adopt; I couldn't have a child come to us as a result of my pressure. So, I shut my lips and took my petition to God alone.

"Would you consider adoption, Chad?" a friend asked my husband.

Our friend's name was Rick who was a Pastor in Tucson of a little church that Chad and I were now attending. Rachel and Rick's twin boys were five years old. We haven't discussed the outcome or the amount of medical procedures we have been through, but Rachel was the one who encouraged me to go to her doctor, scheduled the appointment and was in the waiting room during my first visit, six years earlier. They loved us and we loved them. Chad especially had a close friendship with Rick. Rick was a true believer. His sincerity and heart for the things of God were at his very core. I think that this very spirit that set Rick apart was what Chad was drawn to. On this night, the four of us were enjoying an evening out.

"It's hard for me to process adoption. I just don't have any way to know how it would feel. Truthfully… I am afraid I won't feel connected to the child," Chad explained.

Rick looked at Chad intently, "If I didn't have the boys, I would absolutely adopt."

"How do you know that you would? You haven't been in our position to be able to say you know what you would do." Chad said flippantly.

"When Rachel and I decided to go to the infertility doctor and see what our physical options were, we discussed adoption. We both opened our hearts to it and felt that this would be something we would pursue if God shut the door to Rachel getting pregnant." Rachel nodded, confirming her husband's statement.

Her eyes stared at me, as her husband gently spoke thoughtfully, delicately to Chad. I was paralyzed, afraid to breathe, or make any sound.

"…I am just not confident that I feel as sure as you did," Chad said softly.

Rick leaned in on the restaurant table, reducing the space from him and Chad, "Chad, I wasn't considering how I would feel about the child, but thought about the tremendous opportunity it would be to open our hearts and home to a life, to give a child opportunities it wouldn't otherwise have, to love unconditionally, most importantly share God's love, by teaching through example, and Word His ways and to provide him or her a life in a loving home. You and Andrea could be beautiful parents. God could use you to nurture a child, to experience the life that only you could offer, to witness and be raised by a couple who truly love each other, and to experience the love of the Father. What could be more beautiful and more rewarding than this type of assignment from God, to take a child from tragedy and to give it a life of love and blessing?"

My eyes were fixed on Rick as my throat closed from the lump that was building; I turned toward Chad, afraid of his reaction. I saw my husband, and gasp; his precious heart had been touched and in his eyes I could see he had instantly changed. He put his face in his hands. I immediately wrapped my arms around him. He was ready for that baby that God planned and assigned to us. A baby, our baby, whom God was pointing down from heaven, specifically ordaining, a new distinct destiny in Him, changing its tragedy into beauty, and my mourning into rejoicing. My Father in heaven has waited, not held back, but waited for Chad and me to walk through this process so that on this day our hearts and lives were ready to accept, value and cherish the one whom He has called to us. This child will not be born from me, but I was born, made by God, to be its mother and to become my greatest calling.

Together, Chad and I reached out to a local adoption agency and began the state required classes that qualified us to be eligible. I am asked to put a book together with a letter to the birth mother, along with pictures of Chad and me, our family, home… and nursery. I placed a magazine picture of a nursery I intended to use as the layout, and filled the book with pictures of us, our parents, Esther, Michael and their families. The agent saw the nursery image and asked me if it was an actual picture.

"No, it's from a magazine. I titled the page, 'A dream yet realized' to not mislead anyone…" I answered fast.

"We need to replace that image with a picture of the real nursery," the agent stated.

The words punched my gut hard and I breathed out with a moan. "I don't know if I can get my home ready for a baby before we are even chosen," I said as my chest filled with air and my heart began to beat fast.

The agent was quiet. I waited for her to give me some release from these orders, but she instead stood strong in her silence.

I continued my protest, "I have been trying to have a baby for eight years, already tormented by the current empty room. I don't think I can live with an empty nursery. This will be far too agonizing for me. Please don't make me do this."

Again, the agent remained quiet.

"What is the longest a couple has had to wait on your list?" I asked.

She held her stance without waver in her tone, "We currently have a couple that have been waiting for three years."

I gasped and gripped my heart. "So, I could have this nursery in my home, empty, for three years? Haven't I been tormented enough? Has that poor couple had a nursery waiting all this time?"

"Yes, they have had a nursery set up for three years. Listen, I will put your book in as is, but you need to have a nursery ready. The birth mothers want to see where their baby will be going and the room is important to them," she snapped.

The thought and actions to set up a nursery was punishing. The entire process felt like a cruel joke, where spirits laughed at me, mocked my dreams and were using this to show how foolish I was to think God had a greater plan for me. I had dreamed of setting up a nursery, with its excitement, its promise; yet these joys were not mine. The whole endeavor was painful and cruel. Each item taunted me, scoffed at my years of heartache and trying, called me out on my inadequacies, my bareness, confirming that I was a worthless woman. I felt my very longing to be a mother, and desire to have a child, our child in this empty room was nothing but a foolish dream, unanswered yet once again. I decided to style the nursery in a soft green, light tan and cream. Using the book 'Peter Rabbit', I framed each of its endearing renderings. My mother and Chad helped me paint soft tan and cream stripes on the walls. My father lined my garage and painted the baby's crib a soft green, along with a beautiful matching armoire. My mother and I bought beautiful, deep olive green, silk fabric, which she sewed into drapes that framed the picture window in this now charming little room. She also sewed an elaborate layered dust ruffle in chenille and linen, with matching bumper and crib blanket that carried the soft green and cream into the bedding. After our efforts were done, we all stood back; the room was truly precious.

"Andrea, this room is more beautiful than the image you put in your book; in truth, it's the prettiest nursery I have ever seen," my mom affirmed as a tear rolled down her cheek. We were all tired from our efforts and our ability to hold our emotions now drained. I grabbed the camera and took the required pictures. The impulse to cry had been with me all day. I wanted to curl in a ball and rock back and forth, allow myself to show how insanely crazy I truly felt.

My parents were so sweet to help; however, it was awkward for all of us. In truth, the entire process had such a sting in all our hearts, each one of us were holding back the pain and bitterness of the activity, to have to make ready for a baby that seemed nowhere in our future, after having been deprived, denied, for so many years.

I smiled and attempted to pretend as though my collapsed heart was still in-tact, "If the baby is to be a girl, I will include flowers from Peter Rabbit's garden; if it is a boy, I will add images of Jeremy Frog, Peter Rabbit's friend." The thought of either scenario made my heart leap inside me; yet the room felt ridiculous and foolish.

Within the second week of our state-required classes the adoption agency called, a young girl has asked to meet us. She is seven months pregnant.

Before we met, the agency explained her situation. Her name was Hannah. She was an orphan in Poland as a small child and she and her brother were adopted by a single woman who was an American Ambassador to Poland. Hannah had chosen us along with another couple, and wasn't sure which couple she would ultimately choose until after she had met us. She liked Chad and me because she felt that she and I looked a lot alike. This to her, would mean that the baby would look like us too. She also saw a picture of our nine year old dog, Buffy, and wanted her baby boy to have a dog. The other couple, whom she was also interested in, were owners of a petting zoo, so to win her over would be no easy task. She had been living with her boyfriend at his parent's home when she became pregnant. Her boyfriend's parents were not ready to raise another…. They drove her to Tucson to be cared for at the non-profit maternity home of which she now resided. The agency wanted to make clear to Chad and to me that Hannah was not positive she wanted to give the baby away. She was struggling with the idea and changed her mind daily.

I was extremely nervous, wearing the most maternal looking dress I could find, butterflies twisting in my belly, I sat in the car as Chad and I drove to our meeting with Hannah. Her location choice was Applebees. When we pulled up, the agent was waiting for us. She explained that she wanted us to sit and get comfortable before Hannah arrived. I could feel my heartbeat in my neck, my breath was shallow, air stuck at the top of my chest, making me pant. Each passing second raised my anxiety to a new and excruciating height. I consciously forced myself to take slow calculated breaths, driving my air to sink deep into my lungs, so that my voice could sound natural and my nerves not so visible. A grey haired man walked up to our table. He was from my parent's church. "Hey Chad… Andrea!" he said jovially. I looked at Chad, "I can't…" I plead. The thought of his presence at this crucial and tense hour made me panic. I was too uneasy to even smile. "I'll take care of it," Chad whispered, while patting my arm to comfort me. Chad scooted out of the booth, put his arms around the older man's shoulders and walked him back to his table. Unlike me, Chad was at ease, unaffected by the stress of the moment, he gives the man nothing but a friendly conversation and was able to lead him back to his own table and direct his focus instead on his meal. I feel some of my anxiety leave, but keep looking over at the restaurant entrance to see if a small, petite, girl, seven months pregnant, has entered.

How do I look at this young girl and coerce her to believe that I qualify to be the mother of the child growing inside her. Why did I have to be in this position? Why couldn't I just roll over one morning, tap my husband on the shoulder and then poof: a life begins to form in my womb. Yet, the only option for me to ever have a child means I need to get interviewed, take classes, have my home inspected, beg and plead and prove that I am worthy of this title, the title of "Mom." I want to be chosen, I want this baby. My arms even ached for him.

Fortunately, Chad was back at the table before she arrived. His hand gripped mine and his strength and confidence soothed me instantly.

Light from the sun entered the room and there she was. Her silhouette was all I could see, but her precious belly revealed. My eyes burned and my heart leaped at the sight of that little tummy filled with a tiny baby. She and another agent walked over to our table and Chad and I pulled out of the booth to stand and greet her. She shook our hands and we all sat down. She was beautiful; her eyes, round and crystal blue. They looked like the sky without a cloud to veil their brilliance. She had shoulder length blonde hair and perfect lips that concealed a beautiful, but timid smile. She was so very tiny, smaller than me. I felt like I was huge next to her, yet she was the one pregnant. I instantly felt drawn to her, taken by her beauty, her blue eyes, her soft face. She was shy, meek. The agent talked for a bit, but I couldn't focus. My hands were trembling, so I tucked them between my crossed legs so that no one could see. Then the agent asked Hannah if she had any questions she had prepared. Hannah looked at me, her countenance sincere yet cautious.

She hesitated, "…I love this baby." she whispered. Tears began to fall down her cheek. "I love him so much. But… I, I have struggled with drugs… with cocaine." She was looking down, not giving eye contact to Chad or me. "I don't know if I can trust myself to stay clean, but since I found out about my pregnancy, I have been clean… for him." She looked up and straight into my eyes. I smiled at her, softly, and nodded my head. "I have even taken drug tests for you, so you could know that I am clean, for the baby. However, I didn't realize I was pregnant for a while and I did do drugs then." Her tears flowed stronger and her voice began to crack. My heart left me and I wanted to hold her. She looked so young and so fragile; her beauty within, undeniable. "This is really hard, the hardest thing I have ever done…"

"I respect that you are considering this; wanting what is best for your baby." I said to her.

"I am glad you are pretty." she said to me. "I want my baby to have a pretty mom. …What is most important to me is that he knows Jesus. I want him to know God. I have made mistakes and my mom loves me, but she has made it clear that as long as I continue down this path, she will not let me come home. …But, I think she is proud of me today. I have told her all about you. She feels this is best." She smiled and then looked down. "I loved your adoption album. You have been married nine years?"

"We will be married ten years in November," responded Chad.

"That's a long time married. Did you get married in the church?" she asked as if dreaming of her own.

I smiled at her, "Yes, we did. I wanted to have our wedding in front of God, on the altar and have everyone who was willing to come, come and see the handsome man I persuaded to marry me."

She smiled. Her blue eyes squinted as though she had something important to say, "I came from Poland with my brother, Alexander. I want my son to know his roots and visit Poland one day."

"We will take him to Poland so he can see where you and he came from." Chad answered with a smile and a nod.

"…And I want him to eat cabbage. I really love cabbage," she said.

"I will learn new cabbage recipes," I responded.

"You don't even need to cook it; raw cabbage salad reminds me of home." She paused, looked down and then up at me pensively. "…Please tell him to stay away from drugs. Drugs have made my life hard… the reason I am considering…" she looked down again struggling to finish. "I want, I want him to know I love him so much and that I wanted to keep him; with all my heart I want to keep him." She stopped as tears flowed from her blue eyes.

I looked at her, in deep sincerity, "I promise you this, Chad and I will always honor you in everything we say. Truly, we are amazed by you and have fallen in love with you, as much as we have fallen in love with that baby who is growing inside you. The choice you have made is one of great love and great beauty. You are not making an easy choice, but one that puts that precious life above your own. We will ensure that he always knows your love, your beauty and your sacrifice. He will be proud of you, because we will tell him he should be," I said. My trembling now unconcealed.

She let out a quiet sob and lowered her head to hide her face.

"Can we adopt you too?" blurted Chad.

She giggled, but it is true. Chad and I both had fallen in love with her immediately. She had taken my heart and that of Chad's. She was so young, but so deep, and so beautiful. The agent let us know it was time for them to take Hannah back to the maternity home. We all stood and I reached for her and hugged tightly. She took a few steps away and turned back abruptly, "You are my baby's parents. It is you. I do not need to meet with anyone else." Then she turned back as the agent placed her arms around Hannah and led her back to the front door.

Chad and I sat in the restaurant booth and stared at each other. Our hearts had left and now belonged to that young girl who walked away holding our baby boy.

Chapter 20

"Therefore we also, since we are surrounded by so great a cloud of witnesses, let us lay aside every weight, and the sin which so easily ensnares us, and let us run with endurance the race that is set before us." Hebrews 12:1

JAIL: DAY TWELVE

The night was long and the morning rough. I sat waiting on my bunk, staring at the clock. My bed is made and paperwork in hand. The room is dark as the other inmates are still asleep. It is cold, which is strange; really cold. I take the shredded towel I had in my metal drawer and wrap it around my shoulders as a make shift shawl, while I wait for my release time.

"Ladies!" Deputy Cain screeches. "Ladies!" she yells louder. "Listen up! I saw all your grievance forms… You think they don't show them to me? They do! You are all so good at complaining. You all feel so mistreated because you had to stand outside, so mistreated because you get only two breaks a day. Well guess what, today you get no breaks. How about you learn a lesson and sit on your bunks, in the dark, all day. You will not move, not even for lunch. Once you get your tray, you need to take it back to your bunk and eat it there IN THE DARK. That is what you get for filling out your little grievances."

The inmates are sitting up in their bunks. They stare blankly at Cain as she screams.

"And don't think I don't know who you are!" she points around slowly, threatening each as she passes from one to the other. Her finger points at me, which she stops and holds.

In the inmate handbook, it encourages inmates, when needed, to follow a grievance procedure by filling out the appropriate forms (of which I have no idea where to find aforementioned forms or where to submit such) and to lodge their complaint or grievance to a third party administrative personnel, who are to review each. The jail states that they will follow a formal administrative procedure that has been put in place, where such forms are to be channeled in a confidential process, and all complaints reviewed and investigated. This is what is written; clearly not followed. I did not fill out a grievance form; as I was positive the jail administration was in no way concerned about the safety and health of its inmates, nor did I have any confidence in the procedures or confidentiality they so claimed to keep. My instincts were clearly correct; however, it does appear that my conversation with the male officer getting a chocolate bar might have been discussed in addition to the grievance forms that are now being dispersed and discarded.

I see the second hand hit the twelve and jump to Cain's counter to clock out. She pretends not to see me, so I wait. Without turning her head she slams my badge down for effect and waves me away. "Thank you." I say and smile.

The extreme heat feels like a warm blanket tightly wrapped around my body when I walk outside. I shiver from the cold that now leaving me, as I sit in my beautiful car. It smells of leather and I drench in its warmth. It has deep rich black and brown hues throughout the interior, burled wood dash that stretches across the front, and smooth buttery upholstery that welcomes me as I sit... every inch of it exudes luxury and makes me feel spoiled once again. The goose-bumps begin to disappear from my arms and legs as I take the now familiar trek to my house from jail.

I am glad to be away, even though just for the moment, grateful for the work release and work release program that is offered and ordered by the judge in my case. There are many advances that the jail has taken that seem productive to its officers and inmates. I give credit to city leaders and high level administration who have introduced and implemented such concepts to its facility; by doing so, I continue to be a participating member of this city and community, contributing by paying my taxes, and maintaining my employment while still serving my time. To do anything to jeopardize this opportunity would be counter-productive to me and has ensured that I stay a quiet and submissive detainee.

However, I am deeply grieved by what I see and feel for those whose days ahead outnumber mine and those who were not given the opportunity to work. With great appreciation to God and Esther for the work release given to me, I leave and go to work this day, which seems to fly by. Sadly, before I know it, I am back in my approved sweat shorts, hugging my kids goodbye.

Chad is nearby, but not part or interested in seeing me. I love him. I am still in love with him and want him more than I want anyone else, desperately. My heart is broken, but realize I can't keep protecting it for fear he will hurt me further. I kiss the heads of my precious kids and walk over to Chad. I grab his hand, look into his eyes, still deep blue and bright, but now distinguished, with few lines that crease their sides. He wears a short beard that is dark, a sexy contrast to his blonde hair that lays thick on his head. A light pepper of gray hair mixes throughout his short beard. He still is very sexy, actually even sexier. He is very disciplined in life; working out early every morning. His body is incredibly chiseled and defined. His muscular frame, no longer youthful, but more exquisite and handsome.

"Bye… I love you." I say to him, sincerely and softly. He looks at me, his eyes are wide and surprised, they soften and narrow, "I love you too." he says softly.

With that, I get in my car and head back to jail.

"Can I see your tattoo?" an inmate asks as I change into my red jumpsuit. Lights are on; however, I have been ordered to go see the nurse. The entire block was very cold. The thick jail shirt and pants will be warm, so putting them on was a welcoming thought.

"Yes, of course." I set down the red shirt I was just about to pull over my head and walk over to her bunk in my sports bra and turn around, revealing the artwork that covers my back up to my neck, spreading down to my waist.

"It is beautiful. Are they feathers?" she asks.

I answer, "Yes, peacock feathers."

"What is the meaning behind them? Or did you choose them because they are pretty?" she probes.

"The meaning is 'accepting one's own beauty'," I answer. The power in those words move me. Their significance in my life, real.

"I like that," she says softly.

"Thanks," I say, proud... proud of my back. I exhale with that very thought.

"How long have you had it?" she asks as I walk back to my bunk.

"Just over a year." I say, realizing how momentous this year has been both from the tattoo, the arrest and now jail.

"It is amazing." says the inmate... which touches me.

I do not give off the look of someone who would cover myself with body art; and in reality, had I not had the scars, I wouldn't have.

It was my sister, Esther, who encouraged me to consider the tattoo. She knew how sensitive I was about my scars and felt this might give some relief from the intensity of my insecurities.

The artist, a woman, who had an office in Tucson, but lived primarily in Costa Rica, met with me prior. I had been searching for artists that could work on scars. This takes a special technique. I had contacted specialists in California and other states, but on a whim contacted her because I had seen her work on someone I knew and her talent was unparalleled to anything I had seen before. Although her art was incredible, I was unsure if she could work with a skin texture as uneven as mine.

She was very spiritual. She seemed to be sensitive to people and to life. She put her hand on my back feeling it. She changed my life.

At the next visit, she drew on my back, freestyle. It was her that designed the peacock feathers. I walked to the mirror to see the composition on my body. It was so beautiful. I stood in the mirror staring at this unfinished canvas, where she had taken something so grotesque and transformed it into something that was beautiful; I stared in disbelief. The feather's moved whimsically. There was no order, just feather's that seemed to have fallen and were now laying softly, artfully on my back. They curled and flowed, causing the harshness of my scars to disappear into the wisp and breeze of each feather's form. I couldn't believe their power, their splendor. I looked up the meaning of the peacock and learned the significance, "to accept my own beauty." Maybe, today I can, I thought.

I actually enjoyed the pain of the tattoo. It was gratifying to feel the intensity and unforgiving pain of the needle removing my ugliness. Four hours later, the outline had been permanently placed on my back. The results to my confidence and the way I viewed myself was immediate. It took four more sessions each three hours until complete. That was the end to my self-loathing. Liberty was now mine. For the first time, I wore a bikini and rocked it proudly. I even started wearing backless dresses.

Tattoos don't frequent the country club, but I let it show. Looks of disapproval were constant, but didn't care. They could judge me, or place me in some category they felt superior to, yet they couldn't make me feel ashamed. My shame was gone. Their judgment was a reflection of themselves, a true testament of their shallow and bitter world. The beauty that covered what was ugly was now mine. I had been marked disfigured, but now I am marked exquisite. I had been ashamed, but now I was glorious.

Chad wasn't used to my new found confidence or my bikinis, although he loved the tattoo. All the years we were together, he never seemed to see my scars and always made me feel as though he found all of my body sexy. Now I felt like I deserved his compliments, and agreed with his statements of attraction and desire for me. I now knew and believed the power that my body had on him and I loved it.

Being in jail, I am extremely grateful that I have this tattoo. Without it, I would have had to change clothes in front of these inmates and these guards and reveal my scars. To endure a strip search without its cover would have taken me to an even deeper humiliation and depression. To have had to lay myself bare, show what remained of my cancer, to these cruel and obscene captors would have been my greatest degradation where there could be no repair.

I put on my reds and am led by a young male guard to the nurse's office. The nurse is an older lady with short hair, which is curly around her head. I assume she goes to the beauty parlor once a week to get her curls rolled, and must sleep with her hair wrapped to preserve her parlor do. She wears thick round glasses with light peach frames. She waves at me to sit down next to her desk. The male guard waits at the door. He is friendly. I notice that all the male guards are very pleasant when they talk to me. I suppose my girth is non-threatening, so they feel no need to scowl as the women guards do.

"I need to conduct a TB test on you," the nurse informs me.

She seems very distracted with the items she is laying out on her desk. She doesn't appear organized, but confused, moving the same items from one spot to the other and then back again.

"Please sign this form, here at the bottom." She taps with her fingernail on the paper she has laying in front of me, but still hasn't looked up from her assortment of needles, alcohol and swabs she seems to be puzzled by. "The form just explains that you understand that you will be given a TB test."

I look down at the form and read it while she reassembles her counter.

"This form states that I have received and understand the information given to me regarding the TB test. Where is the information this form states I have received?" I ask.

"No, you are signing the form to say you understand that you will be taking a TB test," she retorts with great frustration.

I pause and look at her. She is angry, now glaring at me. I decide not to let this one go and continue. "I am sorry, but that is not what it says. You are asking me to sign that I have received information regarding the TB test, yet you haven't provided me any such information."

"No, that is not what it says!!" She says vexed, scowling at me through her peach round frames.

I hold my ground, "Do you want me to read this form to you, or should I give it to you so you can read it yourself?" I am determined now. I am done being pushed around and am not going to let this nurse deny me a simple right; it is my body... I have such little rights left, let me have this.

"I know what the form says." She says with her voice raised, slamming both her hands on her desk as one of her tight little curls becomes ever so slightly unraveled near her forehead.

I wait again, watching her anger boil. She stares at me, breathing heavy. Amused, I watch her and wait. I decidedly am not signing the form and can see she can't conduct her test without my signature. Then I add my final recourse, "Actually, I don't think you do know what the form says."

The male officer, who I forgot was there, steps up, "Where are your TB pamphlets?" he says to the nurse.

She continues to stare at me and doesn't' answer him.

"Where are your pamphlets?" he asks again strongly.

"They are on my desk, but that is not what the form says..." she declares, eyes never leaving my face; her anger rising each passing second. The male guard walks over to where we are and begins riffling through her desk, looking for something that resembles a TB information sheet. The nurse becomes visibly irate that the officer is intervening, as he fumbles around on her desk, reaching over her to find it. She grabs a brochure, among a stack that is propped up in a file cabinet in front of her and slams it down on top of the form. The male guard leans in to see what the brochure has written on it, satisfied with its content, he walks back to the doorway and waits quietly once again.

I look down and in front of me is a glossy brochure, with the title, *"What You Need to Know About the TB Skin Test"*.

"Thank you." I say looking at the nurse. She picks up the pen in front of me and holds it in the air so that I will take it from her. I grab the pen and set it back down on the desk and begin to read the brochure.

"This discloses that there is a very slight risk of having a severe reaction to the test, which would include swelling and redness of the arm. It also explains what to look for if positive and what to expect if the test shows negative. This form that you have asked me to sign is specifically noting that inmates who come in for this test have in fact been provided the information in this pamphlet prior to the test. Don't you feel I, and every other inmate that comes in, have the right to read this prior to you sticking a needle in our arm? Do I not have the right to sign that I have received such information, only if and after I actually receive it?" I say, as though I am fighting for the rights to humane treatment from every employee who works in this jail.

The nurse doesn't answer and doesn't really care what the form says. Gaining nothing, I sign the form and pull out my arm so she can inject me, which she does with great frustration and contempt.

"Take her." She brushes the air with her fingertips toward the male deputy, as if shewing away the filth that has entered the room.

With that I stand up and am escorted back to my block.

I really am not an argumentative person, but I don't understand why the staff can't just follow their own guidelines, their own rules and regulations, and why they instead prefer to push people around stepping over the margins of humaneness and the law. In her irritation, she was rough and I can already feel my forearm begin to bruise. I wasn't worried about the TB test and should have just gone along with her explanation of the form, in spite of the falseness of her claims. In the end, I am sure she won't change her assertion of what the form states to future inmates, and most likely I will be the only person who ended up suffering with a bruised arm for attempting to clarify the accuracy of such.

I am back to my bunk. The block is freezing. Some of the inmates have blankets, but many do not... I am one of the ones without. I pull out the old ratty towel from my drawer to use as a make-shift blanket. I get into bed with my reds on. The tiny guard is at her post. She is wearing a quilted down jacket... in Tucson... in August. It is well over 114 degrees outside, but the guards are in down snow jackets. I shiver as I feel the cold bite my face and nose. I pull the towel and sheet over my head which cocoons my breath and warms my cheeks. This calms me and I am able to relax enough to doze off. My head remains under the covers all night. The sheet and towel are frayed enough that lack of oxygen is not an issue; the rips and holes allow me to breathe freely, yet still insolates some heat from my breath.

MAY 2005

Chad and I were able to see Hannah a few more times before her due date. After our first introduction, she had met a young man on the city bus and their relationship became serious. Clearly he could see she was very pregnant, but that did not stop their new romance. Her love for the baby was real and she wanted deeply to be able to keep him. Now that she had a boyfriend, she hoped that this would give her a way. I had daily reports from the agency of her changing decision. My heart felt twisted, turning each day, and my emotions swung high to low like a rollercoaster without vision for what was to come. Her boyfriend clarified that he would support her decision either way, but was not going to help her raise the baby. So, the last word was she was back to following through with the adoption, but had moved out of the maternity home and was now living with him. The agency representatives were picking Hannah up to take her to and from her doctor appointments, so they still had a close account on how she was and what she was doing. Physically, I felt as though I was going crazy, but to those around me I did my best to appear sane.

I had daily visits from my mother and Esther who brought shopping bags full of little baby boy items that they stubbornly and gleefully showered on me. This was in complete disregard to my request to wait until my arms were actually holding him. It was precious and exciting when I held each item, and placed his little clothes in his room. It also felt so frightening, eight years I have been trying, eight years I have wept for this baby. I would question myself, question God, asking if this day would ever be realized, or would I have to watch this dream stay continually out of my reach? It wasn't long before the baby's closet was filled with little boy outfits, and the armoire filled with little socks, shoes, blankets and newborn diapers, all from my mom and sister. My friends were very careful to honor my request of no gifts, no shower, just wait...

Although each day uncertain, Chad and I trudged ahead as though we were days away from parenting; we discussed baby names, mulling over several, but nothing we came up with seemed to fit the baby that was in our heart, nothing engaged my spirit. I picked up the phone book and began reading names in utter exasperation. The name Gabriel touched me when my eyes reached it.

Unexpectedly, I got a call from the agency. Another young girl, who had previously seen our book, had now decided that she wanted to choose us as the adoptive parents for her baby. She too was pregnant with a little boy. My breath, heart and circulation stopped. I paused being confused and unsure.

"What do I do?" I asked. "Hannah wavers every day, but I feel so connected to her."

"You can decide to follow through with both girls, and if one changes her mind, you still have the other; best case scenario, you can raise the boys as twins." she said matter of fact.

This idea seemed bizarre, I paused to process, feeling pressure and uncertainty.

"I can't, in all good conscience, allow these two girls to think that I am going to raise their baby, as the center of our world, and not disclose that I am in the process of adopting another baby at the same time. In addition, there are couples that have been waiting for a baby for over three years, how can I take away one of their opportunities with these two." I said without thinking.

The agent cleared her throat and questioned me, "So, you want to just stay with Hannah and hope she follows through with the adoption?"

I took a deep breath, "Yes… I think so… Wait a moment, Ok?"

The agent sounded confused. "Ok…?" she said.

I held the phone cupped in my hand. Under my breath I began to call out to God, "Jesus, help me! Help me know what steps I should take in this. Help me know what to do… please!"

I put the phone back to my ear, "I am scared. I understand that this could mean that although chosen by two birth mothers, I may end up with not one child… because we put all our hope in Hannah."

"That is a very good possibility…" she said frankly.

We both remained quiet. I felt so uncertain. "I need to call my husband…" I said firmly.

"Of course. I do need some type of answer today though."

"I understand," I said hastily. My hands trembling severely.

Without delay, I dialed Chad at work. He was quick to respond and with great conviction he felt we needed to follow our gut and not open a new door. Our hearts and spirits were aligned, but my fear and anxiety threatened my peace. I paused once again and took a deep breath before I dialed the agent's number.

"I need to listen to my heart. I truly believe that it is to our heart where God speaks. Although scary, we feel that Hannah is whom God is leading us to. The other little boy belongs to someone, God will direct her, but our guts say…" I clear my throat. "…my heart says, it is not me…"

Chapter 21

"And not only that, but we also glory in tribulations,
knowing that tribulation produces perseverance;
and perseverance, character; and character, hope." Romans 5:3-4

JUNE, 2005

Each day drew out, as though an eternity; waiting for the due date, waiting to know if my arms would hold this baby boy, for whom they ached.

"Andrea, he is here!" the agent reported. "He is seven pounds, eleven ounces! He is beautiful. I sent you some pictures on your email. Keep in mind, Arizona law will not let the birth mother sign the adoption forms until twenty-four hours after the birth. So, now we wait."

"Can we come see him?" I ask.

"No, it is best you stay home. Hannah is saying she plans to go through with the adoption, but she is also having a hard time." She says pragmatically.

Chad and I hurry to the computer to look at the pictures. Immediately, the image of this brand new little man fills the screen. We both laugh out loud. He looks like a tiny Eddie Monster; jet black hair and a widows-peak on his forehead. He is screaming with his mouth so wide, his tonsils are visible. His face contorted and scrunched from his unhappy feelings about life. I squealed with glee. He was beautiful and perfect in every way. I loved him so deeply, my very existence wanted to hold him, kiss his baby fingers and toes. Yet, he was still so very far out of my reach. The agony of our distance consumed me and my fear and anxiety regarding the next twenty-four hours became maddening.

Time can be so cruel. Twenty-four hours can feel like eternity and did. We learned that the baby was in the NICU, but the agency was unwilling to disclose the reasons for the move. Something has happened, because CPS is now involved, yet no one was at liberty to tell us what was behind all the activity. I felt as though my mind and body had become crazed with fear, excitement. I was ready to crack. Now unraveled, I was helpless, hopeless, insecure, and could not feel or sense God anywhere. Where was He?

The twenty-four hours finally rolled by, and I waited by the phone, anticipating the end to the eight years of longing.

"Andrea, Hannah said she can't sign the paperwork…" I gasped with a deep groan, then buried my face in my hands, and began to weep desperately. "It is not over though; she just asks that you wait one more day. She is really struggling." She says with concern, but that for Hannah.

"Yes, I am sure she is, I can't imagine her pain, but I am struggling too. Eight years have come to this moment and my heart and body are at hope's end. I can't do this anymore. I just really cannot do this anymore." I set the phone on mute and scream, "Please God, please end this." Then gather myself to answer the agency rep, "Hannah can't keep delaying this process. I will sit by for one more day. One more day is all I can cope with, but if she asks for another day, beyond the forty eight hours, Chad and I need to be out. We need to let her go and make this decision for her. I can't be played with, my heart is too fragile to be strung along any further."

"I understand." The agent replies.

I drop the phone when I hear it click and I rush to the empty baby's room, knowing he is just minutes away, yet I could do nothing to bring him home, to his room, to our hearts, to his family, that waits for him. My knees buckle and I feel my hands hit the carpet. I struggle no more, and let the agony of my soul find escape in one loud, long anguished scream of desperation. Feeling no relief, I then call to God, "Please, please, please God. Please take this from me, this heartache, this longing. I am cracked and my emotions are at their end. Please, God, let me bring him home, my baby, my son… Gabriel."

My phone rings the next day, "Andrea… she is ready to sign! The hospital is releasing him now. She wants, in her last final act, to hand him over to you at a church… at the altar and before God. She will sign the paperwork there and personally hand you your son."

"Do we bring our family?" I inhale.

"No, their joy may be too painful for her; can you and Chad can come alone? I will be there with her, waiting for you." Her words are spoken slowly and methodically. She knows my emotional state and she wants me to hear her every word.

Trembling, Chad and I walk to our car and install, clumsily, the baby's car seat and carrier in the back. We both feel like we are deep under an ocean of emotions, looking up and seeing the sun's light ripple and sway up ahead, but drowning under the waves and current of eight years of sorrow.

We reach the tiny little Baptist Church in the middle of town, with a steeple and wide white double doors. The agent is waiting for us in the parking lot and ushers us into a building that is attached to the side of its chapel. When we walk into the building, there is a table with a few folding chairs in the middle of the banquet type meeting room where the agency lawyer waits for us with papers and pen in hand. He motions for us to sit down in the two chairs across from him.

"Here is the adoption paperwork, I need you to sign here," the lawyer instructs, pointing at the documents signature lines.

I look over at the agency representative that has been working with us and had walked us into the banquet room. "Has Hannah signed?" I ask.

"Yes, Hannah has signed. She is waiting for you. Once you sign this form, you are legally a mother," she says tenderly.

My hands tremble, I hear the agent and am relieved that Hannah has signed and is going through with everything, but I am not processing the depth of what the agent just said, "you are legally a mother." Nothing seems real to me yet. It all still feels so far away and I am afraid that everything is about to fall apart leaving my heart broken and barren again. Once we sign the forms, Chad places his hand over mine to soothe their trembling. We signed without having seen him, but didn't need to. We will take this little boy if he is purple, blue, or green. We love him, more than our own life, we love him.

The agent stands and motions toward a door nearby, "Your son is in here." I gulp and exhale deeply. "My son!" could this be true. I must be dreaming, but have no interest in pinching myself, because I never want to wake up. The agent leads us through a door that opens onto the stage. It dawns on me that we had just left a choir type prep room and were entering the chapel from the stage's side door. We stand on the little church platform as the door closes behind us, and are immediately ushered to the altar steps just beyond a little podium. Hannah is sitting on the first pew, her arms are wrapped around a tiny little bundle, swaddled tightly, with a little face peering out from the cocoon of blanket. Hannah sees me and bursts into tears, the immensity of her grief audible, and her sobs become deeper as she looks down at the little life that she wants so intensely, yet loves so deeply that she chooses this day to do what she felt was best for him; even if this very act resulted in death to her own soul. I felt her heartache, I understood her love. She would never be the same, she would never be able to move on from this moment, she loved him and he would always be a part of her. I am now standing with Chad at the altar next to the church's minister, as Hannah in her immeasurable grief and agony slowly walks toward us holding her son, holding my son.

She stopped as she approached me, her heartache palatable. I touched her arm to comfort her… how can I comfort this young woman. Her pain and heartache so great, I can feel it. The minister rests his hands on her head and prays for her, for strength, for comfort, to give her peace in her anguish, to show her His love. Then he tells Hannah to hand me the baby. She looks at me, her blue eyes are pleading. She again looks at the baby she holds tightly in her arms, then reaches out to me, denying the instincts of her soul and gently places Gabriel in my arms. I look in her eyes that plead helplessly to take care of her son, then down at the baby's face. He is pink and fair, with light blonde hair. Nothing like the Eddie Monster picture I was sent, but precious, beautiful. He seems so peaceful, as he sleeps. He smiles… He smiled… the moment he was placed in my arms he actually smiled. I lose my breath from his beauty. The realization that my son was here, my arms have been filled, my heart's cry has been quieted, God has heard me and answered; this hits me like a lightning strike, and my entire body begins to shake, uncontrollable trembling as my mourning turns to utter joy. I look back at Hannah, back into her blue eyes and spiritually make a promise to be a great and loving mother to this boy. I now begin to sob, for God has answered me, He has brought to me this life, a child of whom He called to me, to us. Hannah stops crying, and she smiles at me. I grab her and hug her, all words have left. Then Chad grabs me and we hold each other, our son between us; our son, Gabriel. I know that the pastor had prayed over us, but I don't remember. I appreciated the prayers, but at that moment my ocean of sorrow was unplugged and the light was now shining over us. In that moment I have never felt love the way I felt love for this baby; it was all consuming, never ending, unconditional. I understood that this child was significant to heaven; my days of longing and crying out to God were days of preparation for me to understand the depth of his value, the preciousness of his life to the Father, nor could my role be taken lightly or given easily, he was worth each year, and every tear. He was worth so much to Hannah, more than her own life. He was my highest calling, the very reason I was made was for him.

Chad did not struggle with his emotions toward Gabriel. He was instantly bonded and his love for his boy was visible. He even wrote his son a poem:

There is A Little Man In My House

Today there is a little man in my house
He is seven pounds, eleven ounces and over twenty inches long
He is my son

Today there is a little man in my house
He eats every two hours and now he is
Eight pounds, ten ounces
He is my son

Today there is no longer a little uncircumcised man in my house
But all is well
He is my son

Today there is a little man in my house
He sleeps during the day and sings during the night
He still eats every two hours and is nine pounds,
Ten ounces and over twenty-two inches long
He is my son

Today there is a little man in my house
He still eats every two hours and sings during the night
He fills the diaper genie every week and can yell louder than Daddy
Did I tell you he is in the ninety-eight percentile for his size
He is my son

Today there is a little man in my house
He still eats every two hours and sings during the night
Grandma thinks he smiled this week; gas is a funny thing
He is my son

Today there is a little man in my house
He still eats every two hours and sings during the night
The books say he will only do this for a couple more months
But I don't seem to care because
He is my son

Today I thank God for the little man in my house
I thank God he eats every two hours and sings during the night
I thank God that he has chosen me to be his Daddy
And I am proud to say that
He is my son

Chapter 22

*"And God will wipe away every tear from their eyes; there shall be no
more death, nor sorrow, nor crying. There shall be no more pain, for
the former things have passed away."* Revelation 21:4

JAIL: DAY FIFTEEN

It is cold and the chill has overcome my body. My neck and back are
sore, exhaustion from lack of sleep makes me feel beaten down physically and spiritually. My nerves are fragile and I fear my reaction to any
hostility will cause my emotions to overreact. I try to get ready to check
out, but my body is stiff from the freezing temperature of the entire
block. I need to have a seamlessly made bunk, yet waiting with the bed
made and no covers to keep me warm is hard. Shivers come over me in
waves and the soreness of my neck and back ache with each spasm. I
can't wait to sit in my warm car and soak in the Tucson heat.

As each minute passes, I feel my body become stiffer from anticipation of the hot sun and my body's defiance to the cold. I feel a pang
of guilt to be able to leave, while so many other inmates continue to
endure this punishment for another day.

The drive home is satisfying, as the hot car brings my body to a relaxed state and the sun penetrates through my tense muscles and chilled
skin. I pull into the driveway and see that Chad's SUV is in the garage.

Startled, I quickly look over to see if instead he took his beloved
"play" car to work, a 1967 Firebird, he lovingly and with a bit of sar-
casm calls "Eleanor." He had purchased her from a client and personally restored her to her current glory. Eleanor is a sexy dark mistress, all
black and chrome, and just as dark and sexy inside, with black interior
and deep red detailing. She flaunts an exquisite custom firebird that was
hand painted on her burly hood. The car is muscular and powerful. As

beautiful as she is, she equals that in the tantrums she gives Chad each time he takes her out. She revs and spits to his delight and then turns off and stalls, toying with his emotions. He also has a 1966 Corvette Stingray convertible. This is my personal favorite. I haven't seen a car more beautiful or carnal than that Vet. Its blue silver paint reflects the gorgeous lines and curves of its impeccable body. So pretty, yet strong and masculine. It seduces all who come into eyesight and plays with the road flexing its strength and speed with one tap to its peddle. The Vet remains on its lift, left alone and brought out only for special occasions to keep running without hiccup. I had thought that I would be the talk of the town if I took the beauty to a charity meeting, but was quickly informed it was not to be left in the hands of valet, nor a full parking lot. I tried to drive it once but realized quickly that she was out of my league and would show her ability to be temperamental to a novice such as me. However, the Vet is more than accommodating to Chad. She is consistent and reliable to him alone, providing all the fun and pleasure he could want in every ride. In spite of the Vet's faithfulness, Chad's heart belonged to Eleanor. That beefy black bird gives him all the frustration and delight in one muscle bound package. I think he loves Eleanor above all others, because he restored her himself. Every inch of her has his personal touch, a two-year process to bring her to where she is today. Now she sits in the garage, next to her sister wife, the Vet. …Does this mean that Chad is home? I shiver from the thought of why.

Hesitantly and on guard, I walk into the house and look around. The kitchen is dark, empty. I am alone. I swallow a mouth full of air and relax my step. After turning on my coffee, I walk while it brews to my bedroom as I rub my sore neck hoping to relieve its stiffness and ache. I open my bedroom door and there sits Chad by the unlit fireplace. I stop paralyzed, startled to see him, moved that he would make an effort to be alone with me, afraid of what he has to say.

"Hi! You startled me." I say surprised. "I saw your car, but thought maybe you had an employee pick you up in the truck." I say in shock, but happy to see him.

"No, I came home to talk to you," he says with a low voice and a serious look on his face.

My heart drops. I want this, but I am afraid of what he is going to say. "Ok…?" I reply nervously.

"Andrea, I don't know what to do anymore. You are just not happy." he blurts as though bottled up and now releasing all his built up pressure. "It seems every time we go through something, you become unhappy. You are an unhappy person and I have to deal with your emotional crazes as you walk around every day as though miserable. So, I just disengage and wait until you decide to be happy again."

"How can you say that?" I vent, "Chad, I am going through hell right now. I have been through more hell than some can survive. I have friends who have to undergo infertility treatments for a year and the world feels their heartache and drama, they go to therapists, are put on antidepressants and then get pregnant and have a healthy baby. I cried one time in your presence, one time after eight years of trying. Tell me one woman you know that would be as easy on their husband and ensure their comfort in hard times as I have for you. Look at me now, I just got out of jail! Still an inmate, yet I just greeted you with a smile. I have slept in jail for fifteen days. I wear a Pima County Jail inmate jumpsuit and am denied the ability to use the bathroom when I need to. Do you know that the highest rate of suicides in jail occurs in the first 24 to 48 hours, which is nearly half of total jail suicides? While others would rather take their lives then face what I am facing, I have you who works to break me even further with your calculated cruelty. You wouldn't even say good bye to me the day I had to check into jail. I had to check into my sentence away from you, away from my kids, frightened and scared with the image of you on that sofa and the sound of your smart and flippant farewell ringing in my ears."

"I was trying to not be dramatic in front of the kids." His answer absurd, but his voice resolute as though completely justified.

"That's ridiculous." I exclaim. I stand rigid, my anger fuming and take two steps toward him. "…Chad, I want to know if you're planning on divorcing me?"

He looks at me surprised, his eyes wide and jaw falls from its clinch. He stares at me, then stiffens, "I am waiting to see if you can be happy again."

I detest what he just said. I feel the ache of my body and the tired-
ness of my emotions become numb and dissipate as my anger rises,
"Chad if you can't be my husband and support and love me now, I don't
want you later. Don't stand by as though a husband to me in the public
eye and then leave me when this is over. Leave me now. Decide to be
my husband after this or don't be my husband today. You are not here
spiritually or emotionally nor have you been while I am going through
this nightmare, so don't act to our friends and community as though
you are. In truth you have been waiting until after it's over to jump ship
when you feel you won't look bad for leaving. Let's be honest, you have
already bailed on this marriage emotionally, so don't pretend you love
me and have comforted me through any of this, because you haven't. At
this point there is no value in your presence, so just go!"

"Really? There is no value in my presence?" He stands, his anger
equal to mine. His eyes narrow in rage. "I am dropping the kids off every day at school while you are in jail! In jail, Andrea!!!"

I can't control myself, my wrath has been unleashed. Without taking a breath I retaliate hard, "I am and have been completely broken
hearted, as you sit there inferring as if I haven't done everything to put
my children first. When have I ever not given my life, strength, time or
sacrificed for those two little lives? I gave up this fight and pleaded out
for you and the kids, so that this whole ordeal could be behind us, putting an end to any more trials, court appearances, or stress that we have
had to undergo for over a year. Don't you dare question my commit-
ment to them. I cry every night thinking of their precious faces, wishing
mine was the last one they saw before school and first one when picked
up. I miss them... I miss these moments with them... terribly."

My fury grows as I hear my voice rise from the release of my deep
hurt and anger, "You know full well that I am a good mother, and I have
laid my life down for my children. I have done nothing to hurt them or
cause them any harm; nor would I EVER. You are using my jail sentence
to discredit me. It's working. I have no credibility... however, let's go
over the facts of my case. The truth is, Chad, you too could have received the same conviction I have. You really cannot cast stones at me.
I have never judged you or questioned you... but I cannot continue to

allow this to be held against me any longer."

My voice cracks and the weight of his insult becomes oppressive, "I have laid out my soul to apologize for the cost that one night has had on my family."

I stop. Chad is staring at me. He has taken a few steps back, but I am not finished… "I choose to take advantage of the work release, so that I can see my children. Every night I check in, I dread the strip search that awaits. I fear how far these guards will take my demoralization, but will gladly undergo any strip search or cavity search, twice a day if it means I can see my kids, if just for a few moments."

I feel my strength leave me as I speak, my voice becomes weaker, and the fatigue of my body comes back and consumes me… but I can't stop… I have too much to say. "I have walked up to those prison doors every night emotionally and spiritually without the love and support of my husband." My voice begins to crack, which kills me to know he can hear my need for him. "When you were not there for me, my friends were. They sent me scriptures, texted me encouragement, reassured me that that place would not define me. Yet, I received nothing from you. Your lack of love and concern for me has been deafening. "

"Now you say I am an unhappy person and throughout our marriage you have had to endure my emotional currents; this coming from a guy who said to me when Anna's adoption was final, that you didn't realize this was so hard on me and you thought I was ok whether she stayed or left! That's the 'emotional' wife you have had to deal with. I have kept my feelings and heartache away from you for seventeen years, so you could live your happy comfortable life and not feel like you have to comfort me. I have walked through each of my life's tragedies and stresses alone, to safeguard you from having to feel my pain. This is the first time I have ever brought you in by telling you how I felt. Jail was my future, jail is my current reality, yet have I balled up and cried, or been too depressed to get out of bed? I haven't missed a beat to our family's daily needs, yours or the kids. I smile every morning and kiss and hug my kids every night. How dare you say I am emotional and bring you down. Chad, I am proud of how strong I have been. You have never encouraged me for being the resilient person I am or praised me for my ability to face such adversity with strength. Instead you rebuke me and worry about yourself citing how hard it has been for you to have had to feel my fear. I am a strong person, I am a happy person. So, your hurtful words, in my most tragic of times won't injure me, because they are not true and you know it… I know it."

My voice now low, it's lost its air, but I am determined to unleash my truth. He can stand there and listen, while I deflate, but he will hear me. "Let's make a list of the worst offenses of entire my life. I really have nothing noteworthy before God. I ask you to look at yourself and think of your life's worst offenses before God, and tell God how much holier you are than me. I think not."

"You know Chad, I have evolved and progressed greatly in the last few years. I am, for the first time, comfortable and confident in my own skin. I have overcome skin cancer, infertility and even jail. I have scars, but all of those scars are part of my beauty. I now see myself, a thirty-seven year old woman, as a beautiful creature. I have bloomed and continue to bloom in the darkest of places… I have found God in my own dungeon. He reached out and touched me in my despair."

Chad's face has dropped. He shows no anger, but pain. A side of me wants to reach out to him, but I won't. I sit on the end of the bed. My anger still real, but my body tired and the ache of the cold night begins to throb. "I am done apologizing. I have paid the price for anything I have done wrong and then some. I have suffered consequences greater than anything I have ever deserved in my entire life; and through it, in spite of it, I stand tall. You watch, after all this is done, my kids will be un-scathed. I have protected them, ensured that they have felt no pressure or pain, no panic or depression. I hug them every day I can. I dream of them every night I am away and not a moment has or will come where they feel I am not here for them."

I begin to cry, "I will not let you sentence me more. I have been punished enough. I am proud of who I am and I am not ashamed of my past or my present. It has helped mold me into the woman I am today."

Chad sits down back in the chair. He looks like he has lost a fight in a boxing match. I stop and then softly, with my last and final burst of energy continue, "Chad, I love you. I will always love you, but I don't want you here physically, yet not emotionally. You make up your mind this day, if you are going to stay, be a husband; if you can't, then leave and we can work out a solution that is best for our kids."

Although Chad has said very little, his face shows his retreat, his shoulders now slumped. He is a fighter, he doesn't give up easy or ever, but today my words were harsh, but true and cut him deeply. I can see he is hurt. "I get so angry." His voice tormented as he wrestles out each word, "I called you that night, Andrea, and asked you to come home. I had a bad feeling, but you didn't come."

"Chad, I was helping my sister. It was part of my job." I respond.

His face stays down, not looking at me as his voice strains and the pain of our circumstances well, "I know… I don't blame you. I really don't. I just feel so powerless, so frustrated. I worry about you and sometimes I feel like there is nothing I can do to protect you."

My heart pulls toward him as I hear the grief and regret in his voice, "I am a grown woman, I don't need you to look after me, I need you to be my husband."

He lifts his head, his eyes narrow and his voice becomes strong again, "You are wrong, I do need to look after you, I do. I am your husband. I need to protect you… That is who I am, who we are. I get so angry and frustrated…" Chad begins to weep. His words are forced and his breath labored. I have never seen Chad tear. He is sobbing. I am taken back and consciously tailor my words. Realizing this is the first time I have seen him tear. For me, now, he sobs. He sobs because he loves me.

His lips are tight and pressed as he speaks and strains for each word, "Andrea, I get so angry. I feel like I can't do anything to fix this. I want to fix it all. I can't go with you, I can't help. If I touch you, I feel like I have betrayed you. My heart is so bottled and I want to lash out. I love you. I really love you. I am so sorry I can't make this whole thing right." His head drops again and I see his shoulders jerk with his sobs. My heart breaks. I have been so angry at him, yet he has been hurting just as I have.

I misread him, and felt he was cold and penalizing me, but in truth he too was tormented. Tormented that he could not help me, could not protect me, could not show his love to me as he wanted to, as my husband, as my champion. He too was broken and powerless. His actions were confusing and hurtful, but a result of his frustration and anger. He never really left my side, he was right there fighting with me. He didn't tell me to stop the fight, to plead out, but supported me when I did. When the prosecution offered work release which included my home office, I agreed. This ensured that my children would see me, so I chose to plead out and not risk jail where work release would no longer be offered. Chad knew my reasons for accepting the plea; although my case was strong and the lawyers wanted to go to trial. Through it, through all of it, Chad supported me, defended me... and I gave up. I gave up to protect my kids from the possibility of my absence, a choice I knew would permanently damage my record and hurt Chad's and my reputation, as well as temporarily cause great hardship on us both. Chad let me decide, he let me make the call and backed me one hundred percent. I understand Chad's actions now; I am sad I didn't. I pulled away too, I was enigmatic. I thought I was being open, but I was questioning him at every beat. Suspicious this would be our end... and it almost was.

"I am not that broken bird you once loved and protected, but a woman with wings that spread. Nor am I that naive little girl, but someone who has lived through a lot and been places you haven't, or will ever." I say this and stand up, feeling my internal strength once again.

"I am sorry. I am sorry I hurt you and made you feel alone." Chad groans from a heart that sounds as though collapsed. "I want this all to be over. I want us back. I want you to be happy. I want us to just grow old together. Can we just get through this and grow old together. I want to just be happy again, with us, and you with me. Will you do that?" He looks at me. His blue eyes red and revealing his vulnerability.

I walk over and reach for him. Softly I touch his face, while tears are streaming down mine. "I love you. I will always be in love with you. Always."

"I love you too, Andrea. I love you so much." He says and looks down, then reaches and touches my hand. We stay still holding this moment, feeling our hearts bleed and repair. He takes my hand in his and pulls it off of his face, bringing it to his lips and kisses my palm

I lean down to kiss him and he grabs me, pressing my body against his. Our faces are both wet and salty from our tears. Our kiss becomes passionate as we embrace each other in our emotion.

I sit down on one of his legs and wrap my arms around him. He begins to lift my t-shirt. I grab his hand to stop him. I feel disgusting from jail and my body still aches from the harsh night. He looks at me with surprise… I smile at him and lead him to the bathroom and turn on the shower. He slowly undresses me and then presses me against his body. I undress him out of his work clothes and lead him into the steaming shower. As the water beats down on us, he kisses my shoulder and back. I turn around and hold him tightly. My heart and body feel as though rising in emotional release and my broken heart now soothed.

NOVEMBER 2006

Life as a new mom was complete and total joy. Chad and I were so enraptured in our son and loved being a family. Many times I would be heading out with Gabriel tucked into his seat, his baby bag full of all his little necessities; yet overwhelmed with the urge to stop, turn around, because something was missing, something familiar. What had I forgotten? I mentally went through my checklist of items needed, but couldn't think of what it could be. Then it dawned on me, that eight year ache was no longer there, the weight of its presence gone. I tried to pretend or ignore its existence; but it never left me. It was a daily sting, a constant agony that grew each month, each year. It was a familiar but a painful companion. Yet now, I was free from its grip. In fact, it had vanished. What was missing was my heartache, now replaced with joy, my mourning turned to dancing. I looked back in my rear view mirror to see his precious face, my son. He was here.

Gabriel was a sweet baby. The first night, he laid next to me in his bassinette. I kept one hand on his tummy to feel him, not letting him go, making sure that this precious life that wiggled and slept would still be there when I woke up. We slept like that until he was too big to fit in his bassinette. I learned to eat with one hand touching him, or one arm holding him. I loved his naps when he would lie on my chest. As he grew, he became adventurous, fun; yet he never stopped being that sweet, soft spirit that captured Chad's and my heart. His crystal blue eyes reveal love and compassion, sincerity and his unassuming nature. Chad and I celebrated him, enjoyed him, adored him. Gabriel and I had a very special bond. I could look at him and see into his thoughts. I learned, through him, that I was a good mother. I was called to be a mother and I was gifted at it. Ultimately, the greatest priority was knowing that my child's life took precedence over my own. I am my child's greatest advocate and it is the job of all parents to be their child's launching pad to become all that they can be in life, to ensure that they learn how to love, how to laugh, how to play, how to care, how to be confident, how to be curious, to stretch oneself, push beyond comfort, to find and pursue what they love, to know and believe in God.

Chad also found that he was an excellent father. Time with his son was his favorite part of the day. He gave up weekend hobbies such as golf or tennis, so that he could be home with his son, with his family, when not at work. He canceled all week night meetings, so that the last hours Gabriel would be awake were not missed.

Chad and I hit ten years married not long after we brought baby Gabriel home. We had so much time just the two of us, we felt no need to be away from our boy. We just wanted to enjoy us as a family. This may have been considered a mistake by some, but I wouldn't change one of those days with our little man. Life was precious, life was in order, our home was quiet and sweet... then came Anna.

Chapter 23

"He gives the barren woman a home,
making her the joyous mother of children.
Praise the Lord!" Psalm 113:9

JUNE 2009

The smell of spaghetti dinner permeated the entire house. Gabriel, Chad and I were sitting down together at the kitchen table, as I discussed with Chad the details of Gabriel's upcoming birthday party.

"I want a Star Wars birthday party!!!" Gabriel interrupted. Chad and I looked at each other and giggled. This was not the first time he requested this theme, nor would it be the last. In fact, he had mentioned his desire to have a Star Wars party repeatedly, throughout each day, and more frequently, as his birthday neared.

"Star Wars it shall be!" I explained. "The country club's new pool and slide will be opening one week before your birthday. I am sending invites to all your friends to come to a pool side Star Wars birthday party celebrating you. At each table I have ordered lightsabers to be at every seat. I talked to the club bakery and they are making a Storm Trooper cake, per your request!" then in a whisper I leaned into Gabriel's ear, while Chad looked on, smiling suspiciously, "Plus, I heard through my Star Wars friends that Darth Vador will be coming too!!!" Actually, Chad ordered the entire outfit, planning to secretely change into it in the Men's locker room… a fatherly effort to make sure his son's dreams come true, in spite of the heat of the June sun. "But don't be frightened, Daddy's friend is a certified Jedi Knight and has been given the authority to train other Jedi's. So he will make sure you and your friends are trained as Jedi's and ready to use your new lightsabers to battle Darth Vador when he comes." Gabriel looked at me with delight and a bit of apprehension from the thought of meeting Darth Vador in person.

"Sounds like a fun day, Gabriel. I can't believe you are turning four! Four is a super big deal." Chad looked over, while Gabriel hugged himself in delight, his little face beamed with enthusiasm. Gabriel had a round face, and little nose, his skin was fare, with rosy cheeks that appeared as if someone had applied with makeup. His hair was short in the back and cut just below the top of his ears, leaving his bangs and top long, just above his eyes, which peered out from his soft blond hair and paralyze its viewer. He had natural blonde highlights that streaked through his light brown undertones. He was beautiful. His eyes captivated Chad and me and every expression and thought could be seen deep into those crystal blue oceans. My heart lifted as I watched Gabriel's eyes dance with excitement. He had been counting "the sleeps" until his birthday. Chad was a secret Star Wars fanatic and delighted in the fact that Gabriel was an enthusiast too. Chad's mother had saved all his Star Wars toys since he was a boy, which have now been given to Gabriel. Chad and Gabriel played for hours on the floor with the little figurines and space aircraft, excuse me: Jedi Star Fighter, X Wing Fighter and of course the Millennium Falcon (a mother to an almost-four-year-old boy needs to know these things...).

That evening, when Chad and I were alone in our room, Chad looked at me, his face much more serious and his eyes pensive, "We are celebrating Gabriel's fourth birthday, Andrea.... If we are going to adopt anymore children, we need to make a decision now. I don't think we should keep putting this conversation off much longer."

I caught my breath, which had escaped me, and lowered my head.

I moved my hand to touch his while I tried to formulate my thoughts. Raising my head, I responded as best I could, "I do want more children. Having siblings is such a blessing. Esther and Michael were my childhood's greatest gift. No one knows me, like those two. I want that for Gabriel. I am just scared to have to walk through the emotional rollercoaster it takes to get chosen again. I am also conflicted, because we are so incredibly happy just as we are. Truthfully, I am scared to interrupt what we have today. We are already so blessed."

Chad began to softly stroke my arm, "I completely agree with everything you feel and wrestle these thoughts too. However, I don't want to postpone this decision any further. We need to go ahead and pursue another child or be done and be happy as a family of three. I, too, am happy as we are, but I feel we need to come to some resolve on this matter," he said frankly.

My throat closed up and my voice strained as I spoke, "I am not sure I want to face the emotions it takes to start the process again, but I am not willing to close the door to another baby."

He let go of my arm, with his voice lowered, "I know, Andrea. I have been thinking about this and I feel we need to consider adopting a child that is in the foster care system. There are so many couples waiting for a baby in private adoption, that waiting list is endless with years of hopeful people, yet few babies to fill its lengths, all while there are thousands of children in the foster care system and such few families willing to adopt. If we are going to do this, we need to look into a child that needs us."

His words hit me like a brick. I cleared my throat and shook my head to clear its rattle. "You are right, but I don't know if I can foster a child. What if they bring me a child, then pull that child from my arms, and from Gabriel's life and heart. I could never say goodbye. Once that child is in my care and my home I will not love and raise them 'as if' they were mine, but because that child IS mine. I know that I am not capable of walking away or emotionally detaching once they are brought to us. They will forever be part of us. I applaud the people who can keep perspective and an emotional distance, but I am not one. I love and give myself fully. I know myself enough to honestly say, I won't be able stay dispassionate or even recover if it ends badly."

"Will you do this for me?" Chad touched my arm again and with the other hand turned my chin so that I faced him, "Will you go with me to the agency to see what our options are? We can go through the foster-to-adopt classes and decide if this is right in our spirits. Then we will know if this is what God has for us. I am not asking you to make any decisions today, just be willing to look into it and allow our hearts to be open to this type of adoption if this is what God wants from us."

I exhaled hard with trepidation, "Ok. I will see what they say and open my heart to the idea… I'll call tomorrow to schedule a meeting with the foster agency and start the process."

Excitement and fear made war in my thoughts and kept me from rest for weeks leading up to our first foster/adoption licensing class.

When we entered the agency's lecture hall, I realized Chad and I stood out from the other foster-to-adopt families. Most were family members pursuing licenses for children of relatives that were living in their homes. The license would give them much needed financial and medical assistance. The remaining individuals, not all couples, were taking classes to offer their home temporarily to children, while getting a small payment in addition to their current employment. I applauded those who were committing their hearts and homes to children who were in need of a safe and warm place to lay their heads. What made us different from the rest, we were there, specifically to adopt and expand our family. The first class went over case files of children that had actually been in the system, explaining the suffering they experienced from their biological home as well as the trauma the night CPS stepped in and took them from their family. The stories were tragic and my heart broke for each child.

Chad and I sat silently as we drove home from the class; our hearts were bleeding for those children, their tragic stories and the feeling of hopelessness from what we had just learned. Nationally, there were approximately 435,000 children in foster care that year. An estimated 249,000 children entered foster care that year alone and 115,000 children were waiting for adoption.

"Chad, you are right. How can I not consider one of these children? God has given us so much. We are so blessed. How could I turn my head and heart away from a child who has nothing? I am frightened that our hearts will be broken if they end up taking that child away, but I cannot turn my back from helping if not just one of these lives."

"I agree. What age are you thinking?" He asked.

"I don't want to interrupt Gabriel's birth order, so I would like to keep Gabriel as our first born. So, I guess infant to two years old? What do you think?" I questioned.

"If I could select an age, I would choose a six month old. That is the best age. The baby is responsive, smiles, laughs, sleeps through the night, isn't quite mobile yet. It's the perfect age," declared Chad.

I laughed. "Six months is a fun age."

"I am sure you want a girl." Chad stated as a matter-of-fact, but was really asking me if that was what I was going to request.

"I would love to have a girl, but I would love another little guy too. Either way will totally be great. The forms we need to fill out requires that we define the ages we are willing to take, should I put newborn to two years old then?" I asked, hoping he agreed.

"That is good, but I think you should say six months only. I don't want to be up all night feeding a newborn," he said with a bit of passion.

I chuckled, "Chad, you only took one feeding shift a night for Gabriel. Seriously, we can lose a little sleep once again for our number two…"

He sighed, then agreed, "Ok, but I still say we ask for a six month old."

Chapter 24

"...Some things hard to understand, which untaught and unstable people twist to their own destruction, as they do also the rest of the Scriptures." 2 Peter 3:16

JAIL: DAY FIFTEEN

As I drive back to jail, my heart is now mended and my spirit lifted. The weight of love denied now gone and I have renewed peace and hope.

I open the front doors of my imprisonment and am abruptly greeted by the small, ugly face of Samil.

There is an inmate in her thirties, tall, dirty blonde hair pulled back into a ponytail and wearing prescription glasses. She has a very pretty face and full lips. She is not overweight but her body is a bit disproportionate and thick on her lower half. However, her face has the look of a Vogue model, small nose, small eyes and full pouty lips. She stands up, throws her shoulders back to reveal her small chest and walks toward Samil's desk, giving him a little extra bounce as she approaches.

Leaning on the counter she beckons in a childlike voice, "Hi Samil..."

"What do you want?" He grunts with a smile. He loves this attention. For the first time I see he has discolored teeth, some grey and blue, others yellow.

"Do you have a snack back there you can give me?" she says in a sulky voice.

"Nope." He snaps, but stands up and walks toward the counter. His voice remains harsh, yet his face beams with delight as he leans down, pulls a brown paper bag and launches it in the air toward the female inmate. She catches it and skips back to her seat proud of her immense power of persuasion.

I am sitting next to an older inmate. "I guess Samil likes her…!" she says sarcastically to me.

"Is that an accomplishment to be proud of?" I retort.

She giggles as the other inmate pulls out her treasures from the brown bag: an apple, bologna sandwich on white bread and carton of milk.

I glare at Samil as he sits back down feeling puffed and desirable.

"He is a miserable, pathetic man," I say seething in a whisper.

The inmate with the snack looks at me with great pride. "He is ALWAYS nice to me…" She says with a grin.

"I can see that…" I respond. How pathetic that she thinks she is being favored, yet has only inflated the pitiful ego of a small man for a bologna sandwich. Her sexual flaunts brought him to his feet but she wasn't even worthy to be handed a brown paper bag, it was thrown at her. How sad that she feels that this is what special treatment looks like from nothing but an imp of a man.

My anger begins to rise as I stare at Samil and his ugly little face. He so delighted in the dirty blonde's attention. His pathetic life outside probably has such little affection or attention from anyone he meets. His deformed features reveal the hell he lives by all who turn away repulsed by his appearance.

How heartbreaking, I gasp. I have hidden my scars so carefully my whole life, fearing that if anyone would see they would recoil from me like the little girls who clawed their fingernails into my gnarled skin in elementary school. I have known the scorn of the juvenile, young and old, in reaction to my body. Yet, here before me is a man, now old, who lives his deformity out every day on his face. Scorned like me, but far worse. His hatred of mankind deserved and the only power or feeling of self-worth is his position at the front desk of the Pima County Jail. He enjoys tormenting those he can, just as he has been, and is being tormented outside these block walls. How can I judge him? I haven't walked in his shoes; yet know the wounds and bitterness that imperfection has had on my own soul. I take a deep breath and my anger leaves and is replaced by a deep sadness for a small boy likely teased, and now a man in all probability rejected and unwanted.

When I arrive at my bunk, my bed is made, but not how I left it. Other bunks near mine have their sheets, books, towel and clothes piled in a heap on top of the thin torn mattresses.

"They had another inspection today," the inmate above me whispers. "I made your bed for you and put away your personal items."

I am touched. "Thank you. That was so nice." What had I done to earn her love, I am not sure, but I am truly moved by her gesture.

"Hey, I know the inmate with the long brown curly hair is out tomorrow. Ask her if she will give you her blanket when she leaves," she says whispering. The lights are down, so our conversation is undercover.

"The one reading the book?" I clarify.

"Yes." She says.

I put my thumb up and mouth, "Thanks. I will ask her."

When I see the inmate she pointed out look in my direction, I wave and use unconventional sign language to communicate my request. She agrees. So, I relax on my bunk, relieved my communication was missed by the guard, and contented that I will soon have a warmer night ahead, bracing myself to face one more night with only my clothes and that ratty towel as my lone source of cover.

I hear a few around me whispering. They are trying to figure out a way to turn off or unplug the floor fan that is running in the middle of our area. With the temperature so low the fan teases us with an additional cold bite every time it passes.

"Ladies!" the tiny guard in her down winter snow jacket yells. "No more talking or I will turn down the air even more... how 'bout another ten degrees? Then we will see if you all still think it is ok to keep talking. Don't think I won't."

The room goes completely quiet.

It doesn't take long for the chill to permeate my body. I try to sleep, but the cold night becomes excruciating. My back is already aching from the metal board; however the pain now intensified as my muscles stiffen and tremble from the cold. Shivers come over me in great waves that cause my arms and legs to spasm from the pain that now infiltrates each muscle. I try to control my body and force it to relax, but it braces with tension into convulsions making my torso and limbs throb from their uncontrolled constriction. My sleep is tormented and sporadic with hallucinating dreams that cause me to jerk and startle throughout the night.

I wake up to screaming and wailing from other inmates in their beds from delusion and with it tormenting visions. Other inmates nearby attempt to wake those up from their nightmares and silence their screams. If only I had something that I could offer to cover them so they could find warmth… find peace. I have been away from the block and away from the cold all day, but these women have been here without break for days. I worry they are becoming ill. Their bodies cannot take this unyielding torture of cold. I grab my extra clothes in my bunks drawer and use to pad my cover, then put my frayed towel over the clothes to not incite the guard. I raise the towel over my head and allow the heat from my breath to warm my nose and cheeks. I am tired and feel myself begin to doze off. Rest is coming… I am grateful.

꜀꜀꜀

Darkness swallows me. It is completely black. A fat man, with a double chin and beady eyes is looking at me. His face is smeared and hidden in a fog. I try to focus but am confused. In the background are lights, strobe lights of red, flashing in the fog that consumes the night. I am afraid. Chad is looking over at me. His face is sad and disappointed. My kids are standing at a window at a distance, their hands are pressed against the glass. I look over at them. "I am sorry," I say to them, then turn back to Chad, "I am so sorry." I begin to cry. He reaches his hand out to me, but when I try to touch his, I can't reach it being pulled away, further and further away. My body is falling, falling deep and spiraling down. The fat man and his haughty face is spinning as the vortex of the world around me begins to swirl and suck me deeper and deeper away from those I love. It pulls me down to a great abyss below. I scream, scream for help… "God, save me!"

꜀꜀꜀

I sit up, pulling myself from sleep. The steel board under me crashes from the movement of weight. My children's faces are in my head. My arms are cold and empty, I feel powerless. My body starts to shake violently, confused and startled, I throw the towel off my face and breathe deeply. The cold of the block hits me hard and my disoriented mind clears as I look around and see the inmates around me. A quiet groan escapes my mouth as I throw my sheet and towel over my face again as I lay back down. Each time I close my eyes the image of the fat man's face looks back at me.

❧❧❧❧

My eyes slowly open. I am afraid to look, but I do… I look. The sky is black, eerily black. The moon glows sickly. It is round and full but the night has overpowered its brightness and consumed its strength and power. The dense fog has erased any stars that would offer any assistance and their sparkle eliminated. Fear strikes through my body and anxiety causes it to quake. I turn to learn where I am and see my house, windows glow lightly, but the house is imposing and unfriendly. My children stand at its window, hands pressed against the glass and their faces stare blankly. Bars suddenly appear and erect over each window. Chains sound loudly as they link across my front door and a large lock appears at their center which offers no whole for a key. I try to run toward it, to pound my fists and claw my way back in, but I am being held by something. I have no shoes and the rocks are sharp. A sharp piercing pain cuts through my feet as I try to run, but it's not my feet or the rocks that hold me back. I look around to see what is holding me and feel my arms yank back further away from my home. I fight its pull and look toward its source. The sound of metal scrapping causes my skin to constrict as I look to my wrists which are painfully being pulled and twisted, striking a piercing sting through my arms and shoulders. I stare paralyzed and powerless as handcuffs clank and pull my hands together locking me in, dragging me away.

❧❧❧❧

My body jerks, gasping for air. I hear deep moaning and look around, then suddenly recognize it was the sound of my own voice wailing. Like the inmates next to me from their nightmares… yet mine are no nightmares but actual tormenting and distorted memories of the horrible day that brought me here to walk these halls.

I grab clothes I have under my towel and wrap them around my hands and feet; which seem to be the areas of my body that all blood has left. I feel faint and dizzy and my eyes see spots, so I shake my head hard to make the blood flow back to my brain. This makes me woozy and I lay down, closing my eyes tightly. Once again, I grab my towel and pull it over my face, curl my body in the fetal position hoping it will help warm if my limbs touch my torso. My throat is dry and its lack of water is making my stomach feel queasy. I breathe deep and allow my exhale to warm me.

꜀꜀꜀꜀

My hands are covering my wet face. I hold them in place as though if by keeping them and hiding my eyes, what looms above me will disappear. I can taste the salt of my tears as their heat dampens my hands and cheeks. "Why are you so sad?" a voice heckles me. "Are you crying?" "I see your tears, you fool." Laughter fills the air. I drop my hands in total despair and look at the faces that laugh. Three ugly men, stand over me. They laugh loud and take turns pushing me. Each makes a comment as they push me backward. In the center is the fat man with beady eyes and a double chin. The other two are younger, one short, with dark hair and dark skin. His mouth is wide open from his laughter. The third covers his mouth as his shoulders jerk sporadically from the humor that has overtaken his spirit. He is fair, white hair with an awkward stance. I lean back from the smell of their foul breath, but the mist of their laughter swirls around my head. The fat one pushes me one last time, which causes my body to fall. My stomach swirls as gravity pulls me down. I turn my head away from the men's twisted faces and toward what is beneath me. My hands brace my fall, and stick to slime that covers a vinyl seat as my body lands hard. I turn and look and see that I fallen back into the back seat of a car. The vinyl is black and there is a pool of dried vomit where I touch. I look up and see claw marks on the car's ceiling. I feel trapped and defeated by the three men who lean in further as I try to scoot back deeper into the car and further away. Each time I move the image of the car and where I am, comes further into view. The car's front seat is separated from me by a cage, so I can't crawl over the seat to escape. I reach for the door behind me and try to open it to escape but it is locked. I panic and feel around for a door handle to release its hold. It offers no escape. The men lean in closer and I look back at them while I coil in the corner between the seat and door. The men stand together, arms linked and I suddenly see their entire form. They wear brown, with large badges in gold that spark and glare. Each badge becomes larger and brighter and grows as I flinch from their glory. My recoil is blocked by the door of the car and the seat that allows no place to hide. Their badges continue to expand and violate what little space I have that remains. Their metal comes up against the skin of my face and I turn offering my cheek as they press against me, while continuing to grow. My breath heats and fogs their splendor, and my face begins to bend and fold from their strength. I try to hold my form, but their might overpowers me. I exhale one last time, surrendering my will and relinquishing my body as the insignia slowly consumes me, I let it swallow me, giving up the fight and my life.

Chapter 25

"Do not rejoice over me, my enemy;
When I fall, I will arise; When I sit in darkness,
The LORD *will be a light to me."* Micah 7:8

JAIL: DAY SIXTEEN, SIX A.M.

I feel shock from a thump to my stomach. I open my eyes in a daze; looking over me is the curly-haired inmate who has placed her blanket on top of me. She smiles and walks away. Her arms full of her sheets. She was supposed to turn in the blanket with her sheets and dump them into the laundry bin. I quickly smooth out the blanket over my sheet to hide any evidence of the handover. The wool blanket is thin and scratchy, but its warmth an immediate relief. I stay under the blanket as long as I can, as I wait for check-out for work release.

Once released, I sit in my car as my teeth chatter uncontrolled, my hair and mouth unbrushed. I decided it was just too cold to leave the blanket for personal hygiene.

I place my keys in the ignition but realize I am in no state to drive. I decide to wait to let my body thaw and allow my trembling to subside before I start my car. The heat of the car is comforting. My teeth chatter and I shiver one strong convulsing wave as I allow my body to relax in my car's warm embrace.

The sun hits my face through my window causing my body to ease. I want to clear my mind of the painful memories that consumed my night. My hypothermic state brands evil faces into my thoughts, and the precious lives I love and care so deeply for, who were hurt as a result. I shut my eyes and let the sun's potency stroke my face, while I rest my head against the headrest. As the cold leaves my body, fatigue devours its place and distorts my senses.

Soon I am able to start the car and take my long trek home, relief is mine as I pull into my garage, excited to take a hot shower and wash the night off. Chad's car is parked and waiting once again. I open the door from the garage to our kitchen to find him standing with a fresh coffee in hand. My heart melts and my defenses become liquid. He wraps his arms around me and I sink into his strength. My teeth and hair still musty from the dreadful night, my body tired and sore, yet his arms are the only place I want to be.

August, 2009

When the phone rang, I instinctively had a strange feeling. I didn't recognize the number. Now that I was no longer pursuing real estate clients, but instead focusing on being a stay-at-home mom to my son, I let most unknown callers go to voice mail. This time I had a peculiar urge to answer.

"This is Andrea," I answered inquisitively.

"Hi Andrea! This is Brooke. I don't know if you remember me, but we took adoption licensing classes together four years ago. …We were adopting a little girl. Do you remember me?" The woman's voice was cheery and familiar.

"Yes of course! How is your daughter?" I said surprised to hear from her.

"She is good. We are all good… I know this call is coming out of the blue, but my friends have just contacted us to see if we knew of a good family that would be open to adopting a little girl. I thought of you and Chad!" she said hesitantly.

My heart stopped. I was speechless. Unable to clear my throat, I gulped the air that had clogged my airway.

The silence made her nervous, so she continued, "…I wanted to call you to see if you were even open or considering more children…"

I pressed through my shock and answered, "Uh… I am so sorry….

I am just so taken back by your call. We just started classes to foster to adopt yesterday, so yes we are open. How old is the little girl?"

"She is six months," she said.

My head started to spin and my stomach turned upside down in disbelief. Chad had just stated that he wanted a child that was six months old the night before. It was all too coincidental.

I started to laugh, "Wow..." Forcing my head and emotions to come back to reality, I tried to ask her more questions... important questions... yet my mind was completely blank, "Um... What is the situation?"

She took a breath and then responded, "Well, the extended family has the baby right now, but CPS has placed her with them. They are looking for adoptive parents, because the couple she is now with are older and they do not feel they can be long term caregivers. They called me to see if I knew anyone that would be a good fit. They really care about her and want what is best."

I am completely covered in cold chills. "I am in shock and touched that you remembered and thought of us! You have no idea how significant your timing is. Why did CPS get involved and where are the biological parents in all of this?" I asked.

"I don't know the details. If it is ok, I will call them and give them your number. They want to meet you and have you meet the baby," she said, cheery again.

"Yes, please give them my number..." I answered, trembling and head spinning.

I sat and stared at the phone after I hung up. My mind was twirling and my heart was beating fast. The timing was so strange and the coincidence even stranger.

It was not long before my phone rang again. It was the family. Our conversation was short, but I felt their urgency to meet.

When they hung up the phone, I clicked over and immediately called Chad. "Hey Babe, what's up?" Chad asked curiously. I didn't call him at work often. This couldn't wait.

"I just got a call from a family with a baby... They want me to come meet them tomorrow. She is in the system, but the extended family can't care for the child long term."

"Oh my!!! I didn't expect this all to happen so fast. How old is the baby?" he asked.

"Six months!!!" I shrieked.

"You're kidding me?!" his voice as shocked as mine when he heard her age.

"No…" I said excited.

He paused then asked, "A boy or girl?"

"A girl." I exclaimed, knowing how bizarre it sounded.

"That's crazy…" he said as though pondering and his mind distant.

"I know. It is so strange." I said excitedly, unable to contain my enthusiasm. "The baby's family has asked me to come by tomorrow to meet them and the baby!"

"My flight home is not until Friday. I can't go with you." Chad reminded me, sounding bamboozled.

I heard his concern and tried to alleviate it, "I know. I told them that you would be away on business. They said they understood that I would be coming alone."

"Can't they wait a day to meet us both?" Chad retorted confused by the hurry.

"I think they need to get things underway now. They want her to get settled as soon as possible so she doesn't have to keep transitioning to different homes and caregivers," I said.

"Are you going to go?" he asked curiously.

"Yes." I answer resolutely.

"Ok… Wow!" He said, after taking a deep breath and the gravity of all that just happened. "This is so crazy. Don't get attached too quickly," he warned, "we need to keep our heads on. I know you… I'll lose you the moment you see her."

"Chad, I'm already gone…"

JAIL: DAY SIXTEEN, NINE P.M.

This time, on the way to the Pima County Jail, I am wearing long sweat pants and a long sleeve shirt, but know I have a wool blanket to sleep under, which calms my tension and brings me hope for a night of actual sleep. As I wait in the waiting room, I am grateful for that dirty, grey, wool blanket that smells of old towels and human sweat, and the comfort it will give me this night. My body is tired and my head not completely clear, but my heart has some calm and my spirit less fearful. Maybe this unexpected peace comes from now knowing what is to come and feeling it won't get any worse than what I have already experienced; or maybe I see the disgrace that surrounds me, yet feel as though it doesn't define me today, but instead I distinguish myself by those who love me and wait for me at home. I still have a long road of this darkness to travel before I discover the light of its end, but I have hope tonight; I have love.

As I ponder and question my spirit's ease, a young man is being escorted out of the jail. He is an African-American man, who walks with great swagger. He has perfected his walk so much so, that one might think he is limping to one side from a damaged or broken leg. The male guard gives him a clear trash bag of clothes and personal items, then told to change in the lobby's bathroom and return his red jumpsuit and rubber flip flops to the bin near the lockers. The look on his face shows me he is being discharged. He is free, and moments away from walking away from this place, with every intent to never return.

I envy that look, but do not wish to take this moment from him. I am happy for him. While he is changing, a young woman walks in and to the front desk. She is young and pretty with dark chocolate skin and jet black hair. She softly talks to Samil, who loudly retorts that the inmate she is picking up is in the bathroom and still waiting for his discharge paperwork. She is told to sit in the waiting area where I am seated. The young man comes out in jeans, a t-shirt and tennis shoes without strings, feeling human again and proud as he walks to the front desk. In his hand he holds the clear plastic bag, while shuffling through it a bit perplexed. He pulls out a wallet and rifles through that too, then places it in his back pocket. He seems upset and waits at the front desk, but Samil intentionally ignores him requiring the man's process to be delayed out of spite. A female guard casually enters the area with what appears to be the young man's paperwork. She is dark skinned and stalky wearing her brown uniform, badge and all the menacing hardware that comes with it. Her black hair is spiked and chopped tight up against her head. She walks up to the young man from the other side of the desk.

"Ma'am, do you know where my cell phone is?" he asks softly and with apprehension.

"Here is the list of items you signed noting what was submitted when you were taken into custody," she responds with great aversion, not looking directly at him, but deliberately looking side to side at inanimate objects that she felt were much more interesting than the person who she now addressed.

"Please sign this form to say you have received all items listed." She points and taps her fingernail on the paper.

"Thank you Ma'am, but listed here is my cell phone and it's not in the bag." He points to a section on the form in front of him.

The guard looks at the form and then turns it back to him, becoming strangely frustrated at a rapid pace.

"Sign here and then initial the items you did receive. Then write next to the listed cell phone that it was not returned at discharge. You can file a complaint, using a copy of this form," she says irritated.

"Thank you Ma'am, but I really just want my cell phone back; it belongs to my place of employment… I need it for work, it has my contacts in it and work schedule…" he explains with a bit of panic.

With her teeth clinched, her lips curled under and voice now elevated and boiling, "I… don't… have… your… cell… phone…" She pauses, steps back from the desk, and exhales as if trying to cool her immense anger. Stepping forward she looks again at the young man to continue her instructions, speaking slowly and deliberate. "I do not have your phone, nor do I know where it went. Please do as I have instructed you: initial each item that you have received and write next to the listed 'cell phone' that it was missing at discharge." Each word is spoken slowly and heavily, as if her way of controlling her anger and attempting to force her emotions to simmer from its uncontrollable rage.

The young man stands in front of her, confused, upset, helpless, "So, all I can do is file a complaint?" he questions. "I... I'm afraid to ask..." He hesitates, but then continues, "Umm... where do I find the form to file a complaint?" His words are short and once finished he quickly steps back as though fearing she is going to throw something at him or dodging a blow of her fist to his face.

The guard takes another deep breath before she opens a drawer, then unable to control her escalating fury, she slams a form down on the desk in front of the young man. He jumps and raises his hands as though protecting his face. The young girl and I jump too, startled by the loud pound she creates.

With that, any further discussion is over, the discharged inmate grabs a pen and begins to fill out the form as instructed. The guard had what she needed and walks away, as the young man continues filling out the complaint form she loudly placed in front of him. He stops and realizes she left. He looks around confused, apprehensive that now there is no one to receive his form or his request to find his lost item. Setting down the pen, he leaves his form on the desk complete, and hopelessly turns around to look at the young girl sitting next to me.

"I guess that is it..." He says to her, "I can go!"

The girl near me stands up and throws her arms around the young man. He smiles, but is clearly deflated.

"Let's go." She says to him, taking his hand and leading him out the front doors.

"I really need my cell phone." He says bitterly.

"I know. We'll figure it out." She says in a soft voice.

With that, they leave.

Today, the group that waits to check in is large. I see a guard entering through the jail doors and realize its Officer Julius again. I am relieved to see her. We all stand up and walk through the metal detector and then to the bathroom. Julius is one of the few that doesn't seem to enjoy this portion of her job.

Once in the bathroom, behind a closed door, I muster up the

courage to say something. "Officer Julius," I say, "I want to thank you for keeping this as professional as possible. I notice the inmates respect you and listen to you. You have earned their respect, and not by being cruel. I work in Human Resources and would consider you one of their most valuable employees. They should have you conduct trainings for the other officers. They could learn a lot from you."

The other inmates hold their breath and look down. Officer Julius is a woman of few words and her facial expressions enigmatic. No one was sure how she would react to my compliment, as conversations between guards and detainees not customary.

"It's really difficult working here." She says looking directly at me. The other inmates let out their breath, as Julius continues: "There is such a 'rah, rah, let's get 'em' attitude; it's part of the training, part of the culture. I don't and won't buy in, which keeps me on the outs of the fraternity. I tell them that they really can't act the way they do... the things they do in here are just wrong. But, hopefully, my days here are short. I am currently pursuing other jobs so I can be done with this place. With the way they act, something is going to blow and I don't want to be part of any of it." She says frankly.

"I do wish that there were more guards like you here, but understand your desire to leave. What other jobs are you looking into?" I ask.

"I have been looking into hospital security jobs. I know a few people in the hospitals that are encouraging me to apply." She explains.

I feel sadness for the inmates who will have to survive without one guard who handles herself appropriately, but Julius should not have to carry this cross. "I think that would be a great environment," I say in support.

"Maybe..." she says with a shrug.

She leads the group back to our block. As I sign my time sheet, the chill that engulfs the block hits me like a wall. I look at Officer Julius and ask, "They have it so cold and there are no blankets. Do you know if there are any blankets somewhere for those that don't have any?"

"I'll go check." She says to me. I see her walk into the 'fish bowl' and look through the same cart I had searched through on my first day. She walks out empty handed and then leaves the block. I had assumed that was the end to her search, but learned later that she not only went to the men's block to search for any available blankets, not finding any, she then went to the main jail, where she was assaulted by another inmate. Her injury so severe she was taken to the hospital for treatment.

Chapter 26

"And we know that all things work together for good to those who love God, to those who are the called according to His purpose."
Romans 8:28

TRANQUILITY, AUGUST 2009

The family's home was a beautiful house set deep in the Tucson hills, with views of the Catalina Mountains and large windows that looked down into the valley revealing the entire city of Tucson. At night the city lights must be breathtaking, I thought to myself as I entered. Everything from carpet to furniture was a bright and unblemished white; clearly the years of child rearing have long since passed and now the home reflected a quiet, cleaner life. I was greeted by an older woman in her early seventies. She was attractive and fit, wearing vibrant colors in linen. Her hair was short and very white. She led me to the kitchen where her husband sat at the breakfast table. He was stout with a full head of grey hair, wearing a bright orange polo shirt that seemed to blend into his round, red face. He looked at me and smiled, a smile that extended from one side of his face to the other. He had a sweet grandfatherly appearance, someone you would want to cuddle up to and hear that everything was going to be ok. The older lady reached out her hand to direct me to sit down at the breakfast table. She turned me to the baby sitting in a high chair with a big piece of American cheese squished in her hand and full uncut grapes on her tray. Her face was covered with food. Pieces of cheese stuck on her nose and cheeks. She was round… too round. Big hazel brown eyes were set deep into her chubby face. Her hair was dark chocolate and looked chopped short in spots and bald in others around her head. I smiled at her and touched her filthy cheek. She looked back at me without expression and shoved cheese in her open mouth.

The older lady sat in front of her with a spoon and baby food. She began shoving it into the baby's gaping mouth at an extremely rapid pace. The baby grunted and growled in ecstasy with each frenzied bite.

"This is Tranquility." She said matter-of-factly.

"Hi Tranquility!" I said softly and moved my hand away from her gooey cheek. I looked intently to see if she recognized her name yet. Her focus was completely on the food that was being spooned at her feverishly.

"It's an awful name. Please change it," the older man complained.

"George, stop!" His wife scolded.

"I am serious. Who names their kid Tranquility? ...And not to mention, this child is in no way tranquil either." The older man's face seemed to be even redder, looking obstinate and sporting an ornery smirk.

"George, stop it now!!" the older lady barked.

"...Are you Tranquility's grandparents?" I changed the subject, but secretly loved the old man's outspokenness.

"No... no!! We are the baby's great-aunt and great-uncle." She explained.

"Oh..." I said as I looked back at the baby. She was now pushing in several green grapes. I leaned in to grab the grapes and decided to not intervene. I was afraid to watch the baby eat, fearing the size of the round grape might lodge in her throat and cause her to choke.

"Her grandmother, my sister, passed away when the baby's mother was very young." The older lady said pragmatic.

"Did you raise your niece after your sister passed?" Wondering what type of personal role she had in the infant's life.

"No Eve was raised by her father. He is not a good man... Eve had a hard life." The older lady continued.

"...which for some reason my wife feels responsible for Eve's 'hard life' and continues to pay the price for it every day." George stated with irritation. His hands were crossed over his chest and resting on his round belly.

"Enough, George..." she demanded, then resumed. "He was cruel to Eve, but he had custody. There was nothing I could do for her."

"Well, now she uses that to manipulate her aunt." The old man grunted.

"What do you mean?" I asked.

"Martha pays for everything for her forty-year old niece, including her clothes, her fines, her evictions, her drugs..." He grumbled, his hands waved as he spoke.

"I don't pay for her drugs!!" The older lady retaliated in a corrective maternal tone.

"Yes, you do!" he said with one of his bushy eye brows up high above the other. "...Well, not directly, but ultimately you do." He snapped, crossing his arms across his chest again.

I reached and touched the baby's head and stroked her course and patchy hair.

"I know... her hair looks awful..." Martha blurted. "Those CPS people went crazy cutting her hair for what they called drug testing. I don't know why they had to cut all over her entire head. It just looks terrible. You should have seen her before; she had cute little brown curls all over, now she looks bald and shaved, like she has some horrible disease."

The impact of that statement set in. Child Protective Services suspected that Tranquility had been exposed to drugs and have taken samples of her hair as close to the scalp as possible, so they could determine the length of time she had been subjected. The fact that her hair was patchy was not the sickening part of all of this, but the realization that this baby had seen things I do not know, felt things I could not understand, and known what life was like not to be safe in the arms of those who are supposed to protect her.

I cleared my throat and pushed back my emotions, "So, her mother lost custody of Tranquility because of her drug use? Where is her mother now?"

"Oh she is here in Tucson. She only struggles with marijuana." Martha snapped correctively.

"Martha, don't be so naïve..." George barked. The older lady gave George a decisive glare and then returned her attention back to the baby who was still being fed baby food.

"What about the others, grandparents, the father, siblings? Are any of them able to step in?" I asked.

"Well, Tranquility's grandfather is already raising Eve's other daughter. She is seven now. He has had her since she was tiny. He said he can't take another. Of course, my sister is not with us and Eve has no siblings." Martha replied.

"The father...?" I asked.

"He is in prison," she said without looking at me.

George sees another opportunity and sounded in, "...But we aren't sure he is actually the father to be quite honest; nor is the father sure either."

Awkward silence consumed the room. The baby continued to eat and maintained the peculiar growling sound while doing so. I stared at the infant and worried for her. Her little face seemed so expressionless; a look of having lived too many years in only six months of life. I wanted to pick her up and hold her, weep over her, caress her face and that shaved and cut head.

Martha broke our silence, "I love the baby, but I have my own grandchildren. I can't take on another child at my age." Her voice cracked and she stopped shoveling food into the baby's mouth. Tranquility made a loud bark sound in protest. The older woman took her cue and continued the unusual feeding process.

"I want a good family for her. My daughters are grown and have children of their own. I am just not able to start over with any children now." She began to tear, but quickly distracted herself by opening up another can of baby food.

I looked over at the six month old baby. She was huge. Her face was wide, her legs thick. She had no elbow, ankle or knee, because they were camouflaged by the multitude of rolls that folded up and down her legs and arms. She looked nothing like Gabriel. Thick dark eyebrows met in the middle of her forehead, creating a unibrow that held a permanent frown over her brown and hazel deep set eyes. She had dark circles under her eyes that gave her a look of hardship and sadness; yet she was just a baby. My heart broke for her, her eyes told a sorrowful story and I wanted to help make those big eyes sparkle as they should, I wanted to take the sadness away and give her reason to know joy and laughter. Martha finished up the last can and walked over to the kitchen where she grabbed a hand towel that was resting nearby. She ran some water over the towel and then returned to the baby. In a rough manner she grabbed the baby and wiped her face and hands, the baby growled and squawked her protests loudly. Then she forced Tranquility's head back as she plunged the hand towel into the crease between the baby's head and shoulders, what was supposed to be a neck.

"You never know what can be in there later if you don't do this after every feeding..." She explained. "Let's move her to the floor?" Martha suggested.

She pulled Tranquility out of the highchair and moved her onto a small blanket on the white carpet. She laid the baby down on her back.

"Do you ever lie her down on her on her tummy?" I asked.

"Oh no, she hates that." Martha asserted strongly.

Tranquility, laid on her back, did not move her head, legs or arms, nor did she try to roll over or reach for a toy but instead stayed flat and motionless. Her face was vacant, the only sounds she made were grunts and that distinctive dog-like growl. Martha brought over a bottle and held it up to the baby's mouth as she sucked. Tranquility made no attempt to touch the bottle, or reach for it, but instead remained in one position with her head against the floor, arms flat to her side and legs frozen, as her eyes peered around the room as though hollow.

"Do you think that Eve used bottle props? I am surprised the baby makes no attempts to hold or touch the bottle yet." I asked.

"I really don't know what her routines were." Martha stated.

"How long have you had Tranquility?" Wondering what the longevity of her stay had been with her great-aunt and uncle.

"Just a few days. I still work as a real estate agent. I am not equipped to work and care for a baby too. It's been crazy trying to juggle both work and caring for an infant at my age. When can you take her?" she said abruptly.

I looked at her stunned... I gathered that my interview was over.

Martha saw my look of surprise and quickly explained, "We have done our research on you. You live in Tucson Country Club?"

"Yes, we have a home there," I answered stunned.

"You are also members of the club, right?" She asked but clearly already knew more than I realized.

"Yes." I answered.

"My daughter runs the children's programs there!" Martha explained.

I looked at her surprised. "Ms. Lydia?"

"Yes, Lydia is my daughter. Your son, Gabriel is in her program, he plays tennis and is involved in the summer kids club," Martha continued.

"Oh my goodness, that is crazy. Gabriel loves Ms. Lydia. She is great." I said surprised and felt as though my senses were spinning as I put faces and people together.

"Lydia really loves you and Chad. She had no idea that Gabriel was adopted until recently. She talks about what loving and dedicated parents you are, one of her favored in the country club. She has seen you parent and told us that if you were open to taking Tranquility, she is sure the baby would have a loving home and a happy fulfilled life," Martha said with assurance.

This completely made me immediately choked up by Lydia's observation and confidence in Chad and my parenting.

"I can't believe how small our world is! I am so touched Lydia said such kind words and would have such a high level of trust in us with members of her own family. I can only imagine how incredibly hard this is on all of you, but as long as Tranquility is with us, you all can still be a part her life as much as you want. We love Lydia. I have met her daughters too. They help out in the kids club with their mom. You have an amazing family." I said with tears in my eyes.

Martha's eyes began to well, but she fought her emotions. "Well, what we really want is to get Tranquility settled as soon as possible and into her permanent home where she can be established and thrive. My daughters are grown with four children each. Neither of them feel they are in a place they can add another child at this point. Lydia loves Tranquility, but this is her cousin's child and she does not feel it is her role to become Tranquility's caregiver. I trust my daughter, we all do, and because of her confidence in you, we all feel you are the best answer for this little girl." I heard her voice break and the sound of her strength weaken. "I don't want her to bond with me, she needs to bond with you."

Her eyes once again filled with tears and this time she didn't hold her emotions back. I could tell she didn't show emotions often, so her tears were foreign to her and to those that knew her.

I placed my hand on her arm, "I agree. I am ready to take her today, but CPS is the legal guardian, so you need to talk to her case manager, and I need to talk to my foster agency representative. I want to be her permanent home, but there are few hurdles that need to be overcome if this is meant to be..."

Chapter 27

"My brethren, count it all joy when you fall into various trials, knowing that the testing of your faith produces patience." James 1:2-3

JAIL: DAY SIXTEEN, ELEVEN P.M.

The tiny muscles attached to each hair follicle contracts causing the hair on my skin to stand up. A reaction from the assault of cold air that strikes me as I reach my bunk. As I lay down, I relax at the weight of the wool blanket and the warmth it provides in comparison to that of the shattered sheet and towel. I am tired from lack of sleep, from nights past, and rest my head on the thin mattress. Soon I know I will be able to doze off, chilly, but better off this night... and better off than some of those who sleep near me...

The sound of inmates coughing, moaning and shifting in their bunks fills the entire block, leaving no still or silent moments. Some cough deep from their lungs and the sound of fluid gurgles from their chest. The cold torture has made its mark on these women's health, creating sicknesses of bronchitis, pneumonia, and fevers evident throughout the block. A woman two bunks down from me moans, as she cough incessantly. It crackles, while her throat sounds closed and sore, causing her rest to be sporadic, as she comes in and out of consciousness. She groans in agony with each breath. Each time she wakes she is startled and confused. She braces her chest from pain as she coughs. I whisper to the woman next to me, who is across from her.

"Please ask her if she will take my blanket. I am so worried about her," I say, whispering and hoping my conversation is not seen.

She looks at me and smiles. She is the woman who reached out to me my first day and held my hand. Her warm brown eyes still show me comfort and appreciation. I see her lean in and touch the sick woman.

The ailing inmate is startled then shakes her head after the offer is made, able to somehow respond with a smile, despite her failing and aching body.

"She has a blanket already. She wants you to keep yours. Thank you though." She says.

"Ok, I hope she can get some rest... and warmth. It sound like its turned into pneumonia. I am worried." I say softly.

"I am worried too. Get some sleep." She answers.

I relax and pull the blanket up high over my chin, and the sheet over my face. I close my eyes hoping for slumber. I am still chilly even with the wool blanket, but am able to immediately fall asleep in peace from its weight and warmth. Tomorrow will come and another day completed.

AUGUST, 2009

Martha did not mess around. Families of children that are in the welfare system do not have the option of looking for, or choosing, a suitable foster home. CPS selects the foster family, yet Martha presented that we were as though kin. Kin has first rights.

We had not completed our foster classes and were not yet licensed at the time, but the case manager arranged a court hearing, where the judge could rule to give us temporary guardianship of Tranquility

The day of the court hearing was no less chaotic. Martha waited for Chad and me in the parking lot of the court house.

"Eve (the biological mother) is here. Beware she is in one of her moods..." Martha lamented.

I timidly looked over at Chad for affirmation. In the past it was the biological mother I needed to win over. In this situation, I needed to win over not just her, but her family, the judge and all the CPS representatives. It was a strange and intimidating feeling walking up to the court room, fearing I will be seen as the enemy to the biological mother and possibly the biological father.

As we headed to the lobby outside the court room, there was a woman in her forties in a tight red shirt and jeans standing with arms crossed and foot tapping near the courtroom doors. Her jeans were too tight which caused her stomach and back to spill over her waistband. The tight shirt extenuated the size of her belly and the roll that the low-waist jeans exposed. Although her belly appeared swollen, I would not consider her to be overweight; however her physique, face and skin, were of a woman in her forties who had not taken care of herself, some-one who clearly lived hard and her appearance showed it. Deep welts were conspicuous on her face and arms that appeared to be raw and frequently picked. Her hair was stringy and short, processed into a dirty blonde. Her face was round like Tranquility's. Eyeliner placed under her lower lids were running, making the dark circles under her eyes more extreme. She had grey round eyes just like the baby's. The two looked so much alike, almost identical. It was like I had peeked just days before into her past, an image of her as an infant, or now fast-forwarding to Tranquility's future adulthood. I gasped as I thought of that fat little baby becoming hard and worn; and silently prayed that I was not looking at the baby's true fate. The woman saw Chad and me walk in with her aunt and charged toward us.

"If you think you are going to take my baby from me, you better think again!" she roared, her finger pointing at my face.

"Eve, stop!" Martha demanded. "These people are willing to care for Tranquility. Instead of shouting at them, you should be thanking them."

"I am getting her back. She is my daughter. You are not taking her away from me." Eve's eyes were crazed and her fury showed that all blame for her current situation was directed at me.

The CPS case worker quickly scuttled over to the escalating alterca-tion and escorted Eve to the corner of the waiting room, attempting to calm her down. I could hear the case worker explain to Eve that her cur-rent actions would not be viewed favorably by the judge. This seemed to calm Eve, so I slowly, and very apprehensively, sat down on one of the waiting room seats, but kept my feet and hands in ready position so I could easily launch back to standing at a moment's notice.

A few minutes passed and Eve strolled amiably over to Chad's and my location, her countenance now open and cheery, an extreme contradiction and change from the demeanor she exhibited just moments prior.

"I am sorry. I shouldn't have yelled, but these people are wrong to take my baby." The countenance of her face quickly changed back to that of fury and her breathing became heavy again. I looked at her as her chest rose and fell at a rapid pace. She was glaring at the case manager and her hatred now directed toward her and not me.

"Can I see her? Will you bring her to me, so I can see her?" Eve questioned me, hopeful.

I answered honestly, but softly, "As long as it is approved, we will ensure that you have visitation."

"Where do you live?" she asked.

"We are on the East side of town," I answered.

"I don't have a car, but can take the bus... So, you will let me see her?" she probed.

"Of course, the judge will rule and we will make whatever provisions possible that CPS and the courts allow. We want what is best for the baby, and right now as far as Chad and I are concerned, the baby needs to see her biological mother," I said to soothe her anxiety.

The court officer called us into the court room and we all stood and walked toward the open door.

"Don't tell her where you live..." the CPS agent whispered in my ear as we walked.

"I won't," I responded quickly.

"I heard you tell her what side of town you live, which is fine, but nothing beyond that," she warned strongly.

"Ok. I will be careful." I whispered as I walked into the courtroom alongside of the agent.

As we entered, the CPA agent motioned for Martha, Chad and me to take a seat on the small bench reserved for public seating. Eve was ushered up to the defendant's chair. The judge hadn't entered, but there was scurry of action coming from behind a side door to the courtroom. The door had a tempered window and through it I was able to see uniformed officers backing up against it. The door opened and the officers entered the room followed by a young man. He was hard but young, in his early twenties, captive to the chains on his wrists and ankles, wearing the notorious, orange jumpsuit. The officers kept their hands against their baton on their belts as they escorted the inmate to his seat. His hair was short and light brown; he was thin, small, but menacing and rough. His arms and neck were tattooed, but his eyes were dancing and show a soft blue color that contradicted the threatening exterior he embodied. He looked straight at Eve and a sinister smirk spread across his face. Eve rustled and waved her arms around in anger, without restraint, while she vociferously voiced her frustration that the court allowed Tranquility's incarcerated father to be present. Her frustration didn't seem to be about his having a voice into the custody of their daughter, but instead her anger that he had cheated on her with his now pregnant girlfriend before he was imprisoned. Eve was quieted by representatives around her. The father was completely quiet, but held the smirk on his face and continued to stare pensively at his forty year old ex-girlfriend; clearly a deliberate effort to taunt her, as he joyously watched her become unnerved under his stare.

The judge entered the room and the court was called to order. Immediately the case manager described to the judge the current guardianship of Tranquility under Martha and George, the difficultly they were having due to their age and their request to place Tranquility under new guardianship, that being Chad and me. Then we were described as close family friends and that the family was requesting that we be considered as though kin, in the care and guardianship of Tranquility, while biological parents fulfilled their requirements for parenting classes, treatment and drug testing. The judge directed her questions to the biological parents. "How do you feel about having the Smith's declared as temporary guardians of Tranquility?"

"They seem like very good people and I know that Tranquility will be in good hands until I can get her back." Eve responded promptly. My mouth dropped and I felt my throat and tongue become dry in shock at her sudden change of heart and new confidence in our future role.

The judge looked over at the father, whom she called Saul, and asked him the same question. He responded, "I am fine with them too."

Saul had now deviated his penetrating gaze away from Eve and was now looking directly at me. It's the first time he had looked at me. His eyes appeared soft toward me, but I was intimidated and felt vulnerable that he had identified me, grasping that he now knew my name and what I looked like. I felt afraid with the idea that I was not only taking his daughter into my home and under my supervision, but in truth, I fully intended to fight for her permanence and adoption. This thought made me terrified of his response to such actions. A strong and uncontrolled shiver ran down my neck and back as I felt his eyes continue to size me up. I looked away from the intensity of his stare.

The judge then asked Chad and me if we were aware that we would not receive compensation for the supervision of Tranquility, nor any reimbursement for costs incurred for her care. We both responded that we were aware of this, and confirmed to the judge we would assume the role of guardian at the request of the family.

The judge ruled Chad and me as temporary guardians, while the biological parents fulfilled their objectives in order for Tranquility to be placed back into their custody. These objectives, or otherwise called the reunification plan, included: drug/alcohol classes and treatment, random and scheduled urine analysis, proof of permanent and safe residency, proof of income and continued parenting classes. As well as Saul was ordered to take a DNA test to establish paternity.

I left the court house in a daze. The caseworker grabbed me as I walked out.

"I have to be honest with you, I am totally shocked the judge agreed to let you take custody, having no biological relationship to Tranquility. I have never seen this happen before…" She said in disbelief. My mind was blank as I looked at her. I was glad I didn't know her skepticism until that moment.

Before I knew it, Martha was at my door with baby in hand. Chad unfortunately had to leave town for another business trip, so Tranquility's first night was going to have to be spent without Chad. I had just enough time prior to go and purchase a deluxe car seat, something super soft, safe with extra cushion so she could easily and happily fall asleep comfortably, a play pen for her to sleep in until I was able to purchase a crib, and a little pink car baby bouncer. It was super cute and made me laugh, but ultimately I wanted to give Tranquility the right equipment that would help her develop her leg muscles so she could begin to pull herself up to standing, give her strength to crawl and to prepare her to begin to walk.

Martha placed Tranquility in my arms and dropped off a few clothes and a highchair. This was the first time I had held her. We were alone. Tranquility looked at me with her eyebrows lowered, pushed together down over her eyes, causing the skin between to wrinkle. Her lips were tense and pressed. She growled at me and pressed her hands against my chest, pushing me away with all her strength. I set her down and smiled; she returned my smile with a furrowed brow while continuing to growl.

The doorbell rang and I could see through my glass front doors my mother and father, giddy to meet my foster daughter.

"The door is open Mom, come in!" I waved at her and beckoned them both to join me inside.

They had big smiles and came in with arms wide open. "She is beautiful Andrea!"

"Really, you think?" I looked at the baby. Tranquility's face now had a blank look, a chilling hollow expression, with eyes that seemed sunk in, encased by dark sad circles.

"Yes, Andrea, of course she is beautiful." My mother said in a corrective tone.

"Well, she has my heart, beautiful or not. She needs me and we want her." I answered softly but sincerely.

My mom inched in closer to the baby, trying to assess the enigmatic gaze the baby exuded. "Can I hold her?" she asked.

"Of course, but I need to warn you, she doesn't seem to like being held." I cautioned.

"I just want to snuggle her as her Mimi," my mom said defiantly.

Without hesitation, my mother moved right in and picked her up. As quick as she was to grab her, the baby's growling began. Tranquility took the affection as her prompt to forcefully push away while growling and grunting as she attempted to get distance from my mother's embrace.

"Well, you can push me away, but I will always keep loving you," my mother said to her, looking into her furrowed fat little face. She giggled at the baby's strength and persistence and kissed her forehead in one last unappreciated and unaccepted smother of love.

My mom set Tranquility down into a sitting position, which she seemed to have mastered, and joined me on the floor to watch. My dad saw the box for the little car bouncer and took that as his cue to begin assembling.

"Thanks, Dad!" I said appreciatively, then looked over at my mom, feeling her gaze. Her eyes looked acutely into mine, prying and keen. I quickly turned and stared back at the baby, knowing my mom could read my thoughts and fears, and without strength I began to weep.

I then whispered, "I sense a long, terrifying journey ahead. A side of me screams at God for making me walk through another emotional and grueling mission to prove my worth to parent. I don't know if I am up to this challenge, Mom." I said and rested my hand on hers for comfort.

"Andrea, I am afraid for you..." There was a pause between us. She moved her hand and placed it on my back, then began to stroke my hair. Still her little girl, but this time she couldn't rescue me. I was an adult who had a long road ahead that only I could take.

"I am afraid too, Mom; but I feel deep in my heart that this is from God... that she is from God. I know this is not going to be painless, but a fight she deserves. He chose her... He chose me for her, for this moment." I said to her and looked into her eyes looking for affirmation to my thoughts, my instincts.

"I fear what will remain of you if she is taken away and back to whatever horrors that await. I am afraid this will kill you, honey." She said with honesty.

"Right now, I look at her and tell myself I will love her as a mother, as her mother, and give her everything my daughter can possibly receive; even if for a short time. Yet today she is mine because that is what she deserves," I said resolutely, rationalizing my determination to my mother.

"Oh honey, I love you so much..." She turned to the baby, tears flowing and grabbed Tranquility's hollowed face and kissed her fat cheek. In an instant the baby defiantly and impulsively pushed her away, "…And we love you too, even if you don't love us back… yet!"

The baby growled loudly as my mother released her face from her grasp. Tranquility resisted the show of love so strongly that she lost her balance and began to tumble backward, her little head falling to the hard floor. We both quickly caught her and propped her back up to sitting position. She greeted our rescue with a scowl.

"Mom, she is only six months old, but I look at her and her face shows a complexity of emotions, fear, suspicion, distrust… frustration… even anger. I know these emotions are not possible at such a young age, but her eyes show much more than any infant I have seen. It breaks my heart," I said in a low voice as if the baby shouldn't hear my words.

My mom looked back at the baby, "I think if she could talk she would tell a story that is sad and tragic. I want to just weep for those six months and whatever she seems to have seen that we do not know." She said.

The baby's countenance now changed back from scowl to deep blankness. The complexity of her pain appeared endless.

"Honey, I forgot to ask you if you have seen the gifts that are lined up at your front door?" she said excitedly.

"Gifts? No!" I said in surprise and confusion.

She grabbed my arm, "Sweetheart, it appears your neighbors have found out about the baby. Your entire front entryway is covered in packages and gifts. I think someone even brought over groceries with organic baby food and diapers."

I stood up and walked over to my front door. My entryway was covered in pink; there were gift bags, ribbons, bows and grocery bags full of items to welcome this little girl into our lives. No one rang the bell, but each quietly set these thoughtful items at my door. My heart erupted from their expression of love and thoughtfulness. My mom and I brought in each gift, card and bag teary over each unexpected precious show of love from friends and neighbors who heard that Tranquility had arrived.

As the morning became afternoon, my mother gave Tranquility a bath, a tradition she had performed for each of her grandchildren, which was carried on and started by my grandmother, Anna, who washed each of us on our first day home. I watched my mother stroke Tranquility softly and lovingly, rub her course bald and chopped hair tenderly and became deeply moved by her love to this little life now in our care. While she caressed warm water over each fat little roll, she sang to her, she sang over her, her voice soft and sweet, telling this baby that she was wonderfully and beautifully made; she sang that God had a plan for her, would protect her and that she was loved by Him. Tranquility watched my mom sing and softly spill water over her, yet the baby's enigmatic gaze told a story unknown, of pain we do not understand; and once again, as it did for Gabriel, my heart left me and she became its keeper. I grabbed her slippery little body into a towel and lathered her with fragrant lotion. I loved the lotion's sweet scent, its smell reminded me of my baby Gabriel and brought my heart and mind back to such joyous days. I then wrapped her snug, with her arms tightly cocooned in her towel so she could not push me away and kissed her little bald and buzzed head while resting under my chin. Her little defenses were now down for the moment as the warm bath had soothed her. I pulled out some new pajamas I had purchased that were soft and luxurious, making her look so sweet, even pretty, like a little ballerina in white and cream. Tranquility stared at me blankly. Her eyes quieted but guarded and suspicious.

"Mom, Dad, I need to go pick up Gabriel from preschool. Do you want to stay here, come with me, or do you need to leave?" I asked.

"I can go with you, Honey. I think Dad wants to run some errands and get some things for the baby." She said as I began to pack.

I reached to pick Tranquility up, looking in her eyes, "Ok, baby girl, time for you to meet Gabriel."

Chapter 28

"And the peace of God, which surpasses all understanding,
will guard your hearts and minds through Christ Jesus." Philippians 4:7

AUGUST, 2009

Gabriel was overjoyed and instantly fell in love with Tranquility. He immediately and instinctively called her "sister." I wasn't sure how to explain things to him and was concerned that title may make things confusing if and when she was to return. Tranquility softened to Gabriel. She seemed to love him back. He showered her with his favorite toys, and all that he loved, and entertained her every second. Putting him to bed was no easy task, he wanted to spend the night with her, her first night; yet they both needed their rest, as it was an emotional day for all. I had set up Tranquility's little play pen next to my bed with a soft blanket for her to lie on. I worried the room would feel strange and she would need comfort throughout the night. After laying her down next to my bed, I called Chad.

"Hey, Babe! So… how is it going? Is she there?" Chad inquired.

I whispered, "Yes, she is here lying next to me."

"How did she do?" he asked.

"She is fine. She doesn't cry; she doesn't really show any emotion," I said looking down at her.

"No crying? That's good!" He said flippantly.

"Not really…" I responded with a hard sigh.

"I guess you're right…" Chad agreed, realizing the irregularity of an impassive infant. "How did Gabriel do with her? Did he get jealous? He has always been such the center of our entire world; this has to be a bit hard on him."

"He has been precious! He adores her. I think he is excited that he can play with someone besides Mommy. His love for her was instant… and is calling her his 'sister.'" I explained with concern.

Chad paused to consider the weight of his adopted son, calling a foster child "sister." "Should we tell him that she is not his sister yet?" Chad questioned.

"I don't know. I didn't expect him to call her that on his own. I think we need to rest on it and then talk when you get back. His heart is so big, it makes me so proud of him; but I also worry about how damaging this can be if it doesn't work out…" I replied.

Chad took a deep breath. I could hear him exhale on the phone. The sound reflected my own misgivings and confusion.

"We will know what to do." Chad answered with conviction. "When I get home I think we should talk to him and explain that she is his foster sister and we are hoping and praying she will be his forever sister."

"I like that." I said with confidence.

"I miss you. I wish I could be there." Chad said tenderly.

"We miss you too… I miss you. You will be here soon enough; maybe the first night needed to be just Tranquility and me… maybe it was meant to be that way. I love you." I said genuinely.

"I love you too. See you tomorrow night," he said.

"See you tomorrow. Travel safe ok? I need you." A message I gave him whenever he traveled.

"I will. Stop worrying, I'll be home before you know it," he said as he hung up.

I set down the phone and looked over at Tranquility. Her eyes were wide open and was clearly awake. She was making a strident and raucous grunt, a sound she had made often. It was a short sporadic type grunt or bark, which seemed to be the only form of communication I heard from her apart from her growls. Setting my head down on my pillow, I laid motionless with my eyes wide open, wondering if she would go to sleep, if she would begin to cry, if she was scared, wishing I knew… Thirty minutes go by and nothing changed. She continued to bark with no intention of falling asleep. I wondered if her circadian rhythm was off. Had she adapted to being awake at night and asleep during the day or was she not used to company and needed to be moved to a room alone to be able rest? I slipped out of bed and opened the double doors into my bathroom, grabbed the end of the play pen and leaned it up to its wheels so that I could slide it easily. Our floors were stone so the play pen slid smoothly. Tranquility barked a few times in her response to the movement. I reached down and caressed her head to let her know all was well, then turned out the lights to the bathroom making it very dark and softly closed the door. Hoping she didn't hear me, I stood by the door with my ear close and listened; within ten minutes I could hear her breathing deep. She had fallen asleep. Without one tear she slept through the night. The night was not as I had anticipated, an infant who couldn't sleep unless left alone in the dark; yet was able to sleep through the night her first night away. This trait was going to make Chad very happy, I told myself.

JAIL: DAY SEVENTEEN, 7 A.M.

The block is now cool, no longer freezing. I sit up in my bunk and glance over at Cain who sits at her desk. She is dressed in her usual uniform, this time without a down winter coat. I look around and see other inmates sitting up in their bunks relieved as I am. Today I do not have work release, not because my work is closed, but due to the limitation of days an inmate can work outside of the jail. I weigh the luck that the day I need to serve full is also the day the cold punishment has ended. The block still echoes throughout from the sound of coughing and sickness, but now those ailing can rest without fighting the chill which continued to exacerbate their condition. I pass on breakfast, staying in my bunk, choosing to instead finish the trashy and ridiculous novel I had begun (no more Sidney Sheldon's left to choose from).

I wait… and wait… then the lights turn on and I become among the many inmates who circle around each sink.

Time only reminds me of how slow it passes when one is barred from the world. I am brought back to the reality that I am a detainee, nothing else. I am an inmate, a criminal. Around me are beautiful wom-en who, like me, have an identity, yet not known to those who stand beside them fighting for access to the bathroom sink and mirror. I have no more significant role in the fight for the sink, than that of the woman next to me as she pushes her way to spit out the toothpaste she holds in her mouth. There is no hierarchy among us, no one smarter, or more beautiful than the other; each is given the same respect, whether she has a full set of white veneers, or just three teeth that remain; or the person with a doctorate next to a woman who never graduated from high school. I would comfort her and she would comfort me. She sees me and understands me in a way that those who have known me my entire life do not; yet we have no knowledge concerning one another beyond this place.

As I walk back to my bunk, I dread the final chapters of the raunchy book I spent my night reading, but at the same time I was frustratingly lured back to it. A male deputy, standing at Cain's desk, yells out my name: "Andrea Smith." I turn, confused, and walk toward him hesi-tantly. "I'm Andrea Smith." I say with suspicion.

"You need to report to medical," he says in a reserved way.

"Medical? I'm not sick?" I say bewildered.

He responds direct and without any pleasantries, "It is a required routine check-up."

"Oh..." I wave my hands forward to signify that he can lead the way and with that we walk the hallway.

"You need to wait here," he instructs and opens the closet door to the small little chamber where I was left my first day. There in front of me sits the small plastic chair accompanied by four dark block walls, and nothing else. The door closes and locks and I am left alone. As before, the small covered window periodically gets pulled aside as others peer in at me. At this point, I am glad that I am no longer cold; for the first time I was able to actually get a little rest the night before, so my nerves have been able to find some recovery. Time has settled me and I am not comfortable with my incarceration, but have accepted it. Despite the fact that I have been locked in this dark room and for however many hours planned, I feel no anxiety; I am confident that whoever hopes to get some type of emotional reaction from me will not, the panic they so anticipate will be unfulfilled. Instead, I sit, close my eyes and let my thoughts and heart take me to another place.

TRANQUILITY: FIRST MORNING HOME

I could hear Tranquility barking in the distance. She was up, ready to start the day. She didn't cry, she didn't call sweetly, she barked. It was like a sharp, angry beckoning. Gabriel heard Tranquility too and walked into my room with his messy bed hair and his eyes squinting from a good night sleep. He jumped into his dad's side of the bed and snuggled up next to me tight. I kissed his little forehead and slipped out of bed to greet the little girl that called. There she laid, she hadn't moved, arms straight down, legs affixed to the very position they rested when I laid her there last night, but her mouth was ajar ready to bark and her eyes wide open.

"Good morning baby girl!" I said softly.

As I picked her up she began to growl and push. She didn't know what she wanted. She clearly wanted to be up, but didn't want me to hold her to get her out of her play pen. Without thought, I instinctively swung her around so her chest faced away from mine, my arm across her body and her face looked out toward where I walked. With her back to my chest, she stopped growling. This was the only position she would accept. The feeling of her chest next to mine was too much affection for her.

As I laid her down, removing her diaper, she began to yell, not a cry, but an irate scream, a reaction that jarred me. I stopped touching her, confused and upset. She was not afraid, not sad; simply angry. She continued to yell, deafening my thoughts, I put my hands over my ears and moved backwards startled. Her diaper was full of her stool. It smelled of a grown man, not of a child. I began to gag and her relentless wails continued. I felt this acute anger toward her. My thoughts became explosive and primitive. I felt my mind detonate and my blood boil. I turned to breathe some fresh air and looked back at the screaming child. Her face was angry, her mouth open and yelling, her hands tight and white making a fists. I realized my face showed of shock and anger: my eyes wide, my breathing sporadic. I stopped, turned my head again to inhale air that was not rank and suddenly felt a warmth come over me, my spirit instantly calmed. This time when I looked at her, as she continued to yell, I could see beyond the wail. Although her shouts sounded angry, I realized they were her cries of survival, an infant with only her scream to defend herself. She was warding off a threat, a threat she had known. She sounded angry, but she was truly utterly afraid. I put my hand on her chest, which she immediately began to vigorously push away with both hands, but I didn't let go. I realized she was frightened. "I am sorry... I am so sorry." Tears began to roll down my face. "I don't know what has happened, but I get it. I get it Tranquility." I changed her diaper, although she never stopped screaming, I cleaned her and endured her fight. I deeply hoped that in time, she would learn that she was now safe.

JAIL: DAY SEVENTEEN, 10 A.M.

The female guard who escorted me on my first day to this side of the jail opens the cell door and is my chaperon once again. The light in the hallway seems brighter than I remember and my eyes squint from its glare. This guard is attractive, yet callousness makes her ugly. She stands at the door without a word nor does she look in my direction. I know this is my cue to stand and follow her. We walk down the jail's halls to the small little bathroom that is regrettably formerly known to me. She props the door open to the hallway, stretching out her arm and hand toward the toilet to signal my next required stop. I walk to the small plastic chair squeezed in between the wall and the toilet and begin taking my jumpsuit off. She stands in the doorway with the door open for all who may walk by to see, but this time I am devoid of any shame; all dignity has now been stripped away and I have nothing left to hold on to. As I follow procedure, I realize that the guard who once clearly enjoyed my emotional response weeks prior now seemed bored.

From the bathroom she takes me from the "Mission" to the main jail. I am escorted by and through many hallways and many group cells with two to four inmates in each; typical jail cells that I would see in television or movies, yet nothing like where I am assigned. After many turns and through many doors I am placed in another empty chamber. This holding cell has more amenities than the one I just left, but still quite crude. I sit on the concrete bench that stretches half the dark blocked room. There are lights overhead and a video camera that is in the corner so that I can be watched in any location of the small cell. There is a half wall at the end of the bench veiling a metal toilet and small sink on its other side. Although I never would have pictured myself appreciating a space such as this, I feel it to be more humane than where I just left. By the toilet is a roll of toilet paper, which I see other inmates have made great use of; spit wads are covering the ceiling and wall. There is a concentration of such around and on the video camera. The door to the holding cell has a large tempered glass window. This window is open to the hallway. Groups of male inmates are lined up in this hallway throughout my stay. They line directly against it. Each group takes great pleasure in peering through to see me as I sit on the bench. They talk to me, but I can't hear them, only the muffled sounds of their words. They like to slowly mouth words so that I can understand them, but I smile and look down and take the fun away by politely ignoring each. The fact that this room has me on display to the hallway doesn't bother me. I find it much more interesting than that of the closet I just left, dark and deprived of anything but that plastic chair. I gather that the main jail undergoes too many health inspections in contrast to the Mission; it probably reports that the devoid holding cell is used only for storage or declared vacant. It just doesn't seem as though it can be legal, a health and safety violation to those who are captive within. This holding cell, although crude, is less shocking; however, to use the toilet would mean the inmates lined up in the hallway would see the upper half of me while sitting and using it. Fortunately, I haven't eaten breakfast nor had water since prior to my check-in the night before, so I have no fear of any such bodily functions to come.

I wait in this room for what feels like a few hours. I suspect lunch has passed. I am hungry. However, at fourteen, I was diagnosed anorexic; controlling or accepting my hunger is something I am quite adept. To me, being able to allow my mind to endure and not be controlled by hunger is a triumph. When life is out of control, I remain in control of one thing I can overcome, my body. However, I am already very thin, and know I need to be careful, as under the current pressures, my close friends and family are watching me intently, and I don't want my exterior appearance to reveal the true depression that consumes me inside.

Chapter 29

"Let us therefore come boldly to the throne of grace, that we may obtain mercy and find grace to help in time of need." Hebrews 4:16

TRANQUILITY: WEEK ONE

Tranquility was scheduled for a supervised visit with her biological mother at the CPS office; her first since in my care. I set out a sweet little outfit for her. As I dressed her, she growled at me, which was less alarming than that war cry she sounded at every diaper change. I was beginning to figure her out. Growling was her rejection of affection, or it may mean she was frustrated about something when not being touched. Her irate screaming was her response specific to changing her diaper, which was her way of dealing with fear, feeling vulnerable and afraid.

My brother and his family had come to Tucson to meet Tranquility and were staying with us. My sister-in-law, Beth, and my niece, Tabitha, and I had planned to go shopping at the mall near the CPS office during the supervised visit, while my brother, his son, along with Chad and Gabriel were going to hit some balls at the driving range at the country club.

I was nervous as I drove with all the girls to CPS. I could tell that Beth was aware of my tension and gently set her hand on my shoulder as I drove. Her kindness moved me and her love felt. She too had been through a lot, having seven miscarriages before her son. Now she had two beautiful children, but her heartache for them not over. Her baby girl almost died from Type One Diabetes at two years old. Her vigilance as a mother saved my niece's life. Now her life and that of her daughter's was full of doctor visits, daily shots and plugs to monitor her sugar. I knew she and my brother battled with their frustration that God allowed this to happen to their baby and the torment to now watch her suffer everyday with the disease. I felt connected to my sister-in-law, because she too knew what it was like to fight to have, long for, and cry for her children; we had this in common.

I didn't want to see Eve. Last time we met, she was aggressive and angry toward me. My sister-in-law and niece kindly waited in the car as I carried Tranquility to the CPS office. The lady at the desk informed me that I needed to wait for the biological mother because no one in the office was available to care for Tranquility during the transition. So, I took a seat and waited. I was nervous, jumpy. I kept a close eye on the entrance door, soon realizing I was swinging my foot back and forth, a result and spectacle of my anxiety. I decided to bounce Tranquility on my knee as a way to take advantage of my nervous jitters. She sat on my knee and continued to look blankly at the world as I tried to get her to smile from my movements.

After ten minutes Eve walked in holding a 44-ounce Thirstbuster, with a thick layer of sweat covering her body. She saw the baby and grabbed her, crying, "Hi, Little Mama! I missed you Little Mama." Her emotions were extremely strong and she was quite overcome with the sight of her baby. I could only imagine my own reaction if I had to be away from Gabriel and felt sympathetic to her.

Tranquility began to growl and the more Eve held her, the louder Tranquility's growling became.

I was taken back by Tranquility's rebuff toward Eve. The baby should have recognized her mother and felt some comfort... I thought. At six months old, babies do start to "make strange" and I had hoped, believed, that some of Tranquility's rejection of me was due to me being a stranger. Yet, she should know her biological mother's smell, her touch and the sound of her voice. I had expected the contact with her mother would soothe Tranquility, but did not.

Sadness came over me as I watched Tranquility's behavior; she was afraid and detached from the people she knew... to everyone. Eve seemed unfazed by Tranquility's spurn, and continued to sob; reaching out her hand she grabbed my arm and pressed me into her and Tranquility's hug, causing me to be part of the embrace. Eve was damp with perspiration. I could see that Tranquility was pushing Eve away with all her might. I wanted to run back to the car and not watch any-more, my emotions were now overcoming me. Each day I became deeply aware of Tranquility's level of devastation and hurt, each day my heart belonged to Tranquility more.

Eve chuckled, "Do you hear her growl?" she said freely.

"Yes. She does that often…" I said surprised.

Eve giggled again, "Yeah, I taught her that," she explained with a smile.

Eve then began to growl loudly back at the baby as though playing. Tranquility furrowed her brow and started to increase the sound of her distain. The moment was strange. There was no joy in Tranquility and the back and forth from Eve with her was sad, not cute. Eve, feeling good about the banter turned to me.

"Will you come to the visit with me?" Eve asked.

"Ummm, I don't know if that is permitted?" I said as the blood drained from my head and face.

An employee had just walked into the lobby to escort Eve and Tranquility to their visitation room.

"Can she come?" Eve asked.

"That is up to the foster mother." The employee clearly giving me an out.

I stood paralyzed, wanting to run, but feeling pressured. In truth, maybe I should go… "Well, if it is ok, I would like to come." I said to the employee and then turned my attention back to Eve, "This way I can ask you some questions so that I understand what Tranquility's routines are."

I really didn't want to go and was extremely nervous that the tide of Eve's emotions will soon turn against me. However, this poor little child had nothing familiar around her, she knew no one, had no toys from home, nor did I know what her daily rituals were before in my care. I had completely changed her eating habits back to organic baby food, while ensuring that her stomach was able to process, before once again introducing adult food in a more appropriate progression.

I quickly texted Beth to let her know that I had been asked to stay and that they should go shopping without me. She immediately texted back.

The employee escorted the three of us up stairs and down hallways with doors, then stopped and stretched her arm toward a room. We entered and in the corner, sitting on a metal chair, was an older man with a notebook and pen. He stood and shook both our hands and explained that he worked for CPS to monitor and supervise the visit.

"I am here only to observe. Please feel free to play with the toys and just focus on visiting with your child. I am not here to interfere, just to supervise and monitor for the court."

He had a thoughtful look about him, with a short scruffy beard that was peppered, the hair on his head was as well, what remained of it. It was thick just above his ears and neck, leaving the crown of his head shinny and smooth.

On the other side of the room was a sofa and next to the sofa was a reclining chair. One wall had shelves with books and toys. Friendly posters and framed pictures are on the walls.

Eve placed Tranquility on her back lying down on the sofa beside her. Then she looked at me and began to ask me questions.

"Does she have a crib?" she asked.

"Yes. My neighbors had their baby's crib in their garage and brought it over for us to use. It is white and very pretty," I said.

"I like her little dress," she said cheerfully.

"Thank you. It is fun to dress a little girl. Having only a boy, it's quite a change to be able to adorn her with sparkles and bows," I said cheerful.

"Thank you for doing this and getting her the dress. I am glad she is with you," she said softly.

Tranquility started to growl again. Eve didn't seem to want to focus on the baby, but more interested in me. I didn't want to interfere, this was Eve's time, but I felt bad that Tranquility didn't have a toy or anything to play with. I wrestled with myself wanting to at least prop the baby up to a sitting position so she could see what was going on.

"This is what I would do at home. She would lie on the couch and I would sit next to her," she explained proudly.

"You had her lie on the sofa at home?" I asked.

"Yeah… just like this." She looked over at the man in the corner and began to snarl at him. "It is you people who get into other's lives and take their children away. You people are the problem. Tranquility was fine. I am her mother and she belongs with me," she sneered.

"I had nothing to do with her removal, I am just here to observe. You really should focus on your daughter. Your time with her should be about her, not me," he admonished her.

Eve's face was red with fury as she turned to me.

Tranquility was now growling louder and I got up and grabbed a little baby toy and handed it to her.

"Oh, I should have done that... should I put her on my lap?" Eve asked.

"I just saw this toy and thought maybe she would like it. However, it would be great if you could tell me her routines. I would love to know what she really likes to eat, if she has any toys that she loves at home and if it would be possible for her to have something of yours that might smell of home that I can put in her crib, something that is familiar," I said hopeful.

Eve picked Tranquility up, who was now banging the toy on her belly, while making more normal baby sounds, voicing a song, practicing her tone. When Eve grabbed her, she startled and dropped the toy. Eve took her Thirstbuster, placing the straw to the baby's mouth. Instinctively I reached toward her to stop her and quickly realized I shouldn't. I cringed as I watched Tranquility mouth and lick the straw. Eve saw her as her daughter, I saw Eve as someone with few teeth, sores covering her body, not living in a place she could care for herself and appeared to be unable to ensure personal hygiene. I had never shared a straw or spoon with my son, because tooth decay is contagious. All adults have some level of tooth decay and by sharing such only increases a child's future levels of decay. Here was a woman with few teeth sharing a straw with a six month old baby. I pulled myself back, but my reaction was seen.

"Should I not share my drink with her?" she asked as I cringed.

"I am sorry, that was just instinctive," I said as my face heated up.

She pulled the straw away, leaving me embarrassed and feeling awkward. I didn't look at Tranquility as her daughter, but mine.

I couldn't help it. I felt like a mama bear protecting her baby from germs, or harm. Eve was her biological mother and Tranquility was her daughter; this I needed to remind myself. Our roles were strange and confusing, but I did know we both loved her deeply. Eve was clearly sick. I could see the addiction and the cost it had on her physically. Her mind was not able to process her deep emotions, making her quick to snap. However, I did see that she loved this baby and wanted to fight to get her back.

"I need to go to a bunch of classes for drug addiction. I am not addicted to drugs, just marijuana," she said defensively.

I nod, but didn't believe her. "You should do everything you can. Do everything they say and prove to them that you will do whatever it takes to get her back," I said.

Her face became tense and frustrated, "I don't want to stop using because they tell me to. I will stop when I decide to."

"You will stop for Tranquility … so you can get her back." I said with conviction.

"You have twenty minutes remaining," the older man warned.

Eve's anger began to flair, "You need to leave us alone. Why don't you just leave?"

"I am here by court order," the older man said without missing a beat.

Eve's face was red and sweaty. Her anger was building and I was starting to feel uncomfortable. "Well, Andrea and I are going to stay as long as we want," she said defiantly.

"No, the court has required that any visitation with your daughter be supervised by a CPS licensed representative. When I leave, you must leave. Do you both understand this?" he said sternly.

"Yes." I respond.

"Fuck you, you asshole! It is people like you…" Eve was yelling, her anger uncontrolled.

I grabbed her arm and shook my head. This did not help her. She was attacking all the wrong people and waging war the wrong way. She was sabotaging herself. Her attack on him would only go back to the judge. She must have known this.

I quickly changed the subject and tried to get something accomplished for Tranquility, "Before our time is up, I want to see if you can look through your house and find something that Tranquility loves and give it to Martha. I will put it in her crib and let her play with it at home. I worry that she has nothing that smells and feels of home, nothing that is familiar. I hope that having something that she recognizes will soothe her and let her know you are not far."

"Yes, I will do that," Eve said, her rage simmering a bit.

I continued, "Also, what does she like to eat? Knowing what she loves would be great, so I can implement those things into her daily life."

Eve thought for a bit, "she loves McDonald's hamburgers!"

"She has had hamburgers?" I tried not to look shocked, but wasn't able to hide my stun.

"Well, I just give her the meat," she stuttered in reaction to my surprise.

This tiny baby eats McDonald's beef patties? I cleared my throat and resumed, "What is your daily routine, nap time, sleep time, etcetera."

Eve paused, unsure. "Umm… well, I lay her on the sofa with me. She likes to eat whatever I am eating." She chuckled as if this was cute and then continued, "she likes to sleep in the dark. No light."

"Yes, I learned that the first night. I was worried that being in a strange new place would scare her, so I put her next to my bed, but she thought that meant it was time to party. She went right to sleep the moment I moved her in her own room and turned out the lights," I explained.

She chuckled again. "Yeah she is like her mom. I like to sleep in total darkness, and if I think there is a party, I am not going to bed."

The older man stood up, "Ok ladies, time is up."

"Fuck that!" Eve roared and stood up aggressively as though she intended to get physical with the older man, who quickly backed up seeing her hostility. I had already texted Beth that the time was ending and knew she would be waiting for me in the parking lot. Innately, in response to the commotion, I quickly grabbed Tranquility and walked to the door. Eve saw and instead of going further with her violent intentions she instead directed her focus over at us. She leaned in and kissed the baby's head. Tranquility responded with a growl.

We all said our goodbyes and I left the room. As I walked down the hallway I could feel that Eve was close behind. I looked over at the older man who seemed to be following Eve. When I left the building and began to walk to my car, Eve had not turned toward the bus stop, but continued to follow me. I stopped and looked at her stressed, not sure how to react. She stood with me, as did the older man, who was shadowing us. I didn't want Eve to walk to the car. My car was flashy, expensive and not something I wanted to flaunt in front of her, nor did I want my sister-in-law and niece to see Eve; I was concerned that the sight of her would affect how they viewed Tranquility. I wanted them to see Tranquility as the precious baby she was. Her biological connection was not what defined her, nor did I want those around her to have the image of where she came in their heads. I want all to see that Tranquility's future was bright and in my arms, she was loved, adored, and right then, while in my care, she was a Smith with all the benefits that come with being a Smith.

My heart began to pound and my throat became dry. I realized there was no way to ask Eve to go away, so I turned back and walked to the car in spite of my reservations. I could feel Eve's breath against my back. Beth and Tabitha looked at me petrified as they realized that the biological mother was behind me. They shifted uncomfortably in their seats and glanced in multiple directions wishing there was a place to hide. I opened the car door and placed Tranquility in the car seat. Eve forcefully pushed me aside to strap in Tranquility herself. I stood back to allow Eve the opportunity to have one more farewell, but realized she was getting frustrated trying to figure out how to secure the car seat straps. Tabitha, who was eleven, leaned in to help, but I shook my head and she quickly slinked back from the scene as instructed.

"I can't figure these fucking straps!" Eve blurted.

"Don't worry, I will strap her in." I said calmly, but feeling anxious.

"Ok… Well, bye 'Little Mama'" She leaned in again for another kiss, but this one on the baby's mouth with an awkward hug, accompanied by the sound of aggressive growls. The moment was very strange and very uncomfortable. My sister-in-law and niece were both looking away, yet only inches from all the drama. Eve turned back and then grabbed me giving me a long hug. It was so generous that she was showing me that type of approval and affection. With my family there, I realized the gravity of Eve's appearance and I felt sad for Tranquility. The clear physical resemblance of the two was undeniable, a hard image to shake once you saw the condition of the biological mother. I felt panicky and wanted that image to be erased, but my spirit fell realizing there was nothing I could do, it was now as real in their heart as it was in mine.

Eve finally left to go to the bus stop as I walked around to the driver's side door. The older man charged toward me in a determined stride.

"That lady is not a good person. You cannot trust her. I know you from your father's church and feel I must warn you. She is manipulative and aggressive. You and your family's life can be threatened at any time. I know this woman, I know her file." He paused as I stood stunned, speechless. He stepped closer and then continued, "This is not a situation you want to be part of. Please, listen to me; this is not something you are equipped for. Do not let her into your life. Do you understand me?" he said with great fervor.

"Yes… Ok. They haven't given me the baby's file yet, so I know very little." I said feeling like someone just kicked me in my gut.

He looked at me with fatherly eyes, but a scolding tone, "I do and I am very concerned for your safety. I am so sorry to scare you, but I need to. Be careful and please reconsider this situation."

Rattled, I thanked him and got into my car. My hands were shaking and I felt my emotions begin to bust through. "I am so sorry. I didn't realize she was going to follow me to my car," I explained to Beth.

She reached over and touched my arm softly, "It's ok. We are fine; are you ok?"

I breathed deeply and looked back at the fat little baby who was sitting with her brows furrowed in the back seat of my car. My eyes began to burn, but I held back the tears as they attempted to rush through. I heard the man, I heard his concern. Tranquility's pediatrician warned me too, saying that this was not a situation or child I should take on;

yet my instincts and my heart were not going to give up or change my mind that this little girl needed me… and I wanted her. I took a deep breath and looked into my sister-in-law's eyes and answered her, "I am ok... We are fine." I turned once more and reached over to touch the soft cheeks of Tranquility's baby face. She quickly slapped my hand and pushed it away. "I'm never giving up on you," I whispered.

Chapter 30

"Do not fear any of those things which you are about to suffer. Indeed, the devil is about to throw some of you into prison, that you may be tested, and you will have tribulation ten days. Be faithful until death, and I will give you the crown of life." Revelation 2:10

JAIL: DAY SEVENTEEN, ONE P.M.

The holding cell door opens by a young male guard. He is well built and attractive. He smiles at me and I return the smile but look down. He escorts me through a short maze of doors and then has me sit on a red painted bench in a hallway. Ahead of me are several rooms with open doors. Inside I can see hospital beds and medical equipment in each. I do not sit long before a young woman in hospital scrubs approaches asking if I am Andrea Smith. I nod and follow her to a room.

She tells me to stand on the scale. "102" she says loudly and walks to a desk and computer and begins to type. A man is sitting on a stool with wheels and directs me to sit on the hospital bed beside him. I do as instructed. He then asks me numerous questions that I had already answered at check in:

"How are you feeling?" he says rather grumpy.

I answer softly, "I am fine."

"Do you have any symptoms I should know about?" He says in a monotone and rehearsed voice.

"No," I say quickly.

He looks at me suspiciously.

"Have you been feeling any withdrawals from alcohol or drugs while here?" he asks, now looking at me closely.

"No." I answer, looking back at him.

He pauses and looks again at me distrustfully. I don't know what he wants or was expecting. Maybe he is used to inmates requesting medical perks, free drugs, pain killers, detoxing treatments.

"Do you have any issues with addiction?" he asks me pensively.

"No."

The nurse is typing my answers on a digital form.

"Have you ever, or have you while detained, considered or had suicidal thoughts?" He asks, now looking down at some clipboard, less interested.

"No." I lied… again.

The doctor pauses again and looks at me skeptically.

I shiver from his aggressive questions. "Do you have any prior illnesses or diagnosis that we should treat or be aware of?"

"No." I say.

"Ok, then we are done. Judith will escort you back to the waiting room," he says as he rolls around his chair turning his back to me.

I follow the nurse back to the red bench. My time with the medical staff was no more than ten minutes. The same young male guard greets me at the red bench and walks me back through a short maze of doors and back to the holding cell with spit wads covering the ceiling and camera. Once again I sit and wait for hours.

TRANQUILITY

The new CPS representative was scheduled to come to the house to meet me, see our home and check on the baby. I had grown comfortable with the agent that was overseeing the case, but now Tranquility's case has been moved to an agent that doesn't place children, but monitors while in foster care. She was bringing the case file for us to finally review. This will be the first time we will see the concerns and actual basis that caused CPS to remove Tranquility from Eve. This file will give me a window to see the life Tranquility lived before in my care.

Through my front windows I saw a hybrid white sedan pull up in my driveway. A young girl, in her twenties, with short curly hair, wearing glasses, Birkenstocks, a full pleated, patterned skirt that ended just below her knee and green t-shirt was shuffling through her car pulling out notepads, folders and a clip board. I picked up Tranquility and turned her into the position she prefered, with her back to my chest, and walked over to the front door, propping it open. The young woman, because her hands were full, pushed the door shut with her hip and looked around at our home as though assessing its circumstance. She then walked toward us and I greeted her with a smile and offered to help with her paperwork. Her face was unfriendly while she let her glasses drop distrustfully low on her nose to look at me from above its rim. She immediately turned and looked up and down the hallway, then back at me. She wore no makeup and, although she appeared to be in her twenties, I could see a few grey hairs peeking through. Above her top lip were dark hairs that she seemed to have no intention of ridding herself of. I asked her if she would like to sit down in the living room. She nodded and I led the way.

As I walked I could feel her looking at me assessing my jewelry, the white linen shorts I had on, my matching heels, and then onto my furniture. I could feel her judgment, criticizing my lifestyle, sentencing me for what she considered indulgences. I detected her contempt, a moral bitterness, from a cynical conclusion she had made toward all those who belong to some social elite life that exists to rob others of their rightful place. My house was clean and orderly. There were no toys around, but many were placed in a large decorative trunk next to my sofa. I sat on the floor with Tranquility and pulled out a soft book from the trunk. Tranquility was instantly pleased and began to bang the book on the floor, causing the pages to crinkle and chime much to her delight.

"I understand you have Tranquility's case file?" I asked.

"Yes…" she looked through her pile of paperwork and paused before pulling out a red folder, thick with content, and then handed it to me. The label had a number and under the number was Tranquility's name, written in block capital letters.

"Should I read it now, or is it to stay with us?" I inquired.

She bristled and again bringing her glasses down to the tip of her nose to stare at me from above their rim, "No you can't keep it, but we will leave it with you for a few days for you and your husband to review. We ask that no one else have access to the file," she said in her most authoritative voice.

I set the file down on the side table. Grabbing a portion of the book, I squeezed the side that made it squeak, the high pitched sound brightened Tranquility's eyes with surprise and excitement. She reached and pulled the little book away to get a good taste of that squeaky sound.

"Do you like that book, Anna?" I asked the baby.

Chad and I had always loved the name of my Grandmother, Anna. It was a name I planned to name my own little girl one day. Its meaning was 'favor and grace.' The stories that I have been told of my Grandmother do not dilute the memories I have of her first hand. My mother, being close to her, ensured there wasn't a week that went by that we didn't visit my grandmother in her home from my tiny years to teens. Her house smelled of apple pie. She was round and her hands worn; she was most often in the kitchen busy kneading dough, rolling it out, cutting into perfection, baking, and ultimately wearing flour on her nose and cheeks. If my parents left town, hers would be the home we would stay. Although she may have been at the stove, no mischief could be earned, with eyes in the sky. Apple pie was her specialty, to please my grandfather, but she also had a fresh batch of cookies that warmed the hearts of each of her grandchildren the moment they arrived.

She never lost her wit, smart and quick, up until her last breath. She had five children and each of those had at least four of their own. We all loved her dearly. During her last days in the hospital all her kids and grandchildren camped the halls and the waiting room, not able to let her go. She touched and spoke to each of her grandchildren, exhorted us each to never leave God's love, focus on the things that matter and believe in our callings. She told me that the tragedy of my birth was no accident and there was a reason for my scars. She encouraged me not to hide. A directive I had, but shame kept me from its path. Her memory and the impact she had on my life was significant and I have always wanted to honor her by giving my own her name and hoped that my daughter one day would be like her, just as I too want to emulate her strength and character.

Chad and I wanted to ease Tranquility into her new name, Anna, and had begun calling her such by intention.

"What did you call her?" the case worker asked.

"Anna... When the adoption is final, Anna is the name we will give her." I said openly and tenderly, looking at the baby who deserved the name of a beautiful and strong woman.

She stiffened and raised her voice, "You can't rename her. You must call her by her current name. I also noticed you have pictures that you have taken of her around the house. You cannot have pictures of her up, nor can you post pictures of her on Facebook, email them or text them."

I sat shocked and sad. I felt my head start to ache and sorrow began to consume me, "I was aware that I could not post pictures or email, but I did not know that she couldn't have pictures up in the home she is living. We have so many around of my son, and I wanted to equal that of her." I said bewildered.

"You need to take those down," she demanded.

I looked at Tranquility and thought that this was unfair to her. She deserved to be celebrated in the home she lived. "Ok. I am sad about the name, I want her to become familiar with her new name."

Her cold demeanor became icy. "She needs to be familiar with her current name. I have reviewed her case file and will work diligently with the biological mother to ensure reunification. It is my belief and intention that it won't be long before Tranquility is able to go back home to her biological mother, where she belongs. It is important that you are aware that this child, most likely, will not be permanent."

I coughed from choking on my own spit. "That is not what I was told at placement. Chad and I were clear that we had no intention of making this a job, but we only pursued foster care to adopt. I was assured by CPS representatives that this was a situation that would end with permanency," I said baffled.

"This child's parental rights have not been severed. The biological mother, if she follows her court ordered steps, will regain custody of

Tranquility. You need to prepare yourself and her for that day," she said with distain.

I felt my entire spirit deflate and sink to a dark, helpless and scary hole of hopelessness. I looked over at Tranquility and my entire body grieved while my heart leaped toward her. What was her fate, what will come of this precious little girl, smelling sweet, in ribbon and toile? What sadness and confusion have I introduced my son to? He had already fallen in love with her and without prompting began calling her his sister. In my heart she was already mine and the thought of her leaving, not having any control of her well-being, not knowing where she will rest her baby head was unbearable. My heart lodged into my throat, yet I needed to give all effort to control my breathing so that my true devastation was not revealed to this calloused and cold woman. I loved this little girl, I wanted to save her, and give her a life full of love and affection, laughter and adventure. Am I to be only a short term moment in her life, each day only preparing her to go back to the very place she was rescued from? My mind began to spin, I had no more words for the CPS representative, but in my despair I stayed on the floor and played with the baby book Tranquility was now focused on. Her little face still furrowed with sadness and anger, but each day I saw that shell begin to crack, she was learning to trust me. She was precious in my eyes, worthy of the world that awaited her, too special to know anything less than the very dreams she decided to make her own.

"Can you show me her room?" the agent requested.

"Yes, of course," I said surprised.

I led the woman down the hall, with Tranquility in my arms and open her door. I had turned our guest room into a pink and white wonderland. Billowing drapes striped in pink and cream, with pink little roses subtly embossed as they cascaded to the floor, framing the white crib as the room's centerpiece. I had taken portions of the bedding my mother and I had sown for Gabriel and incorporated it into hers. It delighted me to know that the deluxe fabric that we both had labored over for that baby I so longed for was not only used by our son, but now Tranquility, who I hope to one day call my daughter. The chenille dust ruffle spread out from under the crib, curling out on the floor as though a pleated cloud.

The quilted blanket had cream chenille, and I added fabric with floral roses in pink, green and cherry. Over her bed lay a scripture that my mother gave me the day Tranquility came home:

> '"For I know the plans I have for you,' declares the LORD, 'plans to prosper you and not to harm you, plans to give you hope and a future.'" (Jeremiah 29:11)

In front of the bed was a tiny little table with two tiny Queen Ann style chairs, sculpted in white, ornate and regal. A little table between, embellished with detailed stenciling depicting a pink crown and all things royal. She had a little plastic tea set and two little white bears ready to have tea. The agent gasped with disapproval.

Tranquility needed to have a diaper change. I felt my heart descend at the thought of her screams that were sure to come, all in the presence of one who scorns. I moved to the changing table and set Tranquility down. The growling began and as soon as her diaper was removed the painful screeching erupted. I held my breath, not from the smell, but to cool my panic as I methodically changed her while she wailed violently. A tear fell down one of my cheeks. I quickly wiped it away and looked over at Tranquility now clean. I smiled to soothe her frustration and let her know all was ok. The agent continued her disapproving expression, while feverishly taking notes on her clip board.

After observing behind my washer and dryer, and inside the cabinet under my kitchen sink, the agent left, noting to me that she would have a different place to inspect every time she came, then left.

I sat on the floor, my mind spinning uncontrollably, trying to find some peace as I played with Tranquility. Every minute seemed to drag, wanting to lean on Chad and tell him the contradiction of the new agent's goal for Tranquility's future, our restrictions with her name and then the issue of her file. I was afraid to open the file and decided to wait for Chad so that we could read it together.

One of Tranquility's little toys rolled around the side of the sofa. I crawled on my hands and knees to retrieve it. As I turned back I realized she was leaning out with her head, stretching to see me as I disappeared around the sofa. I popped my head back, "Boo!" I said with a big smile.

She looked so startled, so I grinned at her from ear to ear so she knew I was playing, hoping I didn't frighten her. Her furrowed brow now instead reached high up to her hairline in surprise. Then across her face her mouth spread into a smile then opened wide as she let out a loud and exuberant belly laugh. It was full of elation and so beautiful; it made me laugh with her. I returned back around the sofa and did it again, "Boo!" Once more, she let out another exhilarating, uncontrolled delicious cackle. We both began to laugh together in a thunderous, abandoned chorus. Tears started to fall down my face as I saw her precious face for the first time bright and happy. Her laugh was the most beautiful sound I had ever heard, sincere, uninhibited, joy. I kissed her head and she pushed me away giving me the old furrowed brow I knew too well. I smiled at her and then went back to my place behind the sofa. Before I appeared, she shrieked with delight at our new found game, her joy of laughter equaled my joy in her. It was a new bond between us, a wall that she had broken for me.

"I love you Anna!" I whispered.

Chapter 31

"Yea, though I walk through the valley of the shadow of death,
I will fear no evil;
For You are with me; Your rod and Your staff, they comfort me."
Psalm 23:4

JAIL: DAY SEVENTEEN, 2 P.M.

I am startled by a male inmate who bangs on the window to the holding cell. He is laughing with great pleasure from his ability to startle me. Other inmates next to him laugh alongside as they see my look of surprise. I grab my heart and feel its ache and wish to keep the memories of my past and make disappear the current reality. The blood in my head leaves my body and my stomach fills with anxious stress, no relief in sight, no way to undo what is done, no way to take this cup from me.

I drop my head in disgrace and look away from the faces that are pressed on the window. They taunt, but any fight I had is gone, all dignity I held has been replaced with shame.

TRANQUILITY

When Chad came home that evening, we sat down to read Tranquility's file.

Chad looked at me from across our dining room table and reached his hand out to touch mine. "We can't keep her, Andrea. This situation is extreme and by doing so we are putting ourselves, our son, at great physical risk. This is not what we thought we were signing up for and far beyond anything we are capable of handling. My job is to protect my family and I can't do this if we are opening our home to everything that comes with this situation. I am calling our agency representative to let them know we need them to find another home for Tranquility. I will not put my family at this type of risk!" Chad said firmly, but softly.

A deep wail erupted inside me, my spirit was in conflict with my mind, my heart in conflict with my spirit.

"Chad, I can't!! Please, I can't let her go. Don't call!" I beg.

Chad looked at me angry and removed his hand, "You can't what? You can't put your son, me, and even yourself, first? This type of violence is more than we understand or have the skills to protect from. Another home where the location and placement is kept with some level of anonymity will serve Tranquility better as well as her caregivers. We were not awarded such, and by doing so have put ourselves, our son and her in jeopardy," he said with great frustration in his tone.

I dropped my head and my shoulders sank, "I know you are right, but please Chad, can we just wait a day or two before we make that call, please?" I plead.

"Every day we prolong this, it will only make things harder. I am not going to wait, I can't." He answered with total resolve.

Chad left me at the table and picked up the phone to call our representative. I stood up to walk toward the baby's room and heard him say our representative's name. My entire body dropped to the floor. Without physical strength to get up, I laid there, on our entryway floor, weeping. My entire soul had deliquesced from heartache. I knew Chad was right and the mother in me would never set up my family, my son, to be in harm's way. My mind supports Chad, her file much too grave to wrap our heads around. The things she was exposed to at birth, the state of her sister when taken years prior, the condition she was in and the things she was a victim to, much more horrifying than we ever imagined, however, it was not her or her past that concerned us, but the biological parents.

Eve and Saul were both confirmed chronic meth users, along with cocaine, alcohol and pot. Eve had been arrested and convicted for force with a deadly weapon and attempted murder after taking a knife and putting it to someone's throat. Saul was a known member of a gang called Crips. He repeatedly had been arrested for burglary and assaults with deadly weapons, all while evading capture. Eve was diagnosed bipolar and when off medication known to become violent and dangerous.

Our only hope was that Lydia or Martha, although in denial of the gravity of Eve's level of depravity, had not disclosed to either the location of where we lived. Although Saul was currently in prison's custody, we knew at any point his or Eve's emotions could easily swing back to hatred toward Chad and me, or when high on drugs they could decide to find, and take their daughter back. With Saul's gang alliances, their addictions and their mental health, we could become victims to our own good will. We felt we had opened Pandora's Box and the only way to close it, to ensure our safety, was to let this baby go to a home that will be protected by the secure foster care system which provided clear anonymity and security. Having been pronounced as though kin, the family had full access to all our information and address; this left us vulnerable.

Chad was right to call, but my heart wasn't willing to let her go. She was mine, I loved her, I would die for her. My body became weak, spiritually, physically, my knees buckled underneath me as I looked toward Tranquility's bedroom door, thinking of her as she lay sweetly in her bed. My body hit the floor, my insides groaned deeply, bursting out in a strange animal like moan as I crumpled. I had intended to walk to Tranquility's room, but had only made it to our entryway when my body gave out. There I laid on our stone floor, next to our front door, imagining the people who were soon to come to take this little girl away. With great distortion of speech I managed to call to Chad as he continued to explain to the representative that Tranquility's time had ended: "Chad... please, if they come, you will have to put me in cuffs or a body bag, because I won't let her go. Do you understand me? One or the other, cuffs or a body bag, I'll fight everyone to my death, because I won't let her go... I won't. She belongs with me, she belongs with us. Please, Chad."

I don't know if he could understand me, my voice was strained and unrecognizable, my spirit was standing over my own body, watching it groan a sound so incredibly unfamiliar, as I laid without form.

Chad turned and stood looking at me. His face was white with shock at my appearance. I pulled myself onto my knees and collapsed into a ball. I covered my face with my hands to hide, but unable to mask my groans, "I can't do it Chad, please."

Chad cleared his throat, as he looked at the spectacle of his wife, "I appreciate your thoughts. I want you to know my concern, but I am going to ask you to hold off on calling the case manager just yet. Give us a couple days to digest the file and I will call you with our decision," Chad said blankly.

I looked up at him appreciatively, grateful he had given me time. I wasn't ready to let go; nor would I ever be.

Chad walked over to me and put his hand on my back, "I feel like I am taking your own child from you," he said confused.

"You are," I cried.

"I didn't realize she was that to you already," he said to me, dropping his knees to the stone.

"But she is, Chad," I said softly as I threw my arms around his shoulders.

JAIL: DAY SEVENTEEN, 3 P.M.

The door rattles and I look through the window. It is the female guard that brought me to this holding cell originally. She stands at the open door and speaks not a word. I get up and walk to the hallway. The long wait is almost complete. There is one more cell that awaits me before I am back to my bunk; yet the one to come is dark and crude. I am led through the labyrinth I had previously walked and toward the block cell with no toilet or window. Going from one lonely room to another, from cage to the next cage. I am hungry, alone all day, sorrow has taken hold of me once again. She leads me back to the bathroom as she props open the door to the hallway and turns on her flashlight as I methodically take off each item of clothing. I drop my head back down below the toilet. My face is now upside down cramped between the toilet and the wall due to its tight space. The floor is dirty and my hair hits the rim of the toilet seat, then drops and rests on its base. I see it land on a dark hair clearly not my own. When I stand, my hair will probably pick it up along with whatever else may be lying on this toilet seat and floor, seen or unseen. There is nothing I can do about it now, so I remain in place and let her perform her procedural assault.

Once she feels the task is complete, she leads me back to the dark hole where I am to sit and stay. The white plastic chair is all that can be seen when the door closes. I shut my eyes and consider my life, my role, my mistakes. Although I have never intentionally hurt anyone, cheated, stolen or lived untruthfully; God is clearly punishing me. I have loved my children, loved my husband, remained faithful, honored my parents, walked His narrow path, yet here I sit. I really don't know what I have ever done to deserve where I am. I have tried purposely, desired nothing, refrained from all, and with joy. What have I done spiritually to be here? I look up to the ceiling, yet everything is dark.

"Have you turned from me, God?" I say, as my cry bounces off block walls and echoes in my ear. I am no longer afraid of the tiny window and its curtain that is pulled and those behind who catch me in my despair. I continue to call out to a God, who seems so distant and full of wrath toward me. "Are you angry with me? From birth you marked me, yet I followed you, I loved you, I served you, I worshiped you. I followed your commands and married one man, in purity, yet you made me barren. By your hand I will never know what it is like to hold life inside me. Then I become a loving mother of two children who I brought home, gave my heart and life to, and you arrest me, you throw me in jail, you make me strip naked and humiliate me. What have I ever done to deserve your wrath, but love You? I never asked You for a perfect life, for wealth, for fame, for a path without some trips and falls. What I have asked of You is to give me a chance to be a mother, to let me stand before my husband and feel not ashamed. I have truly walked the life you have outlined in your Word, yet I have been scorned. I now have a new mark, the one You placed on me at birth I covered, yet now I have been marked, blemished again. This is where you want me?"

My body collapses in my chair. Who am I fooling? I am just that, a fool who calls in the dark to a God who is angry.

All becomes silent once again. I lay my head in my hands and weep… alone.

Chapter 32

*"And the L*ORD*, He is the One who goes before you.*
He will be with you, He will not leave you nor forsake you;
do not fear nor be dismayed." Deuteronomy 31:8

TRANQUILTY

My mom made a dinner. I was excited when we pulled up to my mother's driveway and saw Esther's car parked out front. She had yet to meet Tranquility. I didn't understand why she hadn't come over or done anything to meet the new baby in my life. It was unlike her to avoid me, avoid my children. My oldest sister, Korah, hadn't called or seen her either, but that wasn't different from when I brought Gabriel home. Esther, however, had always been my closest friend, supporter, and beloved by my son. I rushed to the door with Gabriel close by and Tranquility in my arms, excited to see her.

"There's my girl," my mom reached out to grab Tranquility. I see Esther at a distance in the kitchen, being busy. My father walked to the door and grabbed Gabriel, kissing him on the head and then reaching to me, to hold me. His tight embrace made my voice quiver with emotion.

"I see your grumpy face! You can keep giving me that grumpy face all you want, I will still kiss those fat little cheeks because I am your Mimi. Do you understand that Anna, I'm your Mimi." My mother said defiantly as Tranquility pushed her away.

"Actually, we are not supposed to call her by any other name than Tranquility," I explained.

My mother looked at me with pensive eyes, "Is that so? Well, as for me, I can call her whatever I want to, and Anna she is. I know Anna in heaven is looking down at this little girl and telling God a few things that need to happen… or two." She giggled from the image of my grand-mother shaking her finger at heaven's thrown.

I chuckled at her confidence and perspective. My mom leaned in and kissed my cheek, walked over to the kitchen with baby in her arms, to introduce Tranquility to Esther.

Esther was being intentionally occupied and glanced short and awk-wardly at Tranquility. She laughed uncomfortably as my Mom bobbed the fat little baby in front of her calling her "Aunt Esther." I found Esther's actions strange and out of character. I wondered if she was judging me and feeling like we were making a mistake. I also noticed her twins were not present. Was she afraid to have her children around us too? I haven't talked to her about everything, which was so not like us. Not having my sister had been a void, I felt alone without her, like I lost an important and crucial partner. I grabbed Tranquility back and with my other hand stroked Gabriel's hair, who was excited to see his aunt. Esther spoiled Gabriel terribly, with gifts and treasures every time she had a chance. He needed nothing, yet she deliberately showered him with her generosity and love. He had no idea how special and rare it was to have an aunt like her, but to him it was part of his life and one that he clearly cherished.

My mom began to set the table on the outside patio and Gabriel and I joined in the chore. My son took the job of placing the forks at every place mat very seriously. I loved his precious concern for detail. He put great effort into making sure each fork was perfectly straight and sitting just as his Mimi instructed.

Meanwhile, I kept an inconspicuous eye on my sister and could see she was clearly avoiding me. The sting of her rejection cut me deeply. If ever I needed her, I needed her now. Within minutes, Esther and my Dad brought out dishes for the center of the table and we all stood around the table hand-in-hand as my father prayed. To Esther's disap-pointment, she was forced to sit next to me by my mother's instructions. Her stiffness was apparent and I felt my sadness grow.

With Tranquility on my lap I began to feed her while the others dug into their meal. Tranquility had a talent for eating fast, which I was working on teaching her to eat slowly, enjoy her food, to help her realize she did not need to panic and swallow her food with such frenzy. This lesson on a seven month old had not been an easy task, so on this night, it was not long before she was finished with her baby food and sucking on her bottle. In the short time she had been in my care, I had taught Tranquility to hold her own bottle. Pulling her hands to hold it and then letting go. Her frustration with the process was evident, but as soon as she understood the independence it gave her she relished her new found talent. As she sat on my lap with bottle in hand, in my peripheral vision I could see my sister looking over at us. "Ok, let me see this baby," she bellowed. All the air left her chest as though a balloon deflating. I handed Tranquility to her outstretched arms.

She looked at the baby and in return received a furrowed brow and a growl to go with it. Tranquility didn't hold her growl long, as the bottle was just too delicious to give up. I took the break to scoop dinner onto my plate and began to eat, but stopped when I saw my sister's face. She was staring sweetly at the baby, who was looking at her with the same unwavering gaze. My sister's chin was wrinkled and quivering, and her face red with unsolicited tears that flowed from her eyes. She picked Tranquility up submerging her in the air, face to face with my sister's blue eyes looking deep into Tranquility's.

With her voice cracked and labored she said, "You will probably break our hearts… and crush my sister … but I will love you… I will love you, Anna!"

Her face now covered with tears, as my own immediately followed. The weight of my role in this, the terror of loving this baby and the fear of what the outcome could bring was not lost on her. In my sister's eyes I suddenly realized her fear for me. She knew me too well and knew this would likely break me. Her distance was her concern for me. She couldn't bring herself to watch as I lost my soul, yet on this night, she too gave herself fully to this fat little girl and offered her support and love no matter the outcome. Esther felt it too. In that moment, she didn't need to wait for a judge to tell her that Tranquility was ours. To Esther, she was hers.

JAIL: DAY SEVENTEEN, 5 P.M.

The cell opens and I am led back to the block and to my bunk. The lower bunk across from me that has been empty since I arrived was now full. There a new inmate sits. She is young and pretty, with long dark hair that falls down her back with round soft waves. Her skin is extremely fair, lips full, eyes are dark and round, but her most obvious trait is her round swollen belly. She is tiny, slender, making her belly even more apparent than most. As I sit down, I look at her and smile. She has a book in hand and greets my smile in return. I rest my head down and close my eyes. I am emotionally drained and want to escape with sleep.

"Hi, I just left the main jail. They messed up my paperwork and had me in a cell with three other inmates. I hate it here and wish I could go back to the main jail. You can talk there, go to the bathroom, lights stay on with breaks outside. This is hell," she whispers.

I look over at her and nod. Then quickly see that Santanas is stomping toward us, as authoritative as she can muster.

"SSSLadies, ssdo I ssneed to put ssyou in the ssfish bowl?" Santanas slurs.

"No, no, we will be quiet," the pregnant girl responds in a panic.

With that Santanas turns and returns to her post.

"Santanas has been crying all day!!" The inmate on the top bunk drops down to whisper to me while Santanas walks back to her desk.

"What?" I whisper back, keeping my eyes on Santanas as she walks. "Why?"

"I guess the Sergeant got after her. She has been sitting there crying her whole shift and we all have been trying to console her," the inmate informs me.

"Wow," I say stunned.

Santanas has reached her desk and sits in her chair. We all go back to our positions as if we had been reading or sleeping. The hour for break is minutes away, so the room is getting restless. My heart is raw from my thoughts and the hours alone left to myself, but I am awed by the thought that Santanas broke down and in front of the inmates. She is but a woman, outnumbered by a room full of inmates. How ironic that it was in the inmates she found comfort.

TRANQUILITY: FEBRUARY, 2009

After six months with Tranquility in my care, Eve and Saul both were ordered to appear in court for a case review. Chad and I were asked to attend, to be available to the judge.

Every week, every month, sometimes even daily, I received a change in the outcome prediction of Tranquility's permanence. One day I would be told to start packing her bags, the next I would be instructed to wait another month or two. I have gone through three different CPS agents assigned to Tranquility's case and with each a very different experience, from sweet and supportive to nasty and hostile. Chad decided to allow her custody to be in God's hands and He close the doors if need be. Thankfully, he conceded to my sense of her belonging. I was grateful for his faith in my discernment.

Emotionally the pressure of all and the fear of what the next day would bring was taxing. However, Tranquility was thriving. With a little tummy time she learned to roll over, pull herself up, hold her bottle and stand all in one week. In two months she was crawling, and then walking soon after. Her case file had stated they were concerned she had Cerebral Palsy due to under-developed hip muscles; yet with just a little floor time, she proved everyone wrong.

I had sought out counsel from a dear friend who had four children of her own and also fostered many. She was a woman of affluence, who opened up her home to children, not for financial support, nor with the intention of adoption, but only to give these children, while in her care, a loving home. I had asked her, when Tranquility first came, if the baby's rejection of my affection was just a personality trait that I needed to accept and release her to be as she was, or if this was a symptom of her past compounded by the transition to a new home and strange faces.

Her advice to me was to keep on loving Tranquility, understanding that she may not be familiar with affection. If Chad and I continued to diligently show her our love, hug her, hold her, kiss her, she would learn to receive and even maybe, one day, give affection in return.

There were many times I would change her diaper and sing worship songs over her, while she screamed. The act of singing songs to God soothed me and reminded me that with patience, Tranquility would learn to trust me; she would learn that I was safe and would know my response would not change. It took a while, but the screaming stopped, the furrowed brow disappeared, and the growling vanished, never to return. What replaced those things was a bright, sparkly, happy little girl.

Her hair grew out into dark soft curls that haloed her round little face. Her eyes turned light brown, round and full of expression. Her long eyelashes would bat at Chad and make him instantly putty in her little hands. That funny little fat baby became a beautiful toddler. People would stop wherever we went to let me know how beautiful she was. She really was stunning, with a spirit that was strong and unstoppable. She was a star, full of joy, charm and vigor.

My friend's advice was right. Tranquility now hugged big, kissed often and loved greatly. Life in our home must have been so mundane before she entered that front door and it's hard to remember it without her. With her in our lives, there was not a dull day. She was truly my joy.

It had been six months since we last sat in the courtroom, before the same judge; yet it felt more like a decade. The architecture of the room emphasized the severity of the moment. The judge sat high at her desk, wearing her robe as the court reporter sat lower, eagerly typing every word. Chad and I found our seat on the cold bench beyond the area of defendants and legal teams. Both Eve and Saul were waiting, and seeing them caused my emotions to squeeze out the last fragment of peace I had left in my heart. The tension of this moment was emotionally crushing, while the toll from the rollercoaster of whether the baby I loved was coming or going, the multitude of weekly CPS visits and staff changes was now physically evident. My body too slender, my spirit worn; I felt like a rag doll that had been tossed to and fro, with years of worn. In spite of my exhaustion, I was ready to fight with a mother's supernatural strength to go any length or depth needed to keep Tranquility where she belonged, with me.

Eve looked over at me in the courtroom and smiled; the gesture came as a relief. Tranquility had recently gone to the state prison, so that Saul could have a supervised visit with the baby too. Eve was back with Saul and had come to the visit in prison as well. The baby was now twelve months old, but still too young to understand or be afraid of the environment she was taken.

We had continued communication with Martha and assured her that Eve would continue to have contact with Tranquility as long as Eve was healthy, once and if we ever had legal custody. This seemed to calm Eve, who I believed truly loved her daughter.

The hearing began and the judge heard the facts of the status of Saul and Eve. The decision then, as we expected, was to extend permanency another six months to allow the biological parents to perform the same requirements given to them six months earlier.

Eve was ill, beat down by the addictions that destroyed her. I know she wanted to fight and be clean for the baby and would do well for a few months, but inevitably fell into another substantial relapse, leaving her very sick and unable to even attend a visit. It is not that she didn't try, she was controlled by this vice and each time she came up ahead, the cycle of recovery and relapse began again. With every step Eve made forward the case would be extended, permanence further prolonged. The drug induced set-backs had no consequences on the extensions to the severance plan. Arizona's entire focus was and is all about reunification, and if a biological parent showed any signs of "trying," the severance and any permanency plan put off. This methodology creates child "lifers" in the foster care system. Children that were once young and more appealing to potential adoptive parents, are held in limbo, bouncing from one group home to the next, only to lose their chance for permanence and a healthy family life because the state instead continued to give their abuser multiple chances.

Approximately one-third of children who reunify with their parents re-enter foster care within three years. Although the statistics are not good, Arizona won't put the children first, and, instead, put the majority of their resources into parent programs, drug rehabilitation, drug testing, day care, and domestic violence classes; while providing less funding for adequate numbers of agents, the children's schooling, foster care, and child counseling. The result is children continue to linger in out-of-home care as prolonged attempts are made to reunite them with their birth parents. Consideration of the child's need for a permanent home is forgotten, and an alternate permanent home rarely considered. I had walked into this process naïve, each new discovery of its system revealed itself to be grimmer and more and more heartbreaking not just for Tranquility, but for all children that belong to Arizona's welfare system.

The agent representative assured me that it was inevitable, that if Tranquility went back to her biological home, it wouldn't be long before she would be back in the system. They told me that if I did lose custody, that I should not worry because before she turned eight years old, I would most likely have the chance to adopt Tranquility again. This was stated in an effort to comfort me, yet this was no comfort to my heart, no relief to my worries, knowing that she would suffer greater abuse and would return to me a broken spirit once again. This beautiful child who patters around our house, with sparkly eyes, and a bigger than life laugh, would not be the same when returned, but the outcome of a beautiful spirit destroyed by hardship, inconsistency and relocations.

I was jolted out of my thoughts when Eve's attorney stood up before the judge and asked the court to honor Eve's request to sever her parental rights.

My eyes became dry from shock. Staring at Eve as she began to sob. The judge was also startled and directed her attention and line of questioning to Eve.

"Do you understand that by severing your parental rights, you will be releasing Tranquility to the custody of the state to further pursue permanency and legal guardianship? This is a forever decision and there is no going back. Are you sure about this?" the judge clarified, looking strong and commandingly at Eve.

"Yes!" Eve howled. Her emotions so strong, yet completely deflated. "I can't keep fighting. I don't want to fight this anymore. I love my daughter… but I know she is where she belongs. She should be with the Smith's, where she is loved, where she can grow, be happy, with people who will be good to her. I want her to have the life she has now…" she said while her weeping intensified.

Saul's lawyer quickly followed Eve, explaining to the judge that he too was willing to sever his rights. He answered the judge's questions, if he truly understood the gravity of such a decision, with one simple response, 'Yes."

I sat with my eyes still wide, affixed to the two, watching Eve in her grief and sorrow, as Saul sat stoic, but his eyes looked at me softly, kindly, appreciatively. I walked into that court room feeling my emotions consuming me, up into my throat, squeezing the breath out of me, yet now I had this strange blankness, as though my spirit was above the entire room floating, watching, receiving a view from heaven and witnessing God's divine hand. None of this was my doing, but His alone.

Eve sat with a pen in her hand and wept as she signed. She looked over at me with eyes asking me to promise to be good to her girl. I met her gaze and smiled at her to assure her I would. I could see her appeal and at that moment and every day to come she was relying on me to love and care for her baby. She was putting her faith in me with her very soul. I breathed in deeply as I considered the depth and gravity of her entrustment and faith, her love for her daughter, and this being her own unselfish and sacrificial act of a mother for her child. Once again my spirit groaned from the enormity of Eve's and Saul's trust and the months of worry that now seemed to have ended… nonetheless my mind was apprehensive that this was truly, really, not over.

I left the courtroom stunned and confused. I could not feel the presence of God in the room, but knew He was acting. My mind was absent, my heart afraid… did I really hear what I thought I heard?

We soon find out, it was truly far from over…

Chapter 33

"For what credit is it if, when you are beaten for your faults, you take it patiently? But when you do good and suffer, if you take it patiently, this is commendable before God." 1 Peter 2:20

JAIL: DAY SEVENTEEN, 9 P.M.

The block lights turn on; inmates jump out of their top bunks and rustle up from those on lower bunks. I am glad I am assigned to a lower bunk, but with the warped metal boards, those that are on the top have less thunderous noise overhead than those below. The blanket was a blessing the first night, but now the room is back to hot and sweaty. Even the holed and ratty sheet suffocated me from the humid heat.

"When are you due?" I ask the inmate next to me as I lay in my bunk with a novel in hand.

"October," she says and rubs her belly.

She looks further along than that, probably due to her slender frame.

"How long are you here for?" I ask, a common greeting here, like mentioning the weather.

"Thirty," she says with a sigh.

"Days?" I ask and she nods. "That is good. Most are here for several months to years. I am on my last stretch with only a few days left," I say excited, relieved.

"I can't wait 'till I have only a few days left," she responds.

"I am sure these beds are going to be rough on your back. I wish I could do something to help you," I say concerned.

"I feel enormous and, to be honest, I don't know how I am going to get through this," she says with a groan.

"Hi, I am Andrea… I'd say welcome, but that would be ridiculous," I say.

She chuckles, "Yes, I would say it is nice to meet you... but under better circumstances... I'm Sarah."

We smile at each other, a strange bond between us, with all of us. We both disappear to our reading and direct our attention back to our books as our way to escape, but it doesn't take long for the conversation to begin again.

"Do you work?" she asks me.

"Yes," I answer and set my book back down.

"Then you are on work release," she probes.

"I am," I say feeling guilty.

She sets her book down and sits up on her bed. "What do you do?"

"I work for a school." I don't want to explain my job. Working for a school is my best answer and seems to satisfy those who ask.

"You?" I inquire.

"I am not from here," she pronounces.

I look at her now intrigued, "You don't live in Tucson?"

"No." She swings her hair to the other side, it loosely drops over her shoulder and I realize how pretty she is. Her skin is beautiful, her hair shiny, her dark brown eyes are deep and captivating. "I was here visiting my sister with my fiancé... the father of the baby," she points to her enlarged belly, "and my son. He is six." She pauses again as though to mention her son takes her breath away.

"I wasn't pregnant at the time, it was over a year ago, and we were here staying with my sister at her house. It had been awhile since we had been together and, I'll be honest, my sister and I had a lot of wine... we were excited to see each other and my sister grabbed two bottles of red and we sat at the kitchen table and were just being silly, you know, catching up... I probably had four glasses, which is a lot for me. I had already put my son to bed, my fiancé was with him and my sister and I stayed up. We were just being sisters, laughing, talking about the past, our men, our kids, I had no idea how traumatic things would end... When my sister's husband came home, he works late shifts, he asked me to move my car. I guess we had blocked the driveway making it so he couldn't get his car in. He asked for the keys so he could move it and I jumped up and said I would. Without really thinking clearly, I grabbed my car keys and backed my car out. I hit my sister's car as I backed out of her driveway. I was drunk... I have insurance, no one was that upset, because they knew I would take care of the damages. Being a little intoxicated... or a lot... my sister and I were actually laughing... which was dumb.

"I parked the car in front of her house on the street and we went back inside. I felt bad, but that was it... or so I thought. My sister has an elderly neighbor that has been at war with her. He called 911 and went out onto the street and took pictures of my sister's car and mine. We had no idea. A sheriff's deputy knocked at the door. I was in so much shock when my sister opened the door with that old, nasty neighbor standing next to this uniformed deputy. The neighbor pointed at me and said I was the culprit. I am thin, so after four glasses the officer could tell I was intoxicated... My fiancé woke up and tried to claim that he was the driver, but the old man said he had a photo of me. He must have been at the window watching us with his camera. The deputy cuffed me, arrested me and I stayed the night here in the main jail.

"I have had to arrange the time I was to come back and serve. Being pregnant, I knew I needed to just get it done and over with before the baby comes. I can't, or won't serve after the baby is here. So, here I am back in Tucson and back in this jail. I had to leave my son, whom I've never left before, not even overnight... well I guess except for the night I got arrested. I can't even call him. He is with his dad... which is good, but being away this long is really hard. I hate that I am away from him and for this... honestly... it is tearing me up." She pauses, her voice was starting to crack. She sits up straight and stretches, but I realize she was trying to regain her composure.

She continues, "I am sure he is ok, but we have never been away from each other. He's like my little man, my side kick. Before I met my fiancé, it was just him and me. Now I have to be away from him for a month and can't work out a time to call him with the jail. They are being so difficult. He has school, so I need to call him before or after. It's terrible." Her eyes fill up and I see her look around... attempting to stop her emotions. "I haven't been able to talk to him since I left. It's breaking my heart." She looks down so no one can see her face, then wipes her eyes.

"I am sorry. Thirty days for hitting your own sister's car in her drive-way seems ridiculous…" I say with disgust.

She nods and her face becomes hard as she leans in as if to tell me a secret, "Between you and me… I hate Tucson. I will never come back. This town is crazy."

I sit up too and cross my legs as I whisper, "I agree… There is an-other person here I just met who was in her car, at a bar, waiting for a family member to pick her up. She never turned her engine on to drive but had the air conditioning on while she waited. They arrested her, and she too is now serving! It makes no sense, she was doing the right thing, waiting for a ride home," I say appalled.

She looks at me and shakes her head, "That doesn't seem legal?" she replies with a question in her voice.

In Arizona, it is! DUI stands for driving under the influence. However, years ago Arizona changed its DUI laws to cover situations where a person can be arrested even if they are not actually driving. Now the DUI law extends to any persons who are 'controlling' a vehicle. Due to a growing debate, the Arizona Supreme Court attempted to clarify the law's definition, and by doing so stated that actual physical control has nothing to do with the intent of the driver to move or use the vehicle. In truth, Pima County has taken the DUI arrests too far. I think our small minded city officials think they are making money, they use DUI arrests as a source of revenue, and even give deputies a DUI monthly quota they are required to obtain, but when you actually pull the numbers, this whole DUI push bleeds our city of taxpayer dollars, while statistics of alcohol-related fatalities have maintained a high rate and actually increased. So, this push does not seem to protect the general public. I am totally against drinking and driving. I fear for children and anyone who could fall victim to a driver who is impaired; but I do feel that Pima County has taken things too far and are no longer attempting to protect and keep safe the general public, but have completely abused their au-thority and stretched the laws to serve a financial interest. What is most upsetting, is the fines and jail costs, as steep and challenging as they are to the individual, do not cover the actual costs for court, prosecution, jury, and detainment, not to mention the arresting officers, back up officers and costs for blood to be taken at the scene and then analyzed; so in the end, the Tucson hard working people carry the financial weight of the myriad of DUI's being served and the correctional facilities burdened with over-crowding due to these enforced and extreme laws.

"Do you work when you are back home?" I ask, changing the subject.

"My degree is in accounting, but having to take thirty days away and being pregnant was the end to my current employment. I really don't know how I am going to pay these fines. My fiancé and I are struggling already, with this baby coming, losing my job, having to be away for a month..."

"You have an accounting degree?" I ask.

"Yes." She says and looks back at me.

"You are not on work release?" I prod.

"No... wouldn't that be nice? Who is going to hire someone that is pregnant, who has only a 30-day residence... in jail," she says with a chuckle.

I stop, hesitate... but feel it is right and continue with the idea, "my husband is in the process of looking for a CFO. He needs someone in the interim until he finds the right fit. I can arrange a meeting? Are you interested? This will give you work release if he gives you a temporary job. You just need to submit the meeting time and get approval from your Specialist. If you are able to go a bit early to the office, I know my husband will let you call your son from there in the morning."

"You would do that?" she breathes heavy, wishful. "I will fill out whatever paperwork needed and get to that meeting. Thank you." Emotions overwhelm her voice as she speaks.

Our fifteen minutes are coming to the end, and we both lay back in our bunks. Potentially she can call her son, which I know is what she is most excited about. I glance over at her from my book and see that her face has tears that trickle down her cheeks; I know those tears are from her heart taking hold of the hope that soon she will embrace the sound of her little boy's voice that she so desperately longs to hear and the knowledge that she may be able to offer some financial help to her family at home while serving her time.

"Andrea, there is Chapel tonight! Will you go with me?" The inmate who sleeps above me excitedly walks over from the cafeteria tables.

"Yes of course. I would love to!!" I say happy to be invited.

"Go to the CO's desk and sign up. They are calling in 30 minutes," she explains.

I am excited she wants me to go with her… and that she wants to go. I stand and walk over to the desk as the last few minutes of our break ends, yet with each step I hesitate. My heart sinks as I stand at the desk and look at the sign-up sheet. I can't go. My sister, Korah, knows where I am and I know her deep desire for the titillating details of my incarceration, which have been all too consuming to her in the past few months; she cares little for my soul or desire to extend a hand to me, her sister. She has gone to many people excited to inform them of my incarceration, the proud messenger of this salacious fact. I have also learned that she has even solicited officers in her congregation to get my police report, court files, and talk to the arresting officer to gather all the sordid details for her to compile; yet not one phone call or text to ask me if I am ok. She has enjoyed shaming me and has made it her position to defame me to the people who love and support me. This has hurt deeply. My own sister and someone who adopted the title of "Pastor," so much so she even refers to herself as "Reverend," yet treats another like this; she treats me like this… her own. As a minister, she could have shown Christ's love, but instead chose to publically humiliate me. As a sister I needed her comfort, but instead she used my sorrow as ammunition to shame me further.

I can't go to this Chapel and subject myself to the possibility that she has her recruits there, if not them, then past members of my father's church who will also love this role I am now in all too well. Why is it that the people who proclaim to be followers, even leaders, of Jesus Christ are the very people I find absolutely no comfort in my darkest hour, only condemnation?

The deep ache to know my own sister's knowledge of my being here brings her such pleasure is hard to bare. To Korah, my incarceration has been the validation and justification for all her actions against Esther and my parents. To her, it is the symbol that authenticates all that she has done, because of me, she can now label all of us as corrupt, which she has done publically and from her beloved pulpit.

I do care about this young girl who has asked me to join her. Her heart is open and I want to be with her as she seeks out the Savior, but I am just too fragile to subject myself to the risk of the theatrics if one of my sister's disciples, or my father's past members, would incite once recognized. I drop my head and return back to my bunk.

"I can't go…" I tell the inmate.

"Why?" she says surprised.

"I can't. I am sorry. I really am sorry. I want you to go, but I have my reasons and it has nothing to do with you… it's me." I sit on my bunk ashamed, a coward. I watch the two I shared Scriptures with leave as I stay on my bunk. Lights turn off and I lay my head on my mattress, throw my sheet over my head and let my spirit sink further as I realize my place in the church: so defiled, I now hide from it.

TRANQUILITY, APRIL 2010

My apprehension and fear turned out to have weight. I was right to not celebrate the finalization of Tranquility's permanence, because unbeknownst to Eve, Saul, Chad or me, by signing the severance paperwork, it released CPS to contact all family members, immediate and extended, to offer Tranquility to them for adoption. They were asked to take her as temporary guardians when she was originally placed in foster care and they all turned away. Now that she was available, Tranquility was offered again to each with first rights to adopt her for having one thing that I couldn't offer, a biological connection.

Eve was devastated. Her side of the family remained strong and supported Eve's wishes that Tranquility needed to stay in the home she had been for the last eight months. Saul's family, although estranged from their son, now decided they did want her, specifically his mother. This outraged Saul. He explained that his mother did not work, but was living with her boyfriend in a one bedroom trailer. She had a rap sheet that included drug possession and intent to distribute. Saul's biggest concern was the death of his sister. He felt adamant that his own mother was the one who took the life of her daughter and when I questioned the CPS case manager, she confirmed that Saul's mother was listed as the prime suspect in her own daughter's murder.

"How can someone with only a one bedroom, living in a trailer, being a prime suspect in the murder of her own child, who has never even met this baby, be considered a more appropriate choice than me, her foster mother who has been caring for Tranquility these last eight months? I don't understand!" I questioned the case manager pleading for understanding.

"Biological family always trumps foster families," she answered solemnly.

My hands and body were shaking; I was visibly upset, crazed with fear and tormented with the idea that those months I feared for Tranquility's future were now escalated into concern for her life. I shivered at the thought of this bright happy little girl in the custody of a violent and dangerous murder suspect.

"This is how the Arizona law has been written and the procedures have been set. The grandmother has not been convicted and without such, suspicion cannot be considered," the agent clarified. I can tell she too feels powerless over the circumstances and worried about the results that this situation will bring. I moaned out loud, helpless.

The agent continued, "Saul has not established paternity. I have Tranquility scheduled for a DNA test at a nearby lab. I know this will be hard, but you must take Tranquility to the appointment without issue. We need to establish Saul's paternity so that we can prove that she is in fact the paternal grandmother."

As instructed I followed orders and took Tranquility to the DNA lab for a swab. Eve had no doubt that Saul was the father, and I believed her, which meant I was taking Tranquility to an appointment that would seal her fate.

Tranquility's swab was taken, yet Saul continued to fail to appear for his… which I found interesting since he was in prison. How was he able to deny appearing to medical when under lock and key? After several months, Saul missed three court ordered appointments. I don't know how he did this, or what ramifications resulted in his refusal, but I knew he did it for Tranquility. The world will judge those two, but I respected them. When they needed to, they made the hard decisions, fought for and loved with all they could for the life of their innocent little girl.

"Andrea, the grandmother has filed an entreaty to you and Chad, can I read it to you?" the case manager asked.

"Go ahead," I said apprehensively.

"She states that if you will give her grandparent's rights, which includes legal partial custody, with the ability to have access to her via phone and visitation; as well would include annual visits to see her in Tucson and/or have Tranquility travel to her location two times a year, each for a week, she will drop her adoption petition… " The agent set down her paper and looked at me from behind her wide brim glasses.

"No way! Any child of mine is my responsibility to protect and I will determine what and who is in their best interest. I will not give Tranquility's rights away by submitting her to some level of partial guardianship. As a mother, and if given that title by the courts, it will be my job to protect her fully and completely. I will never take her well-being or the rights of her custody lightly. It would be easy to throw caution to the wind to ensure that this fight is over, but the gamble is a little girl's life. That is not a gamble I will take or portion off," I said immediately. Then began to shake, worried I hadn't thought things through.

"The risk you take is that if she is able to establish a paternal link, she will get full custody. You won't even have contact with Tranquility." The agent looked at me with caution.

My body tensed up, my throat and chest became tight, "Chad and I would be willing to have let her have contact if she had approached this differently and with a heart that was looking out for what is best for Tranquility. I have no faith that she has the baby's best interest in mind, and when and if she is my daughter, I will give my parental rights to no one," I said with surety.

"I had a feeling you would say that," she chuckled at my resolve, but this was no laughing matter. I was tormented. I knew it would be wrong if I agreed, but the scary truth was that if paternity was established there would be no going back and Tranquility would be gone forever, to a life Saul had lived, and his sister was taken.

My resolve was that Tranquility deserved better. I would fight for everything she deserved, to the end.

This decision enraged the grandmother more. She called politicians demanding an explanation why her son wasn't showing up to his paternity tests, she called local law enforcement, Child Protective Services, her fight had just begun, but somehow, Saul held out and continued to evade the DNA swab.

Nine more long months of fight for guardianship continued, with daily updates regarding the chances of whether Tranquility will stay or go. Each new and rescheduled paternity test date glared at me from my mental calendar and I wondered if Saul would, once again, be able to avoid, or would this be the time he would be forced by the armed guards by whom he was surrounded. The grandmother launched many personal and physical threats directed at Chad and me.

In spite of all this, an adoption day-our adoption, was set for August 30. Each day felt like a month. I held my breath as each hour passed. We were so close, but instantly this could change or be put on hold with one event, one act, one test. All I wanted was to hear that gavel hit and know Tranquility was safe, she was home and no one could ever take her away. I needed August 30 to come and come fast.

The day of court, the case manager called to warn Chad and me that the grandmother was in town and had threatened to wait for us in the parking lot with what she called "plenty of muscle," and because of this threat, security would be escorting us to and from the court house. I was giddy, no longer concerned of her personal threats, but excited that today my baby girl was truly mine and I hers.

If the grandmother was there with her posse, I never saw. None of us even looked or cared. Chad, Gabriel, Tranquility and I all walked into the court house hand and hand, escorted by security, but fearing nothing. Tranquility danced her way through the court doors dressed in bright pink with sparkly shoes. Her curls that framed her little round face bounced with every step. She was boundless, happy, knew we were excited, but didn't truly understand why. She was one year and nine months, and on this day she was becoming a Smith. The government in all its authority was declaring her ours and she would forever have a father who adored her, a brother who worshiped her, and a mother who would lay down her life for her.

My parents and Esther (my brother in route) walked into the courtroom, where that same judge now had Chad and I stand and agree to adopt, care for, never to disinherit the child, now named Anna Smith. This day, my heart was free and all we went through to come here, she was well worth.

Anna now was the name sake of an amazing and beautiful woman, her own great-grandmother, and with it inherits the legacy of all her family, both her biological and mine. She has and will be given all the rights and privileges of being a Smith; and I will ensure she does. This beautiful child who to me was a bright star, who came and changed our quiet little world and brought us love, laughter, ribbons and bows. Truly loved by all those that called her theirs. It was no longer my job to fight for her place in our life, but my cherished responsibility to challenge her to dream big, because her father and I were here to help those dreams come true.

God pointed down from heaven at this little fat baby and called her to me. My heart and my spirit knew it the moment I laid eyes on her. All thought I was crazy for believing that God would make a way. Nothing appeared to be in our favor, but God wouldn't let me let her go. She was mine and I was hers from the start.

The judge hit the gavel and the heartache, my fight, my worries lifted. It was done. I will celebrate this day until my last and final breath, because this is the day Anna became forever ours.

Chapter 34

*"If you endure chastening, God deals with you as with sons;
for what son is there whom a father does not chasten?"* Hebrews 12:7

JAIL: DAY NINETEEN, FOUR A.M.

"Andrea…, hey… it's Sarah!" I hear my name whispered from the bunk across. I jump and look up. Sarah is dressed, but it is still dark.

"Sarah, what time is it?" I ask confused.

"4 a.m. It's the only time I could get the bus to that side of town and be at your husband's office in time. I don't want to get you in trouble, but I couldn't leave without saying thank you. This means so much to me," Sarah says quietly.

"Of course, I am so happy it worked out. I will say a prayer that Chad is able to hire you. I have a lot of pull, but he won't do anything that isn't best for the company. Good luck." I say, hopeful.

"Ok, thank you. I am so grateful… even if I don't get the job… he said I could call my son today before he goes to school. So, thank you for that," Sarah said as her eyes well up. She wipes her face and turns around and heads to check out at the desk.

I watch her leave and realize she has a whole city block in the unrelenting Tucson heat to walk to get to the bus stop nearest the jail. It is dark and a bad side of town; she is very pregnant and very beautiful. The Tucson heat gives no relief, even in the wee hours of the morning, yet she is a mother who will do whatever she can, just to speak to her boy. I would do the same.

There is no way I can go back to sleep. I sit worried about this lovely young mother as she treks her way through the dark streets of Tucson to a bus. I understand her dedication and would offer a limb to never miss a day of each of my own children's lives, yet here I sit, and no one wants one of my limbs in return.

This sentence has been cruel, tormenting to me, but especially wrong to my kids. I let this happen and I, and only I, am to blame. Being here has caused me to question everything in my life, all my decisions, all my beliefs and, although I have walked with great intentions, I fear I have somehow lost God's grace and favor. Maybe I never have known His grace or favor... maybe He has turned from me since the day I was born and I have only been fooling myself that He loves me and has called me. Survived and salvaged at birth, yet marred and ugly, a life that was intended to be snuffed out at its start.

I feel such an ache in my spirit, unsure of my place in God's eyes. I was given parents and grandparents with such heritage in the Lord, yet here I check in and out of jail every day with nothing to show for the Biblical knowledge and spiritual life I was exposed.

This thought plagues me as I watch the hours pass, until it is my own time for my work release, which comes and the day propels as though a freight train passing by. Memories stand still, life in jail moves slow, but life passes me, and I stand aside and watch it roll by.

Evening has already crept up and I am once again kissing my kids good bye. I feel my hair being brushed aside with a tender kiss from my husband to my neck. I reach my hand to touch his face.

I truly love this man, and know that he loves me in return. I realize that our emotional divide was my own doing. I had pulled away from him; I had closed myself off to him. After seventeen years, I had changed my affection toward him. I left him confused, without a way to truly support me, so he stayed quiet and stood beside me. He never left my side... I had left him emotionally. I was spiritually beaten and afraid of his rejection. He was waiting for me to come back to him. I pray for God to shine on him, to shine on these kids. They are all I love; my whole existence is for them. They are my calling, and I can't think of anything greater God could ask of me.

God has blessed me. Although I walk through this dark valley, I must not fear because He is with me. I am comforted by His rod and His staff, because I know He only disciplines those who are His children. If I had no relevance to Him, He would have released me to my own wickedness. I am still His, He is still calling me, He has not left me. I was comforted in that jail, the first night; my heart was warmed and filled from my despair.

"Thank you, God, for not leaving me and comforting my heart in the darkest of places," I say quietly.

Chad hears me. "What did you say?"

"Oh nothing," I say, embarrassed.

"Andrea, I hired Sarah," Chad says softly.

I inhale deeply. "Oh that is so great. I am so happy for her," I say excited.

"One of my female employee's saw her walking from the bus stop three blocks from the office. She saw that she was pregnant and pulled over to help. Sarah told her she had an appointment with me. It is such a stroke of luck because they connected and my employee happens to live near the jail. She is now going to meet her and to take her to and from work every day. She won't have to walk anymore," He says with great excitement.

My throat shrivels and I begin to choke on my words. "I don't think it was luck…" I look at Chad and smile.

"I am really happy for her," He says.

"So am I," I answer.

I was the only person checking in when Officer Julius emerged to escort me to my block. I was anxious to see Sarah, hoping she was still awake.

In the privacy of the bathroom, and because I was alone this time with Officer Julius, I make her an offer.

"I want you to know that I appreciate your dedication and professionalism," I say sincerely.

"Thank you," She says, her stoic persona a bit softer.

"I know you can't discuss this with me now, but I am going to offer you a job. I hate to take you away from the other inmates, but I know you are looking for something away from this place and you would be valuable to us," I explain.

"I'm listening…" she replies.

"I want you to call me in three days when I am no longer serving.

Look me up at the corporate office of Dove Academy. We have just opened up a south location and the feedback we received from parents in the area is the need for security. We are starting a security department to serve before, during and after school while kids are on campus. Those kids are precious. If having security will help the children thrive, focus on their education and allow them to succeed, it's an expense we believe in. We also believe it will boost our enrollment. I want you to head it up. You will need your fingerprint card and to hire employees that you will train and/or that you feel will be the right team to care for these children. Are you interested?" I ask.

"Yes. I grew up on the south side. I know where your school is. It is right up the street from my parents. I would love a school environment. I can't give you any details and cannot discuss employment here, but you will be hearing from me in three days," She responds.

"Ok, so I will hold the position until then and wait for your call as confirmation that you are interested. I am the Human Resource Director and Chief Operations Officer. I have seen you in action, under the most delicate and hostile of situations and know you will be a gift to the children we serve. You will keep them safe and show respect and dignity to each child, their parents and staff," I say confidently.

She nods her head and opens the door to lead me back to my bunk. She has not seen me dressed in anything but my jumpsuit, but I know she has taken me seriously.

I walk over to my bunk and see Sarah waiting for me with a big smile.

"Congrats!! I heard!" I beat her to the punch in my excitement.

Her eyes begin to fill with tears. She has no words, but I feel her emotions.

I talk for her, "Did you speak with your son?"

She nods, tears are running, she starts to say something, but waves her hands as her breath is chocked by her crumbling heart. I look around to see Santanas who is looking away and take the opportunity to touch the top of Sarah's hand... and hold it.

Chapter 35

"Nor height nor depth, nor any other created thing, shall be able to separate us from the love of God which is in Christ Jesus our Lord."
Romans 8:39

JAIL: DAY TWENTY, NINE A.M.

I can hear the breakfast trays being wheeled in. Today is my last day. Just prior to my check in, my father became very ill. I had gone to the doctor's appointments with him and my mom to see what I could do to help. He has continued treatment while I have been in jail. I have been unable to go with them now, unable to help or be there in love and support to a man I adore, who has loved and been there for me, even now. Korah had gotten wind of his state and untruthfully described my father as having gone "senile" to her church, to his church that he built with his own hands, which, once again, was another dagger she so triumphantly pierced through my father's heart, through all our hearts. I believe that this statement was another calculated attempt by Korah to discredit her family and further justify the conduct of her past and present. In no way was he senile. He has been our rock, but now he is old and it is that time in life we need to be there for him. The pain of knowing that I have had no way to touch him, hold him and be there for him because of these bars, this sentence, has broken my heart. He knows why and that hurts too.

While the other inmates eat their sugar-filled breakfast, I grab the instant coffee I had purchased from the commissary and fill a foam cup up with hot water. I sit down at a long table to enjoy my last cup of instant coffee ever… I hope. Older inmates, who are my age, begin to fill the table around me. They too have only coffee. Today, breakfast turns into the morning's only break. As lights turn on the conversations begin.

"You leave today?" asks one. I know this inmate. She is the woman who walked by my bunk on the first night and placed her hand on my head and whispered, "It will be ok."

"Yes!! I check out at noon!" I exclaim, excited.

"Congratulations," she says kindly.

"Thank you. I wanted to thank you for speaking to me and reaching out to me my first day. You really comforted me," I say.

"You are welcome. We are all woman, and in this together," she says to me. Her eyes are green and her hair dark. She is slender, attractive, mature. She wears no makeup, nor do any of us. What's the point? She has soft curls that rest on her shoulders with gray that sprinkles through its color.

"It is tough in here." I say. "I see those of us who are older keep our heads down, knowing this will one day be over... but the young girls, they become part of it, believe it. I worry about them. They have been beat down so low, they think they belong here and deserve to be treated like this."

I want to hear their perspective. What I do know of these women who sit next to me, is their depth of character in times of suffering, and their willingness to reach out to another, no matter what the other's sins may be, and without regard to the others' place in society. They offer support in spite of their own distress. There is beauty in them, compassion that is not seen often. The world probably will judge each of these, the church will convict and add to their sentence, yet I see beauty, I see God. They are more lovely than many of the women in my country club, whose lives are shallow, befriending for self-benefit, who cheat, despise others and gloat in their own fortune. They have more decency than those in the church who press their clothes, put on their lipstick and walk around judging, while living a lie and hiding their own sin. The world will praise those and detest these.

"The real tragedy is to see that once they are ready to leave, they sabotage themselves extending their stay," another inmate adds, agreeing with my concern. This inmate has also been warm to me too. She would often smile at me, or whisper in my ear to inform me of the rules I didn't know.

"That is the evidence of their self-worth. The officers here are so cruel. I think they truly believe in their superiority. I don't think they see us as human," I conclude.

"They are just scared. We outnumber them, so they manage control with torture techniques and cruelty," the dark-haired woman responds. I realize she is right. It is fear that brings them to do the things they do and the attitudes they have.

"When do you get out?" I ask the two ladies.

"I have one more week," responds the inmate who often smiles.

"I have a couple more months," says the other.

"What brought you here?" one asks me.

I take a deep breath. "A DUI," I answer and cringe at the thought, ashamed of this reality.

"I am here for a DUI too..." Says the other inmate who usually smiles, but this time I see her sadness.

"Are you married?" she asks me.

"Yes." I answer.

"I am too... well, for now. Twenty years for us, but I haven't heard from him since I checked in. Don't know if he will be home when I open my front door." I see her pain. It is deep. "I don't drink... or never did before..." She takes a deep breath, begins to talk, but catches herself. Her eyes are welling up. She takes another deep breath, then she continues, "My son died in an accident. I just didn't want to live anymore. After his funeral I went to a convenience store and bought a whole bottle of vodka and drank it. I have no memory of driving, but woke up sober in jail. That was my first and only DUI and here I am. I guess I did die that day... when my son died..." she wipes her eyes and looks down.

I am silent. I look into her eyes and see the deep ocean of sorrow beneath her smile. She has been comforting me, but her heart is desperate for her own consolation and peace.

"I am so sorry. My heart breaks for you and for your husband. He is probably dying inside too. He lost his boy and now feels he has lost you. Don't give up. Did he tell you he was done?" I ask.

"No," she shakes her head, "we haven't talked about anything... just stopped talking."

I am silent again. I want to weep with her, I want God to soothe her; how I have cried so bitterly because of my predicament and here she smiles and eases my heartache when her own heart is shattered. I have my children, I still feel their arms around my waist and kisses on my cheeks.

"Well through this experience, I learned my husband wasn't going to talk, or hold me, unless I talked and held him. I was angry with God when I got here. I felt this unjust. Now I am just glad that nobody got physically hurt by my hands," I say softly.

"Yes, nobody got hurt, but I could have. I could have..." she is very tiny, with petite features, a small face. Blonde hair that is cut into a bob and curls rounded under her chin. She looks frail. I can't imagine her pain, I want to find a way to comfort her as she so often has me. Her story and her pain so real.

I look around and see Officer Cain at her desk, but looking away, so I move my hand and grab hers.

"I belong here..." she says and looks down at the table as if staring deep into some abyss. "God is not supposed to give you more than you can handle. The death of my son was more than I could handle," she says bitterly.

"God never said that." I reply.

"What do you mean?" she looks up.

"It doesn't say that in the Bible." I pause. "People like to quote that as if it came from the Bible. Tell that statement to all the little children in Africa who are sick, orphaned and living on the streets. I think that we can all agree that they suffer beyond what they can handle. What the Scripture does say is God can give us a way out, when tested, so that we may endure. What he promises is that He will comfort us in our darkness and when we suffer. He is not the author of these things, but the redeemer of them," I proclaim.

She looks at me blankly, as though her heart betrayed by a promise from God.

"I am so sorry. I would want to die too, but I know your son wants you to live and not live here in this place." I point to the walls around us. "You belong with your husband. Together you can remember a son, whose life was short, but he was and is truly loved and awaits to embrace you once again. Let the real promise in the Bible be true in your life and let God comfort you and repair you. He will hold your son until you are there. Until then, cling to the one man who knows your sorrows like no one else, your husband. In each other you can find comfort and understanding that no one else on earth can equal. Together you can find healing from heaven and allow God Himself to wipe away your tears."

Her other hand grabs mine and we both begin to cry. I feel her agony and I can't stop my tears. "Go home and hug your husband. He is dying too. He knows your pain more than anyone and you his. Your son needs that from you. You are so strong to walk through this and still be breathing. Don't die with him, live for him. Ok?" I say, my voice forced, tangled from my emotions, but my message is strong.

Her tears flow deep and her breath short and sporadic. She looks down at the table to stop her deep emotions from taking over. I want to hug her, but can't.

Cain calls out loudly that the break is over and lights turning off. I walk back to the bunk that soon will be someone else's, but before I reach it, I look back at the one woman whose pain is beyond my own, she is walking to her bed, she turns to me and whispers, "thank you" then sits down on her bunk, her metal prison, never to see each other again.

I absorb that this is end of my days in jail. Excited to leave. My sentence has been served. But sadness fills my heart for lives and relationships that I am leaving here. I want to help all of them, as they have helped me. We don't even know each other's full names. No one intends to ever contact the other. We will walk away from this, and each other, as closure from hell.

It's only a few hours before I need to start packing my things in a plastic bag and take my sheets and blanket to laundry. It will be nice to see my mattress bare; an awaited symbol of my soon coming absence. Whatever joy I thought I would feel is now dim. I want to just cry, cry for those that are still here, for their tragic stories, for the lives that are hurt because of circumstance, choices, addictions and this place. This burden is so great and the heartache so severe; I can't imagine my life and perspective will ever be as it was before I met these women. I pray I hold each in my heart and remember them as precious and beautiful, each with their own story; each with their own heartache, but each willing to reach out, love and comfort another.

Chapter 36

"…but God is faithful, who will not allow you to be tempted beyond what you are able, but with the temptation will also make the way of escape, that you may be able to bear it." 1 Corinthians 10:13

MEMORIAL DAY, 2011

The sky was eerily dark, with no moon and not one star on this Memorial Day night. Total blackness filled my rearview mirror with only the periodic glow of red from my break lights. I didn't realize how blank and sinister the sky appeared, nor the depth of the night's darkness while at my sister's house. Anna's adoption was final and I was so excited to be going into a summer with my family, no longer carrying the weight and fear of her future. We could, finally, just be happy and complete. It was nine thirty at night and my kids should be in bed. Esther lived in the country club too, just two streets up from me. I had a terrible feeling, but considered what haunted me must be the strange and unnerving sky that hung over as I drove home from the employee party. I do not have a lot of friendships with most of my sister's employees and know the many terminations I have had to make in the last two years have had its impact among those I work with; resulting in people keeping their distance. So, I found great comfort in holding babies of new mothers. Their precious little fury heads and sleeping sweet faces was all the company I needed. Esther's house was beautiful with a sizeable grass lawn, canopied by beautiful mesquite trees that gave shade to the adults, a large pool which invited children of all ages and to top its grandeur, a twenty foot outdoor movie theater ensuring her yard to be a true paradise for young and old. The employees were able to sit back and watch as the kids played ball, or swam in the pool, while others sat and watched a Disney movie in the soft grass. The party had started at four, and most had left around 8 p.m. with only a skeleton crew who remained to help my sister tear down.

As we were cleaning, the doorbell rang. Esther went to the front door, while the rest of us stayed in the kitchen or backyard attending to our chores. Suddenly we heard the rod iron fence rattle and we all startle as a uniformed sheriff's deputy reached over to unlatch the fence and enter into the back yard, then stood in the yard with his hand resting on his weapon; gasps of shock and confusion from the few of us woman could be heard. Esther's Chief Educational Officer jumped from her seat, turned toward the officer and asked if she could help him. I stood still and frightened. Then another deputy reached his hand over the fence and awkwardly fumbled as he unlatched and entered my sister's home. This one much less fit and quite a bit older than the first intruder. He was clumsy and made quite a racket as he too invaded the property with his hand on his weapon. Esther, alarmed by their unprovoked and disturbing actions, quickly ran outside after leaving whoever was at her front door.

"Kim" she called to another employee, "can you turn down the movie speakers?" The movie was over and the screen was displaying its credits while the Disney theme song played.

"What's going on?" the CEO asked Esther and then returned her attention back to the deputies who were marching toward us, hands still on their side weapons.

"They said they had a noise complaint!" Esther responded.

"It's not even 8:30!" she questioned and grabbed her phone to see if the time displayed confirmed her internal clock.

"It doesn't need to be past 8:30 for us to respond to a noise complaint," the old and out of shape officer interjected in a barking manner, then started to change the conversation. "I like your yard! Is this your house?" he asked while he stomped toward us with his hand on his weapon.

"Thank you. Yes, I live here," Esther answered awkwardly.

"I'd love to have a Superbowl party here," he continued.

"Yes, a Superbowl party would be fun..." she laughed uncomfortably, frightened of his posture and concerned he had entered without provocation. "Ok, so the music is off, is there anything else I can do for you officer?" she said sternly.

"What kind of party was this?" the older and overweight deputy continued.

"An employee party for teachers and their families," My sister answered, sounding confused and concerned.

"Have you been serving alcohol?" he interrogated.

"It wasn't that kind of party…" Esther responded. "Is there anything else I can do for you officer?"

"I have a few more questions." He said with a smirk.

They had nothing to say to us to explain their reason for entering, other than a noise complaint, which seemed suspect that a noise complaint gave them authority to enter someone's home without invitation or cause. Esther's CEO tried to lighten the mood by teasing me. "Don't worry, Officer, we will keep Andrea under control from now on." She said with an awkward laugh.

"Oh yes, Officer, arrest me now. I am known for my disorderly conduct." I said jokingly as I walked back inside to help in the kitchen and finish the cleanup. I heard everyone laugh and had no idea what I had provoked. I assumed the drama was over and the deputies were leaving, having seen that there was nothing but a bunch of women cleaning up from a family event.

"That is Andrea Smith?" the older deputy asked.

Jennifer, Esther's CEO, responded hesitantly, "Yes?" Then he pointed at me for confirmation, "The blonde?" he asked.

"Yes…" Jennifer answered becoming increasingly uneasy.

I had stopped by a neighbor's Memorial Day pool party earlier that afternoon, prior to Esther's work event. I was still in a bikini, cover up dress and wedge high heels I had worn for the neighborhood get together. I wasn't exactly in a teacher typical outfit, as my heels were high, my neckline plunged and the bright color of the bikini exposed. I had planned to change, but I was running late and decided it was best to just get to my sister's on time.

I looked back outside while washing a dish and realized that both deputies were still outside talking to Jennifer and Esther.

I began to worry. What more could they want? What exactly were they looking for? Esther was a Superintendent of elementary schools, her life would not be very exciting to law enforcement nor would anyone who had attended. The party consisted of a bunch of people dedicated to education, who work long hours and when they are not working, can be found attending to their own families. After a few more minutes I finally saw Esther escort the deputies to the gate, a much easier route than that which they entered.

Once the deputies were out of her yard, Jennifer and Esther joined me in the house.

"What was that all about?" I asked.

"I don't know. The older one was at the door, when the doorbell rang. I think the other was at the fence when I was answering my door. He asked me to turn down the music, and said I would. Then I saw him go around the side and walk to my fence too!!" Esther explained.

"Can they trespass onto private property without cause?" I questioned. "You had already agreed to comply without issue. What were they looking for?"

"I have no idea…" Esther responded.

"He was being a bit disturbing about you, Andrea," Jennifer added.

"Me?" I said startled.

"He asked me if you were Andrea Smith, had me point you out and made me repeat your name." she recounted.

"How strange! Which one?" I said shocked.

"The fat one." She said concerned.

I found it all to be odd, but quickly blew it off. I walked to my car, and realized they were still out front. I passed the two sheriff cars and crossed the street to my beautiful sports car, which also didn't resemble something of a teacher's typical mode of transportation. The convertible top was down, as I had left it parked, so instead of opening the car door, I leaned over the passenger's side door and set down the Tupperware of leftovers I had been given of rice and chips. While walking past the older deputy as I returned, I felt uneasy, but I quickly forgot all about the two once back inside.

The house was quickly cleaned and the yard put back together.

"That one deputy is still out there!" one of the employee's said in alarm as she looked out the front window.

"That is so strange. It's been over an hour. What is he doing?" Jennifer said as she too walked to the window.

"Nothing… just sitting there!" Esther walked to the window to see too.

"Well I am off. My husband has been texting asking me to come home. I need to go." I said to the women as they peered outside. "Bye, see you in the morning," I said as I left.

"Bye. Thanks for helping," Esther called out, then looked back toward the deputy that waited.

The night was still very hot, the skin on my leg's stuck to the leather of my seats, while in contrast my hair blew loosely around my face and shoulders, cooling my upper body with its gentle wind as I took my two minute commute home. I couldn't get over how creepy the night's sky felt. I knew Chad was anxious and would be happy when I finally got home. He was supposed to come to Esther's, but had decided to keep the kids home after a full day of swimming, to get them tucked into bed and rested for school the next day.

I began to turn into my driveway but saw police lights in the distance from my rearview mirror. I stopped and pulled to the side of the road as it raced to pull up and park behind me.

I waited and looked through my side mirror to see walking up to my car the same portly older deputy that invaded my sister's home.

"You swerved. I saw you swerve right here. Are you aware of that?" He stood at my door. I loved having the convertible down, but at this moment I felt exposed. His chin was up, so that he could look down at me in a superior stance. The position only brought my attention to his fat under chin that jiggled with each of his over emphasized words.

"I was pulling into my driveway. This is my house." I pointed to my house, which we are parked in front of.

"License and registration," he said, his jovial Superbowl conversational side now gone. Instead his tone set to a more super powerful persona, deeper voice and words spoken in quick and harsh snarls.

"Here is my registration. My driver's license is in my house." I pointed again. "I didn't leave the neighborhood, so I didn't take my purse."

"Get out of the car," He said in a strong voice. My heart started to beat hard. Suddenly I realized this wasn't a routine traffic stop, he followed me home. He waited for me out front of my sister's house and followed me until I began to pull into my driveway. I never saw his headlights, no one was behind me. Yet he saw me pulling into my driveway. Were his headlights off? The only time I saw him was when he turned on his top lights at quite a distance. Was he following with his lights off?

I opened my car door and stepped out, now terrified. I knew I should always have my driver's license with me, but would that qualify for a ticket or was it arrest worthy? Wouldn't this just be a fine?

"Have you had anything to drink?" he asked.

"Yes. I had two glasses of wine in the last four to five hours," I answered honestly.

"I am going to do a field sobriety test," He declared.

"Ok." I am scared, not about passing, but from the amount of authority and power this one man held. I felt helpless and frightened. I wanted Chad to see me through the front windows, hoping and praying he would come out.

Another deputy pulled up, his lights flashing too. The dark night now filled with flashing lights and I began to worry my little girl would wake up scared, her bedroom window not far from our position. I didn't want my kids to see this. "Oh please, God, don't let them see this." I cried under my breath.

"From one to ten, ten being the highest, what do you feel your level of alcohol is now?" the deputy asked, while the other sat in his car.

"Two." I answered. He scribbled that down, set his notes on his hood, then picked his paper back up and scribbled again.

The other deputy walked over. He was the younger deputy that also scaled my sister fence.

"Deputy Antipas, what's the problem?" The young officer asked.

"I am conducting a field sobriety test. Did you bring a camera?" Antipas barked.

"Yes," the young deputy retorted.

"Ok go get it, now," He demanded in gruff voice, making his neck jiggle from the low vibrations.

"Stand on one leg and count from one, one thousand, to ten, one thousand."

"Okay, but it is really hard to walk in these shoes on the asphalt, let alone stand on one foot," I explained.

Of all days to be wearing Christian Louboutin five inch wedges. I wore them to the neighbor's pool party. They were crazy fun, but not really something teacher's would appreciate or even recognize; my sister made a comment as soon as I walked in. "You came in Louboutin?" she laughed. My outfit made me feel uncomfortable earlier, now it was turning against me.

No one could stand on one leg in these shoes. I am a master of the heels, however, wedges may be more comfortable and great on flat surfaces, but on anything unlevel, even I, a lover of all things heeled, will fall. An expensive and painful shoe, of which takes special skill and dedication to master. To stand on asphalt on one leg, impossible.

But I try... I lift my foot and begin counting, "One, one thousand, two, one thousand, three, one thousand, four, one thousand..." I made it to four before I set my lifted foot down to regain my balance. Impressed with myself that I was able to stand for that long. I guarantee that Antipas in all his superiority couldn't stand with both his feet down in these shoes and count to one without falling, let alone on one foot as long as me. Thinking I have made my case, I smiled at him and said, "Ok?"

"We are not done here..." he said aggressively. "See the reflection of my head lights on the road. I want you to walk heel to toe following the light as your line, hands to your sides, then pivot back, and heel to toe back."

"Can I take off my shoes? There are a lot of loose gravel and rocks on the asphalt that will trip me in these shoes."

"Take off your shoes if you want," he answered. My heart was pounding and my hands tingling. I took off my shoes and glanced at the front windows of my house, hoping that Chad would see the commotion, praying the kids won't.

I walked over the streak of light that the deputy's head lights made on the road between his car and mine. I felt sharp pain on the heels and balls of my feet from loose rock as I stepped. My instincts were to stop and grab my foot from the pain, but I clinched my hands into fists and endured to prove my sobriety.

"I said hands to the side," he barked.

I stopped and looked at him. "Are they not to my side?" I was holding my fists tightly at my sides bracing myself from the sharp pain of the rock and the sting of the asphalts heat on my bare feet. His demand didn't make sense to me, my arms were not out for balance, but kept secure to my hips.

I swiveled as directed and turned to continue back. I made not one misstep or even a slight stumble. I had to have passed. There was no way anyone would consider someone drunk who could stand on one foot in Louboutin's, and walk barefoot on asphalt without stumble, yet I did not feel any ease in his intentions of finding the truth about my condition. The other deputy finally walked back and was standing by Antipas. The young deputy set his camera on the hood of Antipas' car.

Antipas then got a small flashlight and asked me to look side to side, while he shined it in my eyes. The other deputy stood by Antipas' car at a short distance.

"I've never been pulled over before, or ever even had a traffic ticket. This is very scary!" I said as he flashed the light in my eyes and pressed his head uncomfortably close to mine.

"You've never had a ticket?" he said as though surprised.

"No," I answered.

Antipas growled loudly, "Samson!"

The young officer stood up into attention, "Yes?"

Antipas then told Samson to ask for my information while he typed it in his car. Antipas left while Samson had me recount my address, social security number and full name.

Then Antipas divulged that he was calling in for an on sight blood test, and while he does this Samson was to escort me to the back seat of Antipas' car and remain there with me.

I walked with the younger deputy to the back seat of the patrol car. I sat down to find the vinyl seats sticky. It was a cage. Dried vomit touched my hand. Tears began to burn my cheeks. The young officer didn't close the door. I looked over at my house and at the windows, fearing the kids were peering through. I felt helpless and unable to do anything to prove myself. I was afraid, frightened. I wasn't scared when he pulled me over, but the reality of this man's intentions were becoming clear. I had no rights, I was his to toy with and humiliate as long as he wished, and as severe as he chose. The heat of my tears ran down my face.

"I want my neighborhood to be safe. I have children of my own and need these streets to be free of any harm as they play... I understand you are just doing your job, but don't you feel this is excessive. I have had only two glasses of wine in the last five hours. That is it. Clearly this is not right," I pleaded with the younger deputy.

"Then you understand we are protecting your children and the children in this neighborhood. Children live here, we can't have people driving around putting them or anyone else in jeopardy," He scolded.

"...But I am not drunk and am not putting anyone in jeopardy! He waited until I was home. If he had concern, wouldn't he want to pull me over before I hurt anyone? Why wait to pull me over when I was turning into my driveway... if he felt I was a threat to anyone's safety?" My tears fell as I let my heart bleed before this young man. "I am a mother, an adoptive mother and certified foster care provider. If I get a DUI, I will never be able to foster or adopt again!" tears began to flow deeper and harder.

"Well, you should have thought about that before you drove after drinking," he said in a smirk.

I felt so helpless, so defenseless. Fear had now overcome me. For the first time, I knew what it was like to be truly afraid, even terrified. They could do anything they wanted, say anything they decided and I could do nothing about it. I didn't understand why or what Antipas was getting from this. What was his advantage to circumvent a charge? This had nothing to do with safety or the truth. He waited for me and now used the fact that I was attempting to turn left into my own driveway as "veering over the center line," as reason to pull me over. Our streets didn't even have a center line. I trembled realizing my inevitable doom and his clear plot.

"I saw Deputy Antipas when I drove past his car. I wasn't concerned he was there, because I didn't think I was doing anything wrong. I only had two glasses the entire night… two glasses from 4 p.m. to 9:30 p.m., how could I be drunk?" I said beseeching a man that had no emotions.

"Well Officer Antipas thinks you are. Let the blood test say whether you are or are not," He countered.

"Do you have the camera?" Deputy Antipas asked as he walked over to the back seat of his car.

"I put it on the hood," Samson answered, pointing his finger to the front of the car.

"Get it and take her picture," Antipas demanded as if his superior. The other deputy left and I was alone once again with Antipas. "Why are you crying?" He taunted me. "I see that you trying to hide your tears from me." I said nothing and shook my head. There was no use in talking to him. He was on a mission and was making a sport of my sorrow.

Another deputy walked over. He was short with dark hair. I looked through the back window to see this new deputy too had parked his patrol car, behind Samson's, with its top lights blazing. My entire street was now flashing with the lights from the three cars which strobed the street, bounced off the eerie sky, flashing their colors onto mine and my neighbors' houses. What a spectacle I have become and what fun it was for those who held me.

"I am here to take your blood. Will you agree to a blood test?" the short deputy asked.

"Yes." I stretched out my arm.

"Have you been read your rights?" He asked.

"No. Am I being arrested?" I questioned.

"I have read you your rights three times. Yes, you are being arrested." Deputy Antipas shouted. "I read her rights three times!" He slammed his hands on the side of the car angry and defensive.

"I am being arrested?" I asked again, tears rushed my face.

"Yes, you are under arrest," the short deputy says jeering. "I guess this fact has been explained to you now four times…. Ahhh… This makes you cry. It not the end of the world?" The short deputy said with a condescending chuckle.

"I have a family, children. I know what this will mean to them… and I fear this will also mean we cannot adopt. It will be my fault, once again." I whispered. I couldn't stop my tears. I wanted to, but couldn't. I was surrounded by men who enjoyed watching me cry. They continued to joke and make fun of my tears, commenting that I was "emotional" in efforts to incite me and find more to use against me.

Antipas walked away, while the other stuck my arm. "He didn't read me my rights…" I whispered.

"You have the right to remain silent…" the short deputy sang.

"…I have the right to an attorney, if I cannot afford one, one will be appointed to me…" I said over him. "I know my rights. I thought I passed my field sobriety and would only be taking the blood test to confirm as a precaution. Am I going to go to jail tonight?" I asked.

"Do you want to go to jail?" the short deputy taunted me. "I can take you to jail right now if you want to go." I wiped my tears and did not respond.

My confidence was falling, sinking deep and far from my soul. Everything I believed and was secure in, now gone. Safety, laws, protection was only a statement, not a reality. My life, my truth, my well-being was in the hands of these men.

"You're very emotional…" He jeered again. I realized I needed to stop talking and keep my head down. Of course I was upset, who wouldn't be? This was a horrific moment in my life. I could see that he and Antipas were trying to provoke me. Antipas returned and began to chime in with the short deputy who continued to harass me. They were taunting the wrong person, I am not aggressive, I had no desire to fight them. I didn't care about them or their thoughts or attitudes. I was devastated. Chad and I both had a deep sense that our home and heart needed to be open to another child that was in the system; this time older, whose rights were severed and nowhere to call home, no one to call their own. The ache in my heart deepened as I thought of how God had closed my womb, now He was closing all doors to ever having more. I am a good mother, why has this too been taken from me?

The short deputy finished drawing my blood. My arm became red and began to bruise immediately.

"Who can take your car?" Antipas asked.

"My husband is right here, this is my house… We can even leave the car here. It's parked in front of my house…" I said.

"Samson, go to the door and ring the doorbell. See if you can get her husband to take her car and park it in the garage," he ordered.

"Can we just leave the car here? I don't want to wake my kids. This will frighten them. They don't need to see this," I implored.

Samson turned to look at Antipas, yet Antipas barked at him for hesitating. "Go get him," he demanded.

"My shoes are still under your car..." Antipas had forgotten that I was barefoot. He then decided to let me get out of the car to get my shoes. Samson walked to my front door and rang its bell, it didn't take long for the door to open. I strong quake came over me as I searched the windows, fearing the children were looking through. Chad opened the door, he looked around, saw me, then observed the three deputies and their three patrol cars that flashed brightly. My spirit sank as I considered how he kept texting me to come home. He just wanted me home. It was only 9:30 when I left my sister's; who would have thought my short drive would end like this. My tears began to flow again. I was so relieved to see him, but also so very ashamed.

Samson and Chad walked over. "Baby!" I said and began to cry again.

"Your wife was swerving right here…" Antipas began as he pointed to the road in front of my driveway. Chad passed him, without even acknowledging the deputy in front of him, showing no interest in anything the deputy had to say. Chad grabbed me and hugged me tight. Antipas turned around and walked back over to catch up to Chad, cleared his throat and began his rhetoric once again:

"Your wife was swerving. She swerved right here on this street, so I pulled her over…" Antipas described.

Chad wasn't listening, and begun talking over Antipas as though insignificant. Putting his hands on my face, "You ok?" he asked.

"Yes! I can't believe this is happening," I said mournfully.

Antipas' cleared his throat again, "As I was saying… your wife appears to be over the legal limit. My guess is she is between .08 to .10. Not a lot, but possibly enough. I need you to take custody of her car."

"The keys are in the ignition, Chad." I said.

"Okay." He answered me, still looking at me and not acknowledging the deputy. He walked over to my car and got in, then parked it a few feet away in our garage. He left the garage open and returned to me, and held my hand.

"I don't have enough evidence to arrest her tonight, but she will need to appear in court. Here is her charges and paperwork." He handed the paperwork to Chad.

"Then we can go?" Chad asked.

"Yes… We did take her blood and once processed it will show she is over the legal limit," he said with confidence.

I was in total shock Antipas had now decided to let me go home. Chad put his arm around my waist and together we walked up our driveway and into our garage. Chad quickly closed its doors and we walked to our bedroom. Saying nothing, I changed into a t-shirt and crawled into bed. Chad got in with me and grabbed me again, holding me tight. I sobbed in his arms. "I am so sorry, Babe!" Chad said softly.

I turned my head to him and struggled to say the words, "Did the kids wake up? I was so worried they would see me outside… like that…" my voice broke and only a breathy hiss followed.

Chad began to stroke my hair and then he wiped the tears under my eyes that flowed deep and thick, "No. They never woke up. They are sound asleep in their beds. Don't worry about them, they are fine. I had no idea either. I heard the doorbell and looked outside. It was only then that I saw..."

"I am so sorry. I am so so sorry Chad…" My body became limp and my tears were joined by sobs.

"Did you see the officer when you were driving?" Chad asked.

"Yes, I drove past him. He was out in front of Esther's house." I replied.

"Why didn't you wait until he left?" Chad questioned.

"Because I didn't think I was doing anything wrong," I moaned.

"I understand. I am so sorry, Babe. It will be ok. I'll call around to-morrow to get a referral for a good lawyer. There is no way that blood test is coming back high. No way." Chad said as he stroked my hair.

"I feel terrified, confused, harassed for sport. I was so scared... I have never been so scared. Most of all, I am sad. Sad because I was hoping to have our first summer where we could just enjoy ourselves and my heart could be at peace for once. I thought that I had no more issues to conquer, no more fights to endure, now that Anna's adoption is final. I was just so looking forward to a summer together as a family where my heart and spirit could be calm. I haven't felt peace in so long. Now I have this to face and whatever trial and fight that will come from it." I groaned as my heart that had just begun to heal became shattered once more.

Chapter 37

"We are hard-pressed on every side, yet not crushed;
we are perplexed, but not in despair; persecuted, but not forsaken;
struck down, but not destroyed." 2 Corinthians 4:8-9

JAIL: DAY TWENTY, ELEVEN THIRTY P.M.

As the clock hits eleven thirty, I throw the items in my drawer into a plastic bag, return the books and Bible and bundle up the shredded towel, sheets and blanket, and drop them in the laundry bin. Then I sit and wait.

It isn't long before Officer Cain calls my name, and demands I sit in front of her desk. She pulls out that same plastic chair she propped on my first day and sets it in the middle of the room. I, like my predecessors, was far too excited, far too happy that my sentence was at its end to be affected by her hostility. I was minutes away from having my penalty served and my life back... but as I wait the weight of it all begins to press on my chest and overtake my emotions.

A male officer enters the block. "Your paperwork?" he says to me. I hand the paper that shows my last day. "You ready to get out of here?" he asks kindly.

"Yes," I say.

"Ok, follow me." he responds.

I grab my bag of things, stuff I didn't care about anymore, and followed him down the hallway.

He has me stand against a wall near an office with many screens and a big desk. The officer leaves and walks into the office.

I wait alone, as regret consumes me. Too many nights and mornings away from my husband, away from my children. Such pain and humiliation this has brought on my parents, my husband and, one day, to my children. I know now that even one glass before getting behind the wheel is too much. Too many lives at stake on the road and at home to ever take that risk again. I have felt justified, been angry, considered myself entirely victimized by the system, but I must take responsibility. I will never drink anything, not a sip and get behind a wheel again. The fact that I did that night is my doing and I am truly sorry.

My parents have loved and supported me, without fail, and kissed my face the day I checked into jail; it stings to consider their love and support for me, when I know how deep this all has hurt them. I love them so much and never wanted to cause them this type of pain.

The heartache and strain this has put on my marriage is another regret. Life has thrown so many boulders in my path, yet my husband has loved me through them all. Why he still loves me I wonder. He could have walked away, but there he stands, by my side. How can I feel forsaken by God when I consider the people who stand with me and love me: my brother, Esther, my parents, my husband, and my dear friends. Yet my greatest love and ability to keep perspective came from Gabriel and Anna. I leave this place and value them even more than I ever have. Each person was so important to me before, but now I realize how truly precious they all really are to me. When all had been stripped away, they became what really mattered, their love and my love for them.

The officer returns. "Let's get you out of here," he says, but stops and sees that my face is drenched with tears.

"Are you ok?" he asks.

"Yes, I am just so happy it is over, sad I put my family through this, but happy to be back and be able see them all in just a few minutes." I say honestly.

"Ok, I want to make sure those are not tears of fear. You are not afraid of someone who is outside, who may hurt you?" he questions.

"No, but thank you, Sir," I say.

We walk to the waiting room and I head into the bathroom and remove my red Pima County jumpsuit, rubber size eight shoes and put on the sweat shorts and t-shirt I had in my bag. Samil is at the front desk. I get to leave this place; here he shall remain. I unlock my locker, put on my shoes and grab my purse and stand at the desk to submit to him one last time for my keys. The male officer has me sign the paperwork to declare that I received all the items that I checked in with.

"Looks like your jail fees are already paid in full. Good job. You are done. Don't come back!" he says.

"I hope I never see you again," I say and laugh. The officer smiles and chuckles. With that, I turn and walk through the double doors. I am really done; this is over. I walk outside and the hot sun hits my face. The cicadas have moved on, the sound of their song has gone. I stretch my face toward the sun, close my eyes and lift my arms toward the skies. Freedom feels good.

☽☽☽☽

"Mom, I am driving home!" I declare to my car's Bluetooth speaker.

"Andrea, Dad and I have been holding our breath until today. When can we see you and just hold you?" she says with joy.

"Breakfast, tomorrow?" I ask.

"We'll be there!" she answers with enthusiasm.

I try to hold my emotions but blurt out what I cannot contain, "I love you!" I say a bit too loud.

"I love you too!" my mother responds.

The phone clicks.

Once again, I can't stop the tears, as I take my last and final trek home, the official end to my incarceration. The tears flow like a river and wet my face, my neck and my chest. I'm done crying. I don't want to cry anymore. I have cried enough… yet they continue uncontrolled.

I have had a rare chance to witness humanity become vile. I have been stripped of dignity, humiliated, demoralized, and made sick… because the court says this is what I deserve.

I have also had the privilege to meet and witness the beauty of the human spirit among women who had nothing but the ability to offer a hand of comfort, in spite of their own risk. The beauty in these are beyond anything I have seen… and from those that society wants to pretend do not exist. Yet if we could see Jesus in the flesh, who would he be comforting?

*"I was a stranger and you did not take Me in, naked and you
did not clothe Me, sick and in prison and you did not visit Me."
Then they also will answer Him, saying, "Lord, when did we see
You hungry or thirsty or a stranger or naked or sick or in prison,
and did not minister to You?" Then He will answer them, saying,
"Assuredly, I say to you, inasmuch as you did not do it to one of
the least of these, you did not do it to Me."* Matthew 25:43-45

I truly feel, that in human form, Jesus was in Spirit next to me, holding my hand. He used that beautiful woman to touch me when I was
lost and in despair.

Can the church touch and help these women who are broken and
shattered like me? Has the church become full of the same religious
leaders called Pharisees and Sadducees whom Jesus called a brood of
vipers thousands of years ago? A quest focused on personal gain or is
their motivation inspired by the beautiful Message that they have been
given the platform to teach? Do we as a people, as a faith, show grace,
compassion and forgiveness, or political intolerance, hypocritical judgment, and distain for those that appear to be less perfect? Is many of today's "ministers" a mirror image of the pharisaical leaders who lectured
about God, yet rejected when He stood in front of them in the form of a
Man? To call oneself a Christian, by definition, you are calling yourself
"Christ Like." Are we, the church, really "like" Christ?

As a child who grew up sleeping under a pew, surrounded by members of the church; I had not one of those who claim to be leaders reach
out to me in my hour of desperation, yet received only rebuke, ridicule
and condemnation.

There are many in the church that are good men and woman, who
truly love God and by loving God, they inherit His love for others. There
are multitudes of those that truly show grace to those in need and comfort to those that sorrow, just like Christ. Yet I know and have met many
religious leaders, who are the first to pick up a stone and cast it at another, while they themselves are immoral in secret, they lie, cheat and
steal in ways that hurt more than if they took my purse. As a Christian
community, our voice has been infiltrated by political intolerance and

our public image stained by hypocrisy and pretense. The very message of Jesus Christ has been contaminated with their dogmatic and legalistic doctrine.

My God died and shed the same amount of blood for the woman that laid in jail next to me as He did the deputies that walked the hall and banged on our bunks with their batons. So many may feel that if only we, the inmates, could live a justified life such as them, we too could walk in His grace. Yet when I looked into the eyes of those women, those inmates, I saw my God and realized He was there among them. Yet, their hopelessness grieves me.

Who is bringing them to a Savior; who can show them their true value in His eyes? The echo of the words spoken by their captors and the condemnation of the religious has become true in their hearts and minds. They have accepted and believe the words and treatment of others as their fate… and their value.

My eyes are open and my heart has been touched. I believe in the Church, in a church that truly is like Christ. I believe in love… God's love. If we truly became more like Jesus, we could touch so many, heal countless hearts and change our country, and our world.

As I pull into my house, I exhale deep, because today I am not alone… my beautiful husband waits for me! I can't be fast enough. I run into the house and into arms that are spread wide and open. Chad picks me up and walks me as though a bride into our bedroom, placing me on the soft feathery bed I so missed. I am a mess, but it doesn't matter, he loves me as I am. My head is greeted by a pillow… a pillow! It engulfs me and I roll my head back and forth enjoying its cushion.

"Make love to me, Chad!" I summon.

He smiles at me lovingly, "That, I can do…"

♪♪♪♪

Once Chad headed back to work, I walked around the house and put things in order as I wanted them… back to where everything needed to be. I make my bed and putter in my kid's rooms… I am home. I stand and stare at my bathtub. A bath, hot and steamy, calls. I turn the faucet and watch the stream as it crashes and fills. While it runs, I throw the ugly sweats I have on in the trash; I am done with them and done with where I wore them. I walk back to my bath, once filled and step in, slowly resting in and letting the water engulf my body. The heat overcomes me and I close my eyes, leaning back to let its warmth consume me.

In spite of my joy and the freedom I feel, my spirit feels as though broken, pieced together, then shattered again, with only a glue gun in hopes that once repaired there will still be beauty… if I can just find all the pieces of my broken soul. I thought, hoped, trusted my hardship was over once Anna's adoption final, believing that when the judge hit that gavel, it was going to be joy and celebration, sadness no more. This thought frightens me. I pull myself up, gasp for breath, as the water crashes around me, and brace my heart as I cry out, "Dear God, what suffering will I have to face tomorrow?"

Although I want it desperately, I know that life doesn't offer happily ever after. So, I ask myself, what torment lies ahead?

"Jesus, please, my heart can't take another trial." I scream, then press my eyes shut, and drop my head below the water. I force myself to hold the air, but soon my body takes over, beckoning me to submerge so I can take a breath. I open my eyes while under in protest to my lung's campaign. Above me, my hair billows, moving and swaying as a cloud above my head, as though a flower blowing to and fro in adversity's wind. It remains soft and yielding, even beautiful as it moves. I was told that the most beautiful of roses will bloom not in the gardens of the rich, where the sun always shines and there is no sorrow, but one that grows in darkness, wild and strong and truly beautiful. Roses such as this, their glory cannot be matched, even if their only company is weeds and darkness.

I sit up, and breathe deep, then rest my head on the bathtub's rim. Steam rises from my face and hands.

Should I hold my head down in shame, as some have professed, or should I see myself as a woman who bloomed and grew in adversity?

I let the water drain, step out and grab a towel and stare in the mirror that is covered in steam. My image distorted and the mirror's clarity fogged. I decide to leave it and get dressed without its truth. I stand in my closet surrounded by my collection of high heels and fancy dresses. I can't wear them, not sure I can ever wear them again. I grab my flip flops and throw on linen shorts and a t-shirt instead. Today I can pick up my kids and with joy I drive. They are excited when they see me and I them. We return home and I immediately begin to start dinner, as if life was as it always has been.

After dinner, which was "normal," yet precious, the time for my kids to prepare for bed comes before I am ready. Anna soon runs out in a new nightie. "Mommy, see the nightgown Grandma gave me?" she says as she twirls in front of me. The nightie opens into a wide and beautiful flowing flower. Anna, delighted by the rising skirt, loses her balance and starts to rock head first towards the wall. I reach out to her to stop her and realize she is just fine. I start to tell her to stop spinning, for fear she might get hurt, but change my heart and instead encourage her to twirl.

"It's beautiful Anna. Keep twirling, I love to see you twirl!" As my daughter whirled around the house, hair spinning and nightie flowing, I thought nothing could be more spectacular then to see her dance down my hallway, twirling with excitement and joy. She could not be more beautiful, more special. She stops and looks at me and laughs that loud and unbridled laugh that is distinctly hers. I so love her laugh. It is such a special laugh, it makes me laugh too. It seems like yesterday, she sat, a chunky little baby with a permanent furrowed brow, who for the first time softened and with that big smile soon followed that beautiful laugh. My eyes burn again because I realize, it was me who taught Anna to laugh.

"Eight thirty, time to go to bed!" Chad announces. This makes me a bit sad, but a privilege to be present. This was the time for me to head out to submit to my judgment's order, but tonight, I didn't have to leave. That order has been served, and now I can tuck my son into bed and kiss him goodnight. I can get into my own bed, slip into its sheets, pull my down comforter over my shoulders, up to my chin and rest my head on a soft pillow. All these daily tasks and routines, no longer mundane, but privileges.

"Andrea, let's go to California this weekend. I think it will be nice to go, be together, and just get away," Chad suggests.

"I would love that." I close my eyes, tired, drained. It had been months since I had slept through an entire night. This time, this night, I will rest. I breathe out and look over at Chad to savor his presence. He is lying next to me, staring back.

"Are you ok?" I ask.

"I missed you, Andrea. I hated going to bed every night without you next to me," He says and then touches my cheek.

I begin to tear, surprised I had any left. "I am not going anywhere, Baby. Close your eyes, it's all over, I am here to stay." I scoot over to his side and throw my arm and leg around him and rest my head on his chest. "Tonight, we both rest well," I say hopeful, and sleepy.

Tomorrow, I won't be afraid to look in the mirror and wipe away the fog. I can and will look at my reflection and face myself as the woman I am today. One side of me wants to hold resentment toward all those that gloated over me, broadcasted my failure, treated me harshly, and took joy in making me small, but I must forgive them all.

Matthew 5:43-44

"You have heard that it was said, 'You shall love your neighbor and hate your enemy.' But I say to you, love your enemies, bless those who curse you, do good to those who hate you, and pray for those who spitefully use you and persecute you."

I can't control other's behavior. What I do have control of is my own soul and my own mind. Every day I hold on to my anger, I forfeit the peace that could be mine.

Scripture says Wisdom is calling us. God is a God of Wisdom and order; he created night and day, seedtime and harvest, summer and winter. Part of this order is that which we plant, we will reap. There are penalties for all that we do, consequences for what we sow. My father always told me, if I plant an orange seed, don't expect an apple to grow. I have planted weeds in my soul which was bitterness and unforgiveness, and then wondered why depravity and grief was all that surrounded me. Everyone must face the destruction that we root and also the virtues. Yet to forgive others who have wronged us, or wronged those we love is never easy. These last days, I realize I need to look deep into my heart and truthfully ask for blessing and not destruction for those who have hurt me. I must pray for each, that God does not hold them accountable or penalize them to the depth that they may warrant. In fact, I pray that He shows them grace, just as God has been gracious to me. I pray that He is merciful to them, just as I cried for mercy. If I can do this, then I know in my heart I have truly released them. I forgive the guards, the deputies, Korah, and place them all into God's hands. I do this for me… because forgiveness is the most liberating gift I can give myself.

As sleep begins to overtake me, I ask myself, although circumstances of my life may have felt to me higher than the heavens and wider than east is to west, yet have I not been resilient, haven't I overcome each? I am not bitter, or ruined but see the joy and beauty of each day, and believe in the hope of tomorrow. Am I ashamed and hiding from my experience, or have the scars in my life become a part of me, molded me and made me an even greater person than what I was yesterday? My scars are part of me, they are a part of my ugliness, but also my beauty. My infertility is my story, a true moment of heartbreak, where I laid my life before the Lord and cried out to Him. He answered me, He turned my mourning into dancing. He took me "the baron woman" and made her house, my house, a home filled with the sound of children's laughter. I have been condemned and gone to jail, I have been confined to a dark cell and grouped in a hole without a blanket to warm myself, yet I found comfort and beauty in that darkness. I was alone and found friends. I was rejected and found God. Are these things that I have faced black holes in my soul, bitter edges that are gnarly and hard, or have they softened me? Like the cancer left an angry scar, but today I love the beauty that it brought and now I can and will unveil it.

I am a woman who, if someone told me that I was beautiful, would whisper to myself, "but they don't know about my scars." I have been a woman who hid her imperfections and learned to pretend. I have been a woman who has clung to a scarlet letter that exposed and revealed that I have been "accused" and "condemned." Moreover, I have also been a victim. Yet, do I want to be that victim, condemned and hiding or do I want to be that heroine who has overcome? Should I shrink back and wallow in my self-pity or be the one who rises above, prevails and grows stronger? I choose to be the heroine. My scars, my scarlet letter, is indeed ugly, like an ugly coal strapped around my neck; I can wear that or look deep inside and see the precious gem that is within. The adversity that I have faced is not who I am but what has made me greater. Yes, I am scarred… but scarred beautiful.

Where They Are Now

Sarah continued to work for my husband, until her release. She came to work early every day to call her son before school. I had lunch with her on the last day she served her sentence to celebrate. She returned home and had a beautiful baby girl. Officer Julius was hired and continues to oversee the security for the south-side school. Days after my release, five Pima County Jail guards were caught on tape assaulting individuals, unprovoked. The five Correctional Officers were arrested on felony assault charges and booked into the same Pima County Jail, of which they were employed. In addition, the sheriff's department put a total of ten correctional officers on administrative leave following the incident. The judge in my case has been reprimanded by the Arizona Commission, who found her to be guilty of misconduct violating six provision of the Code of Judicial Conduct, now totaling four public reprimands on her record. Among them includes *unjust actions in courtroom* and *improper sentencing*. She is currently under investigation by the Attorney General's office. To this day, Korah has yet to speak to me. My sister, Esther, continues to touch countless children with three charters and seven schools and hopes to expand and provide quality education to children throughout Arizona... and maybe beyond. My parents are healthy and very present. My mother is now thirteen years cancer free and my dad continues to show great improvement in his health. He is once again the vibrant and loving man he always has been. Chad and I are blissfully celebrating 20 years married. Our kids continue to grow and thrive, becoming distinct and special individuals. Each stage, each day, a true blessing.

CPSIA information can be obtained at www.ICGtesting.com
Printed in the USA
LVOW09s1452170415

434929LV00018B/56/P